INTRODUCTION TO THE SCIENTIFIC STUDY OF EDUCATION

This edition published by Lector House in 2024

ISBN: 978-93-6138-299-4

Lector House LLP
Registered Office: H. No. 96, Block C, Tomar Colony,
Burari, Delhi – 110084, India
info@lectorhouse.com
www.lectorhouse.com

INTRODUCTION TO THE SCIENTIFIC STUDY OF EDUCATION

CHARLES HUBBARD JUDD

2024

LECTOR HOUSE LLP

INTRODUCTION TO THE SCIENTIFIC STUDY OF EDUCATION

BY

CHARLES HUBBARD JUDD

PROFESSOR OF EDUCATION AND DIRECTOR OF
THE SCHOOL OF EDUCATION OF THE UNIVERSITY OF CHICAGO

PREFACE

This book is the result of eight years of experimentation. In 1909 the Department of Education of The University of Chicago abandoned the practice of requiring courses in the History of Education and Psychology as introductory courses for students preparing to become teachers. For these courses it substituted one in Introduction to Education and one in Methods of Teaching. This move was due to the conviction that students need to be introduced to the problems of the school in a direct, concrete way, and that the first courses should constantly keep in mind the lack of perspective which characterizes the teacher-in-training.

In the years that have elapsed since 1909 the conviction has gained almost universal acceptance in normal schools and colleges of education that the History of Education is not a suitable introductory course. Psychology has grown in the direction of a scientific discussion of methodology, and the demand for a general introductory discussion of educational problems from a scientific point of view has often been expressed by teachers in normal schools and colleges. In this period the writer has had frequent opportunity to try out various methods of presenting such an introductory course. The results of this experience are presented in this volume, which is designed as a textbook for students in normal schools and colleges in the first stages of their professional study.

The teacher who uses this book can expand the course to double the length here outlined by introducing schoolroom observation and supplementary reading. The questions and references offered at the end of each chapter and the references in the footnotes are intended to facilitate such further work. A set of questions is given in the Appendix as a guide to classroom observation.

The obligations which the author has incurred in the preparation of the book are numerous. Almost every member of the Department of Education of The University of Chicago has at some time or other given the course to a division of students, and all have contributed suggestions and criticisms with regard to the organization of material. Special obligations should be noted in this connection to Professors J. F. Bobbitt, S. C. Parker, F. N. Freeman, H. O. Rugg, and W. S. Gray. To Professor E. H. Cameron the author is under obligation for suggestions made after reading the manuscript. To the authors and publishers whose works have been drawn upon for extensive and numerous quotations, special thanks are due for courteous permission to use their material. Finally, it is to the students who have from year to year passed through this course that the largest obligation should be acknowledged because of the suggestions which their reactions have given to the writer.

C. H. J. Chicago, Illinois

CONTENTS

CHAPTER VII

GROUPING PUPILS IN CLASSES

CHAPTER VIII

THE TRADITIONAL CURRICULUM AND ITS REORGANIZATION

CHAPTER IX

SPECIALIZED EDUCATION VERSUS GENERAL EDUCATION

CHAPTER X

EXTENSION OF SCHOOL ACTIVITIES

CHAPTER XI

PRINCIPLES INFLUENCING THE ORGANIZATION OF THE CURRICULUM

CHAPTER XII

INDIVIDUAL DIFFERENCES

CHAPTER XIII

PERIODICITY IN THE PUPIL'S DEVELOPMENT

CHAPTER XIV

SYSTEMATIC STUDIES OF THE CURRICULUM

CHAPTER XV

STANDARDIZATION

CHAPTER XVI

METHODS

CHAPTER XVII

CLASSROOM MANAGEMENT

CHAPTER XVIII

SELECTED ADMINISTRATIVE PROBLEMS

CHAPTER XIX

PLAY

CHAPTER XX

HEALTH SUPERVISION

CHAPTER XXI

SCIENTIFIC SUPERVISION

CHAPTER XXII

THE SCIENCE OF EDUCATION

CHAPTER XXIII

PROFESSIONAL TRAINING OF TEACHERS

LIST OF ILLUSTRATIONS

Page

LIST OF TABLES

THE SCIENTIFIC STUDY OF EDUCATION

CHAPTER I

EXTENDING THE PUPIL'S VIEW OF THE SCHOOL

The pupil's view limited. Conservatism in the community as a natural consequence. Demand for a broad scientific study. Beginnings of the science of education. Effectiveness of studies of retardation. A study of high-school courses. An experimental analysis of a fundamental subject. A study of the relation of education to general social life. The scientific study of educational problems. Exercises and readings.

The Pupil's View Limited

Most people think of school matters from the pupil's point of view. When they learned arithmetic and grammar, or later when they studied algebra and Latin, each course was presented to them as though it were a perfect system. The teacher did not confide in them that arithmetic probably ought to be revised by the omission of many of its topics, that formal grammar is a very doubtful subject, and that both algebra and Latin are on the point of losing their places as required subjects. The pupil sees the front of the school scenery; the machinery behind is known only to those who conduct the performance.

It would be possible to multiply indefinitely examples which show that the pupil's view of the school is very limited. What pupil understands the duties of the principal or the superintendent, or of the still more remote and mysterious board of education? Where does the daily program come from? Who decides about text-books? Why are school buildings commonly planned with large study-rooms? Most of these questions are never thought of by pupils. Everything in school life seems to have a kind of inevitableness which raises it above question or even consideration.

Conservatism in the Community as a Natural Consequence

The narrowness of the pupil's view would have less serious consequences if it were not for the fact that the pupil becomes in mature life a member of a board of education or adopts teaching as his profession. Then trouble results, because there is machinery which must be kept running if schools are to be efficient, and this machinery suffers if intrusted to the hands of those who do not understand its complexities.

One school superintendent, who encountered vigorous opposition to the introduction of changes in the course of study, wrote as follows:

> The average American citizen whose schooling was limited to the primary and grammar grades looks with reverence upon the subjects there taught, and refuses to concur in a change of the course of study for the elementary school. Associated with the average citizen is a heavy percentage of the teaching faculty of both elementary and high schools throughout the country.[1]

Another superintendent, who was more successful in bringing about reforms, makes this statement:

> People are more conservative in their attitude towards educational innovations than toward new adjustments to meet the demands of changing modern life in any other field of activity. Each adult is inclined to overvalue the particular type of training he received and to regard with suspicion any change which will tend to discredit this sort of training received at such an expenditure of time and money. The schools are, therefore, the last institution to respond to the changing demands of modern life.[2]

Demand for a Broad Scientific Study

If schools are to be progressive and efficient, they must be studied very much more broadly and comprehensively than they can be from the pupil's point of view. The suggestion naturally arises that this broader study is a part of the professional duty of the teacher. So it is; but it will not be enough merely to exhibit the intricacies of education to teachers. The whole community must be shown by scientific methods that the school is a complex social institution, and that its conduct, like the conduct of every other social institution, requires constant study and expert supervision. In this movement of opening the eyes of the community to the needs and nature of education, the school officers must be leaders; but their methods must be impersonal and exact.

Beginnings of the Science of Education

During recent years the demand for a thorough and comprehensive study of schools by scientific methods has led to a number of investigations which can be offered as an optimistic beginning of a science of education. It would, indeed, be

[1] Report of Mrs. Ella Flagg Young, Superintendent of Schools of the City of Chicago, for the Year Ending June 30, 1915, published as a part of the Sixty-first Annual Report of the Board of Education, p. 25.

[2] Special Report of the Boise Public Schools, by Superintendent C. S. Meek, June, 1915, p. 57.

far beyond the truth to assert that science has settled all the problems of teaching and of school organization. There is, however, a very respectable body of fact which has been clearly enough defined so that it can in no wise be set aside. In certain details the requirements of a scientifically valid educational scheme are known and can be described. The method of studying schools can safely be said to be established. It is the work of the future to take up, now this problem, now that, and by progressive stages to work out a complete science of school management and classroom organization.

It will be the purpose of subsequent chapters to define fully certain of the leading problems with which the science of education deals. The remainder of this chapter will be devoted to a brief statement of certain typical studies, which will make more concrete and definite the contention that the pupil's view of schools is narrow and that the teacher's view must be extended, as must also that of the community at large, if educational conditions are to be improved.

Effectiveness of Studies of Retardation

First, we may refer to investigations which have been made of the rate of promotion of pupils through the grades.

Whenever a pupil fails to complete the work of a grade in the appointed time, it is evident that there is some kind of maladjustment. The pupil may be incompetent to do the work required of him because he is mentally deficient. On the other hand, it may be that the work is ill chosen and in need of revision. The following statement from one of the leading students of education in the United States describes with clearness the problem and the progress made in meeting it.

> Just ten years ago the distinguished superintendent of schools of New York called attention to the fact that 39 per cent of the children in the schools of that city were above the normal ages for their grades. This aroused widespread investigation, which showed that similar conditions obtained in other cities throughout the country. Soon studies of this phase of educational efficiency showed that the same conditions which resulted in our schools being crowded with retarded children also prevented a large proportion of these children from ever completing the elementary grades.
>
> About seven years ago this became one of the most widely studied problems of educational administration, and in the past four it has been one of the prominent parts of the school surveys. During the entire period hundreds of superintendents throughout the country have been readjusting their schools to better the conditions disclosed.
>
> In these seven years the number of children graduating each year from the elementary schools of America has doubled. The number now is three quarters of a million greater annually than it was then. The only great organized industry in America that has

> increased the output of its finished product as rapidly as the public schools during the past seven years is the automobile industry.
>
> It is probable that no other one thing so fundamentally important to the future of America as this accomplishment of our public schools has taken place in recent years. There is every evidence that this is the direct result of applying measurements to education. If the school survey movement now under way can produce other results at all comparable with this one, we need have no fear for the outcome.[3]

The quotation does not tell us how the reform has been worked out. That is a long story. In some cities better teachers were needed and have been employed. In a great number of cases the course of study has been revised. Sometimes smaller classes have been provided. So on through a long list of details, one might enumerate the reforms which have resulted from a careful study of the one fact that pupils in the schools were older than they normally should be.

A Study of High-School Courses

A second type of study can be borrowed from the reports of the North Central Association of Colleges and Secondary Schools. This Association has as its practical purpose the inspection of the secondary schools and colleges of the northern states from Ohio to Colorado. The inspectors of high schools in seventeen states brought together in the report of 1916 a number of exact statistics regarding 1128 approved schools.[4] One set of these facts may be selected for special comment.

The number of units, or courses, offered in high schools has increased rapidly in recent years. Especially marked is the addition to the school program of technical subjects, such as home economics, manual training, and commercial courses. The report here under discussion states that in all the approved schools of the association there is an average of 21.13 academic units, that is, units in such subjects as languages, history, mathematics, science, and English; and an average of 9.41 units in technical or vocational subjects.

When we examine the individual states, we find that Minnesota, which has a large state fund, much progressive legislation on high schools, and a vigorous state department of education, shows averages of 23.87 academic units and 12.65 units of vocational subjects. South Dakota, where the school system is new and economic conditions are much less favorable, has averages of 17.62 academic units and 6.46 vocational units. The more striking differences are those which arise not from economic conditions but from clearly indicated differences in educational policy. Ohio has an average of 22.24 academic units, which is high, and an average of only 7.26 vocational units, which is low. On the other hand, Kansas has 22.9 academic units, or just about the same as Ohio, and 10.13 units in vocational subjects.

[3] Leonard P. Ayres, "School Surveys," *School and Society*, Vol. I, No. 17, April 24, 1915, pp. 580-581.

[4] Proceedings of the Twenty-first Annual Meeting of the North Central Association of Colleges and Secondary Schools, Chicago, 1916, pp. 97-121.

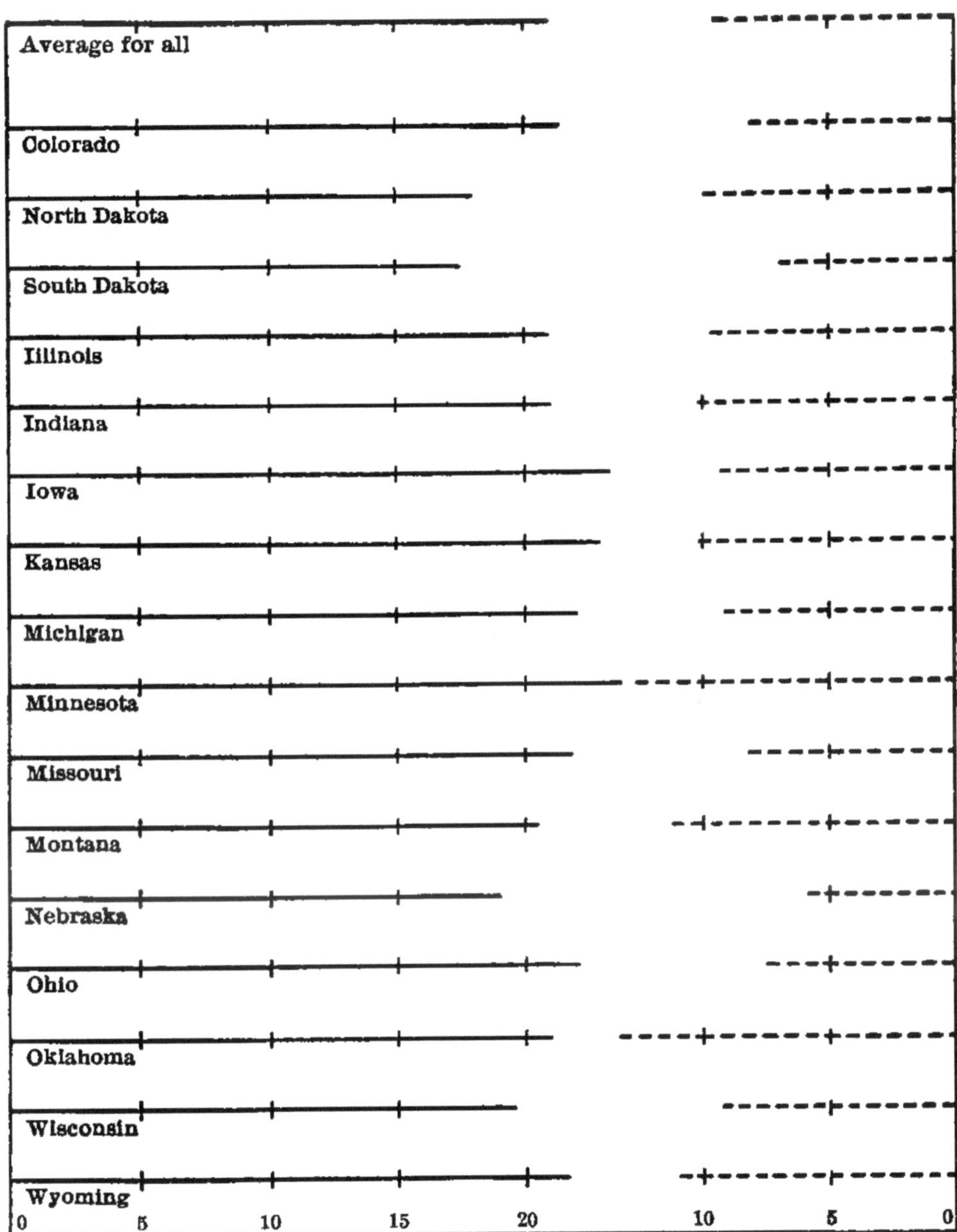

Fig. 1. Average number of high-school units in the approved schools of the various states of the North Central Association

The full-drawn lines are proportional in length to the number of units offered in academic subjects; the dotted lines, to technical subjects

Finally, if we carry the comparison into still further detail by examining the schools in a single state, we find in Ohio one city with a high school of 870 students offering 18 academic units and 5 vocational units, while in another city, where the student body numbers 710 students, the school offers 24 academic units and 22 vocational units.

The comparisons are illuminating in several respects. It is probable that most communities are ignorant of the fact that their own high schools differ from others. The publication of definite facts with regard to the practices of schools would stimulate wholesome thinking on school problems. The whole life of a school depends in very large measure on the course of study. When there are such wide divergences as are here indicated, there is clear evidence of differences in educational policies in different states and communities. At the present time the accepted policies are often the products of tradition or accident. They should be made subjects of careful study and either confirmed or revised.

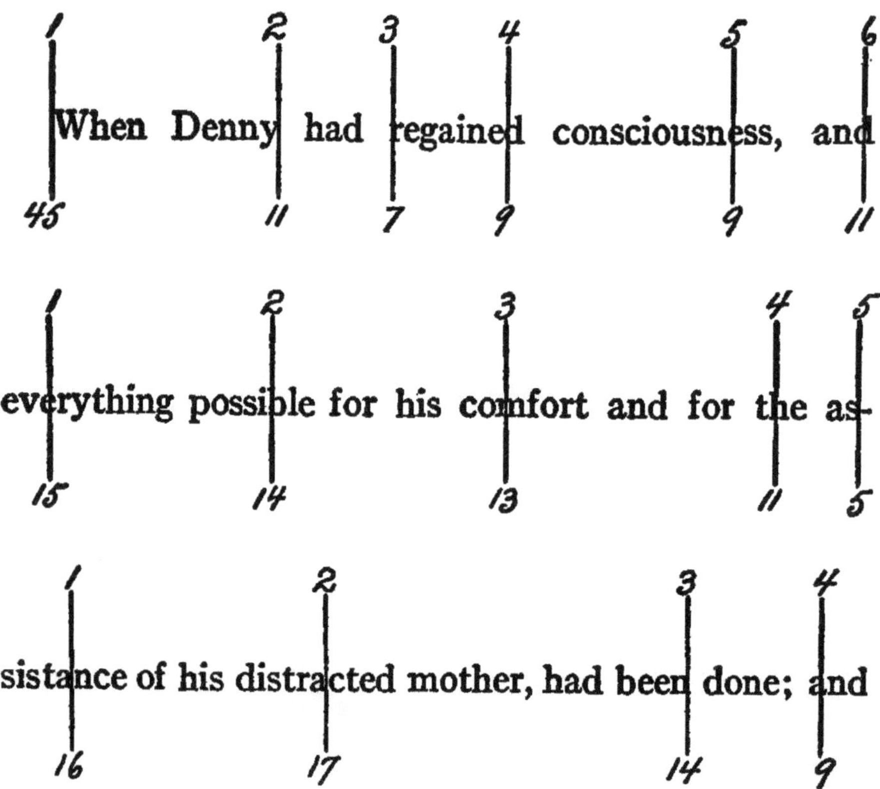

Fig. 2 A. Pauses made in silent reading

The vertical lines, Figs. 2 A, 2 B, show where the eyes of an adult reader paused during the reading. The numbers above the vertical lines in the two figures indicate the order of the fixations

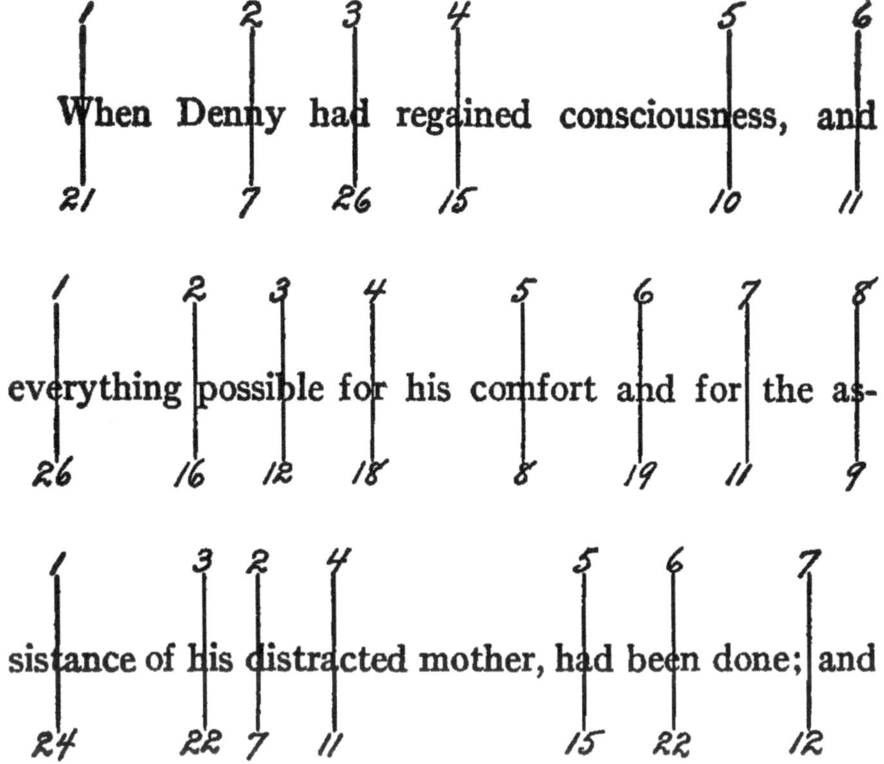

Fig. 2 B. Pauses made in oral reading

The numbers below the vertical lines, Figs. 2 A, 2 B, indicate the duration of each pause in fiftieths of a second. (To reduce these figures to the unit adopted in the text multiply by twenty)

An Experimental Analysis of a Fundamental Subject

As a third type of scientific study we may take certain recent laboratory investigations of reading. Reading is the most important subject taught in the schools; yet there are the widest differences in the results secured with different pupils. It is the duty of the schools to find out what constitutes the difference between good readers and bad readers, in order that both classes may be improved.

The method of these studies consists in photographing the reader's eyes as they travel along printed lines. The number and length of the pauses are thus determined. It is found in general that competent readers see more at a glance than do poor readers. Furthermore, it is found that different types of reading are radically different; thus there is a marked difference between oral and silent reading. The importance of distinguishing these two types of reading lies in the fact that most of the teaching of reading in the elementary schools is by means of the oral method. Most of the demands of later life, and all of the demands made upon pupils when they study textbooks in geography and history and the other subjects of the school course, call for ability in silent reading. The results of investigations can be briefly stated in the following averages: the average numbers of pauses per line in oral reading for adults, high-school pupils, and elementary-school pupils, reading passages of different grades of difficulty, are 8.2, 8.6, and 8.1, while the corresponding averages for silent reading are 6.5, 7, and 6.3. These figures mean that the eye makes more pauses along a printed line when the reader is reading orally than when he is reading silently. Oral reading is therefore a more laborious, difficult form of reading. Furthermore, the time spent in each pause is greater in oral reading. The averages in thousandths of a second for oral reading for the three classes of readers are 380.8, 372.9, 398, while the corresponding figures for silent reading are 308.2, 311.1, and 314.[5] These figures show that oral reading is slow as well as laborious.

It would require more discussion than is appropriate at this point to bring out the full meaning of such facts as these. Enough appears on the surface of the results, however, to make it quite evident that the school ought not to emphasize oral reading in the upper grades as it does to-day. The daily oral-reading drill in the seventh and eighth grades imposes on the pupils a slow, clumsy form of reading at a time when they ought to be cultivating the power of rapid silent reading.

It is by means of investigations of this kind that each of the subjects of instruction is being examined, and as a result schoolwork is increasingly developing effective methods of cultivating children's intellectual powers. The work of analyzing each of the subjects will be slow and will require the coöperation of many investigators, but in several subjects, especially in the elementary schools, an encouraging beginning has been made.

A Study of the Relation of Education to General Social Life

A fourth and final example can be borrowed from studies made in the city of Minneapolis of the opportunities for trade training in that city, of the number of workmen needed in each of the trades, and of the kind of preparation required for efficiency in each branch of labor. An industrial and educational survey of the community was undertaken for the specific purpose of adapting educational organization to the practical needs of the community.[6] Such a study recognizes the fact that the school is but one among many social institutions and that the school must find its proper place in community life through a thorough scientific study of other more general social activities.

The Scientific Study of Educational Problems

Here, again, it is by no means asserted that the solution of the problem of training workers for the industries has been found. It can, however, be stated with

[5] William A. Schmidt, An Experimental Study in the Psychology of Reading (Supplementary Educational Monograph of the *School Review* and the *Elementary School Journal*, Vol. I, No. 2), p. 43.

[6] Report of the Minneapolis Survey for Vocational Education, *Bulletin No. 21* of the National Society for the Promotion of Industrial Education, 1916.

complete assurance that both the school and the community will proceed with greater intelligence if the facts are carefully canvassed in advance.

The spirit of patient, detailed scientific study is more and more dominating the schools. There are some who, impatient at the labor involved in such studies, would rush forward to radical experimentation. Fortunately, even such rash reformers are becoming convinced that they need to keep records of their results in order to prove the success of the changes which they have made. As a result, they too are taking on some of the forms of science, though they do not adopt the full program of patient study of conditions.

The result of a scientific movement such as is under way in education will be the cultivation of a broader conception than was ever possible from any individual point of view. The pupil's view is narrow because he comes in contact with the school only at the point of application of educational methods to his own life. The scientific view of education is broad because it places the school in its proper relations to other social activities, because it defines the relation of the pupils and teachers to one another and to the material used for instruction, and because it opens up all the results of school work to full inspection and evaluation. This broad scientific view is the one which the teacher and the community at large should adopt.

EXERCISES AND READINGS

In every school certain changes are introduced from time to time in spite of the conservatism of the community. Let the student find examples of (1) new courses of study, (2) new methods of appointing or promoting teachers, or (3) new forms of organization, such as the junior high school or departmental teaching. After discovering innovations, let him find how they were brought about.

What are the usual forms of school records and reports known to the student? How could records be made of more value? Suggest methods of presenting the facts of daily attendance so that they can be readily interpreted by a community. What are some of the interpretations that ought to be put on failures and nonpromotions in different kinds of cases? Is repetition of a course desirable for a pupil who has failed? Are failures more common in required courses than in elective courses? When a required course is described as essential to the education of everyone, what is meant?

Let the student test his own rates of reading. How should a college class differ from a high-school class in ability to read? Go to a library or study-room and watch the people read. Report the differences between individuals.

The readings which are most stimulating to students who have never faced the problems of school organization are those which call in question present school practices.

DEWEY, JOHN. The School and Society. The University of Chicago Press. This is one of the most stimulating demands for a reorganization of the school which has ever been written.

ROUSSEAU, JEAN JACQUES. Émile. D. Appleton and Company. This is a book of great historical significance. It is an indictment of formalism in education and a vigorous advocacy of naturalism.

SPENCER, HERBERT. Essays on Education. D. Appleton and Company. This is a demand for a thorough reform of the school curriculum. It is now nearly sixty years old, but it is modern in its spirit.

CHAPTER II

SCHOOLS OF OTHER COUNTRIES AND OF OTHER TIMES

The comparative and historical methods. The American textbook method of teaching. Independence of thought based on reading. European schools caste schools, American schools truly public. Influence of European schools on the educational system of this country. Report of the visiting committee of Taunton in 1801. Adoption of the German model. Results of the adoption of the German example. The reorganization of American schools. Origin of the high school. Education of girls. Higher education free. American public schools secular. The school system and its domination of the teacher. Exercises and readings.

The Comparative and Historical Methods

The scientific methods of studying school problems, which were illustrated in the last chapter, can be supported and supplemented by a comparison of the schools of the present with the institutions of earlier times, and by a comparison of the schools of different countries with one another. Such comparisons seldom serve as an adequate basis for the reorganization of school practices, because the conditions in one generation and in one country are so unlike those of others that direct transfer of methods of procedure is dangerous. Comparison serves, however, to set in clear perspective the characteristics which distinguish each situation from every other. If an American wishes to see the school system with which he is familiar from a new point of view, the comparative method furnishes a kind of outside station from which he may look back and see facts which were by no means clear in their meaning when viewed from near at hand.

The American Textbook Method of Teaching

One very impressive difference between the schools of the United States and the schools of Europe is to be found in the fact that class exercises in our schools are commonly based on assignments in textbooks, while in Europe the chief method of instruction is oral exposition by the teacher. The word "recitation," which is often employed in describing a classroom exercise, is an American term. It originated at the period when devotion to the textbook was even greater than it is now,—when the pupil was expected to repeat verbatim the passage from the text.

In British books on education the word "recitation" appears only when referring to American practices, and usually takes the form "the American recitation." In the German educational vocabulary the word has no equivalent.

The unique American method of reciting lessons learned out of a book can be contrasted with the European method by taking a concrete case. If one goes into a geography class in a German school, one finds in the hands of the pupils no book, except that in the schools for the richer classes there may be an atlas; commonly the wall map serves. The teacher lectures on some section of the country, and follows the lecture by questions which the pupils answer. The advantages of the European method are that the pupils become trained, attentive listeners, and are able in answering questions to talk coherently for long periods, imitating the continuous discourse of the teacher. The disadvantages are that the information supplied is limited by the individual teacher's training, and the pupils cultivate little or no independence in the collection and sifting of information. The influence of the teacher is always dominant—often oppressively so.

Independence of Thought based on Reading

The contrast here pointed out is one of fundamental importance. It can be adequately understood by a study of the history of American schools. When the colonists came to New England they were bent on securing for every individual independent personal contact with the truth. They had left their European homes because there dominating authority always stood between the individual and the sources of truth. One of the first acts of the colonists, therefore, was to provide for the training of every boy and girl in that power which would make him or her independent, especially in religion. The early legislation shows unequivocally this motive. Thus in 1650 Connecticut passed a law which had a preamble very much like that of the Massachusetts law of 1647. The preamble is as follows:

> It being one chief project of that old deluder, Satan, to keep men from a knowledge of the Scriptures, as in former times, keeping them in an unknown tongue, so in these latter times, by persuading them from the use of tongues, so that at least, the true sense and meaning of the original might be clouded by false glosses of saint-seeming deceivers; and that learning may not be buried in the grave of our forefathers [the court decreed that whenever a township increased to fifty householders they should employ someone] to teach all such children as shall resort to him, to write and read.

So strictly did the early schools devote themselves to reading that arithmetic and, in some cases, even writing were neglected in the exclusive cultivation of the one art of reading. Later generations of American teachers and pupils have experienced a great expansion of the content of the course of study, but the method of instruction has always been predominantly the reading method. The large number of supplementary readers used in history, in geography, and in nature study keep up the traditions of a school which was from the first a reading school.

The social consequences of this emphasis on reading can be seen in the fact that public opinion in America is controlled largely by an appeal to the people through reading matter. The importance of this kind of public opinion can hardly be overemphasized. In a democracy there must be ability to form independent opinions, and this is possible only where there is the widest training in reading.

European Schools Caste Schools, American Schools Truly Public

A second characteristic of the school system of the United States which distinguishes it from the systems of Europe is described by the phrase, coined in England, "the educational ladder." There is no limit in the American system to the possibility offered the individual pupil of going on to higher institutions. The boy or girl who has completed the elementary course can go on to the high school and from the high school to the college and university. This is not true anywhere in Europe. There the school systems are sharply divided into two wholly different and distinct lines of advancement. The children of the common people go to one school; the children of the aristocracy and richer classes go to a different school. The school for the common people is limited in time and opportunity, and does not lead into the universities. Thus the *Volksschule* of Germany, which gave instruction before the war to 92 per cent of the total school population, is an eight-year school, teaching only the common branches. The pupil who enters the *Volksschule* cannot look forward to entering any one of the professions or any civil-service position. He cannot be transferred from the upper grades of this common school into the secondary school. The common school of Germany is a social instrument for the perpetuation of a caste system. The common people know their place because they learn it when they enter school.

The European school for the aristocracy, on the other hand, is organized from its earliest years with a view to preparing its pupils for the higher callings. It is difficult for the American to understand how distinct this school is from the common school. The term "secondary school" is sometimes applied in educational writings to both the high school of the United States and the aristocratic schools of Europe. But the secondary school of Europe is entirely different from our high school. It takes little children in the lower grades and carries them through. Thus the German *Gymnasium* takes boys of the age of six. These are received into what is called a *Vorschule*, or preliminary school. After three years in the preliminary school the pupil begins his nine-year course in preparation for the university. In some of the states of the German Empire the pupil may be transferred into the *Gymnasium* from the earliest grades of the common school, but from this point on there is no commerce whatsoever, in teaching staff, in course of study, or in pupil constituency, between the common school and the school of the aristocracy. The division in France is quite as strict. In England transfer in the later years of the common-school course can be made, but only on the basis of examinations.

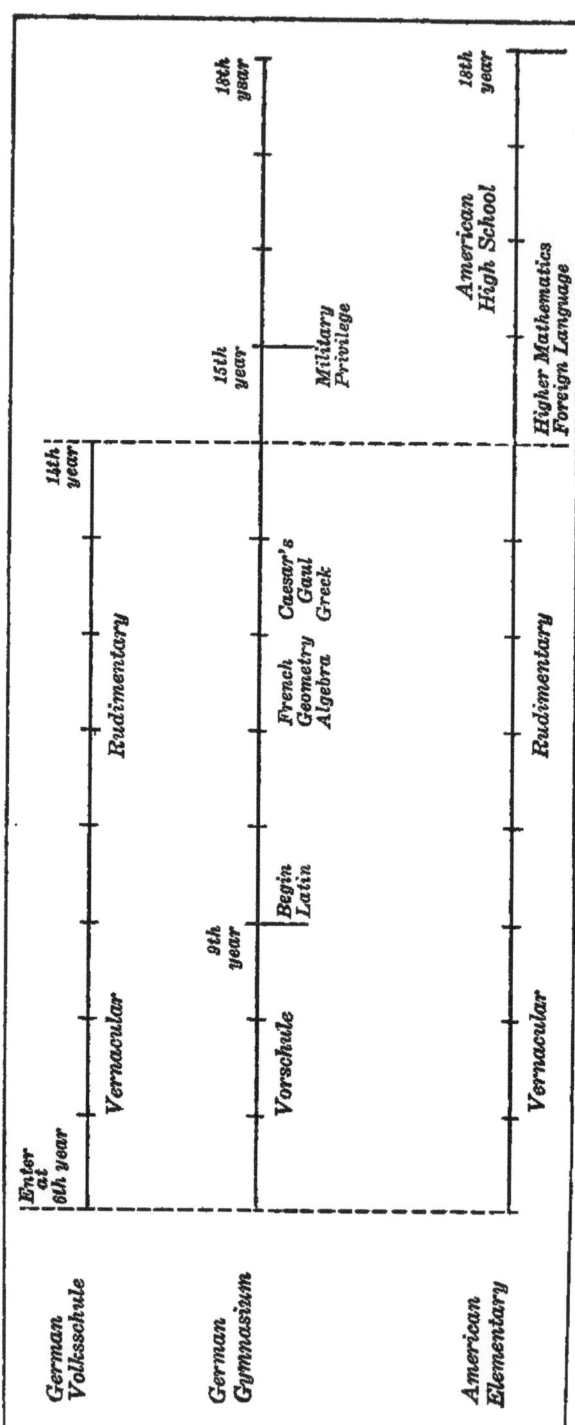

Fig. 3. Diagram showing the organization of German schools and American schools

The subdivisions of the lines indicate a year in each case.

Certain of the important items of the curriculum are set down under the years in which they are first introduced.

The social consequences of such a division within the school system need no detailed exposition. The hard-and-fast lines of caste are drawn very deep in any country where the boys and girls are marked from the beginning of their training by separation in opportunity.

Influence of European Schools on the Educational System of This Country

It is not enough that we should see this contrast, however; we must learn its fuller meaning by looking into the history of our own school system. The fact is that we have not broken entirely away from the traditions of Europe. Our elementary school was borrowed directly from the *Volksschule* of Germany, and many of the readjustments which we are making to-day are nothing less than efforts to shake ourselves free from that disjointed scheme of education.

The time of this borrowing of the German *Volksschule* is clearly marked in our history. In the first three decades of the nineteenth century American schools were at a low level of development. A vivid picture of conditions in 1801 can be given by quoting from one of the earliest school reports that we have. The superintendent of the city of Taunton, Massachusetts, in a recent report reproduced this interesting historical document, of which we may quote certain sections in order to show the kind of school organization which prevailed at that date.

REPORT OF THE VISITING COMMITTEE OF TAUNTON IN 1801

> The committee chosen by the town to inspect the schools beg leave to report their situation and examination. . . .
>
> January 6th, 1801. Your committee visited a school kept in Rueben Richmond's house instructed by Mrs. Nabby Williams of 32 scholars. This school appeared in an uncultivated state the greater part of the scholars.
>
> On the 26 of Feb., visited Mrs. Nabby Williams' school the second time and found that the scholars had made great proficiency in reading, spelling, writing and some in the grammar of the English language.
>
> Nov. 10th, the committee visited and examined two Schools just opened; one kept in a school house, near Baylies works, of the number of 40 scholars, instructed by Mr. Philip Lee. This School we found to have made but small proficiency in reading, spelling and writing, and to be kept only six or seven weeks; upon inquiry why it should be taught no longer, we were informed that the ratio of school money for this School was and had been usually expended in paying the Master both for his service and board, and in purchasing the fire wood which is contrary to the usual custom of the town.
>
> The other School, visited the same day, was kept near John

Reed's consisting of the number of between 30 and 40 Scholars instructed by Mr. William Reed; This School, being formed into regular classes, appeared to have made a good and pleasing proficiency in reading, spelling, writing, some in arithmetic and others in the Grammar of the English language. This School's share of school money is expended to pay the Master for his service only, so that the School will be continued three months.

On the 8th day of December they visited a School kept in a School house near Seth Hodges, in number 30 Scholars instructed by Mr. John Dunbar. This School appeared in a good way of learning, and to be kept four months.

* * * * *

On the 22nd of December your Committee visited two more Schools just opened, one in a School house near Samuel Pett's of the number of 40 scholars instructed by Mr. Rufus Dean, and to be kept three months. This School appeared to be in a promising way of learning in reading spelling and writing and to be regularly taught.

The other School is kept in the home of Mr. Paul Chase and taught by Mr. Nicolas Stephens, consisting of 30 Scholars, and appears quite in a good way of learning especially in Spelling for scarcely a word passed a scholar misspelled, in writing some did very well and others in arithmetic appeared attentive.

January 8th, 1801 visited two Schools for the first time, one in the home of Mr. William Hodges of the number of 37 Scholars, instructed by Mr. Lovet Tisdale, the other in the home of Mr. Daniel Burt, of the number of 25 Scholars, instructed by Mr. Benjamin Tubbs. These Schools appeared in good order and attentive to their learning.

* * * * *

Feby. 26th, visited Mr. Dean's School 2 times, the Scholars were crowded into a small room, the air was exceedingly noxious. Many children were obliged to tarry at home for want of room and though the school was kept only a few weeks they were deprived of its advantages. A want of books was the complaint. The committee were anxiously desirous that this evil might have a remedy and were of opinion it may be easily done. The Scholars appeared to increase in knowledge & claim our approbation.

March 5th, visited two schools, one kept at Mr. Aaron Pratt's of the number of 30 scholars instructed by Mr. Philip Drown. This school appeared quite unimproved and uncultivated in reading and spelling, some of them did better in writing. This uncultivated state did not appear to be from a fault in the children but, as

> your committee were informed, from the disadvantage of having had masters illegally qualified for their instruction; of which class is their present master unauthorized by law.[7]

The situation here described was typical of all the settled towns. How much worse it was in sparsely settled districts one can easily imagine. Briefly put, one can say that up to 1830 schools throughout the country held short sessions in the middle of the winter when the pupils were otherwise unoccupied with home demands. There was no supervision except by visiting committees, no course of study, little or no material equipment, and small outlook for a higher education.

Adoption of the German Model

During the decade 1830-1840 there was an effort, especially in Massachusetts under the leadership of Horace Mann and in Michigan under John Pierce, to improve the common schools. In an illuminating historical treatise on this subject Mr. F. F. Bunker has reproduced some of the evidences that the changes made at that time in the schools of America were largely influenced by German models. The following quotations indicate how the movement began:

> Charles Brooks, a man whose influence in Massachusetts was great, and who may be said to have prepared the way for the work of Horace Mann, did very much to disseminate knowledge respecting the Prussian system. He was primarily interested in establishing a normal school after the Prussian model, yet, during the campaign which he carried on for this purpose between the years 1835 and 1838 he did not limit himself to the consideration of the normal school alone, but sought to acquaint the people with the details of the German system of elementary education as well. His account of the return trip from England, which he made in company with Dr. H. Julius, of Hamburg, indicates the esteem in which he held the Prussian system:
>
> A passage of 41 days from Liverpool to New York (with Dr. Julius) gave me time to ask all manner of questions concerning the noble, philosophical, and practical system of Prussian elementary education. He explained it like a sound scholar and a pious Christian. If you will allow the phrase, I fell in love with the Prussian system, and it seemed to possess me like a missionary angel.

* * * * *

Just at the time that Charles Brooks was laboring so diligently to incorporate in the Massachusetts system the results of Prussian experience, another man, John D. Pierce, in Michigan, also an enthusiastic believer in the preëminence of the Prussian organization, was laying the foundation for an educational system in his own State and building into it the best features of Prussian practice. It was mainly because of his suggestions to the chairman of the committee on education

[7] Reprinted in the Report of the School Committee of the City of Taunton, Massachusetts, for the Year Ending December 31, 1915, pp. 68-73.

in the convention that framed the State government in 1835 that the article in the constitution respecting education was framed and provision made for the office of superintendent of public instruction. Mr. Pierce was appointed to the superintendency in 1836 and at once began the work of preparing a plan for a complete school system.

Before framing his recommendations, which were submitted in 1837 and which were approved for the most part, he visited the schools of New England, New York, and New Jersey. Prior to this, however, he had learned of the Prussian system through an English translation of Cousin's report. This report of Cousin's was first made known to the English-speaking people by Sir William Hamilton, who, in the Edinburgh Review, July, 1833, commended the report highly and quoted at considerable length therefrom. The next year (1834) that part of the report which treated of Prussian practice was translated into English by Mrs. Sarah Austin and appeared in London. A New York edition of the same translation was issued in 1835 and widely distributed. It was a copy of this edition which, falling into Mr. Pierce's hands, profoundly influenced him in framing the system he later submitted to the Michigan Legislature. In describing his entrance into public life Mr. Pierce speaks of this circumstance:

> About this time (1835) Cousin's report of the Prussian system, made to the French minister of public instruction, came into my hands and it was read with much interest. Sitting one pleasant afternoon upon a log on the hill north of where the courthouse at Marshall now stands, Gen. Crary (chairman of the convention committee on education) and myself discussed for a long time the fundamental principles which were deemed important for the convention to adopt in laying the foundations of our State. The subject of education was a theme of special interest. It was agreed, if possible, that it should make a distinct branch of the government, and that the constitution ought to provide for an officer who should have this whole matter in charge and thus keep its importance perpetually before the public mind.

Mr. Pierce's indebtedness to Prussia for many of the ideas which he worked out in the system which he organized is thus set forth by a later superintendent of the Michigan system, Francis W. Shearman, who, writing in 1852, said:

> The system of public instruction which was intended to be established by the framers of the constitution (Michigan), the conception of the office, its province, its powers, and duties were derived from Prussia.[8]. . .

RESULTS OF THE ADOPTION OF THE GERMAN EXAMPLE.

It is a striking fact that all this borrowing had to do with the common school. Nor was it inappropriate at that period that emphasis should be on the school for

[8] Frank Forest Bunker, "Reorganization of the Public School System," in *Bulletin No. 8,* United States Bureau of Education, 1916, pp. 21-23.

the common people. In the young states there was relatively little higher education, and the need was great for an improvement of the common schools.

The consequences of this borrowing were momentous for our history. There are two characteristics which our American schools of elementary grade took on in imitation of the German model, which characteristics have determined in large measure their subsequent development down to the present. In the first place, the German common school was strictly a vernacular school, and, in the second place, it dealt only with rudimentary subjects. The *Gymnasium*, or the school for the aristocracy, was not a vernacular school. Latin and Greek and modern foreign languages were taught in even the lower grades of the *Gymnasium*. Furthermore, the *Gymnasium* alone taught such "higher" subjects as the higher mathematics, while the common school confined itself exclusively to arithmetic as the rudimentary branch of mathematics. In point of time the German *Volksschule*, as noted above, conducted a course eight years in length. The pupils completed this course at fourteen years of age, when they were confirmed in the Church.

The common school was the institution which America borrowed in 1830-1840. The common school was set up in the United States as an eight-year school devoted exclusively to the vernacular and to rudimentary subjects. But the American system developed. The length of the school year increased, and the number of pupils who are ambitious to go on into the higher schools has enormously increased. In 1917 we were told by the Commissioner of Education of the United States that more than 1,300,000 of the young people in this country were in the high schools. Even now, however, the eight-year vernacular rudimentary school of Germany has its stamp on our American life. As a rule our American schools do not permit a pupil to study foreign languages in the lower school, even when we know that he is going on to high school. The general exclusion of languages is due to the tradition that the elementary school is a vernacular school, not to inability on the part of pupils to learn languages. We will not permit algebra to be taught in the elementary school, because algebra is not a rudimentary subject. To be sure, we have had a hard time trying to keep arithmetic in its position of exclusive domination of the elementary course. We have grafted into the arithmetic all kinds of economic information about insurance and banks and foreign exchange. We have exercised our ingenuity to the limit in inventing examples of a complicated sort in order to keep the pupils in the upper grades at work in arithmetic. But through it all we have been kept from a rational development by adherence to the tradition of the German common school,—the tradition which treats higher subjects as the exclusive property of the aristocracy.

The Reorganization of American Schools

The day of reform is, however, at hand. Social pressure has gradually been making it evident to all that in America the elementary school cannot be a caste school. The people are demanding that pupils who are to have only a limited schooling be admitted to some of the higher subjects. Furthermore, there are enough pupils who go on into the high school to make it evident that the American scheme should be organized not with a view to distinguishing between the elementary school and the high school, but with a view to combining the two into a continuous institution.

Within the last five years there has spread rapidly a movement known as the junior-high-school movement, or the intermediate-school movement. This is essentially a reform of the seventh, eighth, and ninth grades, and consists, first of all, in the introduction into the course of study of material which formerly belonged to the high school. In the second place, this movement recognizes the maturity of pupils in a variety of ways. It adopts a form of discipline which throws responsibility on them. It departmentalizes the teaching and offers electives, thus securing the advantages of specialization. The movement promises to reorganize our whole school system in such a way as to give us a new kind of national education. America has at the present moment a closer approximation to a continuous educational ladder than any other country, but the ladder needs a little splicing. With the present enthusiasm for national development the splicing is likely to be facilitated.

Origin of the High School

The foregoing statements extracted from the history of the elementary school may be supplemented by references to the history of the high school. The first schools of secondary grade in this country were patterned after the classical secondary schools of England. The Boston Latin School and the Hopkins Grammar School of New Haven are examples of early foundations of the kind in question. These schools were vestibules to the colleges, and the boys who attended them—for they were schools for boys—were looking forward to one of the learned professions, usually, in the early days, to the clergy.

The Latin school charged tuition, as do all the European secondary schools to-day. It was an exclusive school. It was not a part of the popular movement toward general education. In an important sense it was a vocational school and illustrates the general fact of history that higher schools always had a vocational motive back of their organization, whereas the people's schools of elementary grade were at first always missionary enterprises intended to spread religious training rather than vocational training.

Parallel with the Latin school and growing out of an entirely different motive was another institution which was very much more genuinely American in its character. This was the academy. The academy was often a boarding school to which boys and girls alike went for an extension of their education. Later the village in which the academy was situated took it over or made arrangements to pay for all the pupils, and it became a free academy.

There were some other experiments in the extension of school opportunities. In New England, the oldest and economically most forward section of the country, a ninth grade was added to the elementary school. There are to-day in Maine, and to some extent in other New England states, elementary schools with a nine-year course. But the ninth grade never succeeded. It was cramped by the German definition of the elementary school as a vernacular and rudimentary school. To try to spend nine years rather than eight on the three R's was not productive. The academy, on the other hand, knew no limits of this kind. It reveled in such subjects as French and music and literature and history.

At last the Latin school and the academy fused in the American high school, and the high school took its place at the end of the elementary-school course. The influence of the academy in determining this form of organization was very great, for the academy was from the first connected with the elementary school, while the Latin school was in its early days an institution quite separate from the common school both in its organization and purpose.

Education of Girls

These sketches of school history could be supplemented by other discussions. Perhaps it will be well to comment briefly on the unique American attitude toward the education of girls. In Europe girls have only very recently been given opportunities of higher education, and even now the opportunity is limited to the few. We have undoubtedly made the mistake in this country, in our enthusiasm for equality of opportunity, of administering to girls a course of study originally designed for their brothers. In due time we shall learn how to give to girls an education suited to their needs, but there can never be any question among us about the wisdom of a higher education for women.

Higher Education Free

It has also been noted incidentally that with us all education is free. This has not been attained without much discussion and much legislation. We shall later have an opportunity to treat more at length the fiscal policies of American schools. At this point it is enough to note that American schools are what they are because they are free.

An interesting contrast can be drawn here between the practice in England and in the United States. In England vast sums of money make a free education accessible to certain selected individuals. The higher schools are not free to all comers, as ours are, but a bright boy—it is usually only the boy—who can pass a competitive examination is given a stipend, which provides his tuition and often enough more to get books and, if necessary, pay for transportation. The English theory is that it is the duty of the public to pay for selected boys, but not for boys in general. To the American it seems a little hazardous to select the leaders of the nation by competitive examinations given to eleven-year-old boys. On the other hand, the English think of our plan as wasteful because we postpone selection longer than they think we should. The contrast here pointed out is enough to draw our attention to the unique attitude of American schools, which are free to all and in this sense far more democratic than the higher schools of any European country.

American Public Schools Secular

Finally, we may point out that our schools are secular. Some of our own fellow countrymen do not believe in secular schools. We are familiar with the practice of organizing parochial schools. France and England have in recent years purchased secularization of their schools after long and bitter controversy. Germany gives instruction in religion as an important part of every course of study. In some sections of Germany the distinction between religious beliefs is carried into the school organization in such a way that one finds public schools set aside for the children of this and that sect. In all schools the pupil has a right to instruction in his own particular type of religion.

In the United States the complete democratization of the schools has been possible because differences in religion have been rigidly excluded. There is a common body of knowledge which can be administered in public schools without involving religion. The decision for such a separation was made long ago in this country and is one of the characteristic facts in our school system as well as in our general civic life.

The School System and its Domination of the Teacher

The facts outlined in this chapter ought to create in the mind of the reader a vivid notion of what is meant by the words "school system." The schools of America or any other country have a kind of colossal personality. The teacher who teaches a fifth grade or a sixth grade or a high-school class does not determine the character of the education given at these points in the system. To be sure, the teacher can do his or her work effectively or inefficiently. The special methods employed may be well or ill adapted to their ends. But above and beyond the individual teacher is the system which controls the pupil's progress in many subtle ways and determines all the main lines of his training. The teacher who would succeed must understand this larger influence. Especially is it necessary that the teacher who aims to contribute to the rational development of the system through the scientific study of detailed problems become acquainted with the present characteristics of the system and comprehend something of the conditions which have produced these characteristics.

EXERCISES AND READINGS

Among textbooks there are such striking differences that the student will be able after even a superficial analysis to see that their authors had very different ideas about the use of texts. Find a textbook which is intended to give the pupil a start in a study rather than a complete discussion of the subject. Find a text which is intended to be learned rather than merely read. What parts of a textbook are addressed to the teacher and constitute teaching devices rather than material for students?

Contrast the ways in which different teachers use textbooks. Are there teachers who neglect the book very largely? When should a teacher lecture? Find specific examples of lessons which can best be taught (1) by questions and answers, (2) by written work, and (3) by lectures.

With regard to a given high school it is important to find out when it was established. What was its first course of study?

With regard to courses for girls, it is interesting to inquire how far classes in an elective system are chosen by boys and how far by girls. Why are conditions as they are?

The foregoing questions are asked on the assumption that the contrasts presented in the chapter are of value only when they make students keenly aware of the facts in their own environment. The facts of history are valuable chiefly because of the light they throw on the present.

BROWN, E. E. Making of our Middle Schools. Longmans, Green, & Co. This is the only history of American secondary schools.

BUNKER, F. F. "Reorganization of the Public School System," in *Bulletin No. 8*, United States Bureau of Education, 1916. This shows how our present school system was organized.

FARRINGTON, F. E. French Secondary Schools. Longmans, Green, & Co.

FARRINGTON, F. E. The Public Primary School System of France. Teachers College.

JUDD, C. H. "The Training of Teachers in England, Scotland, and Germany," in *Bulletin No. 35*, United States Bureau of Education, 1914.

MONROE, W. S. "Development of Arithmetic as a School Subject," in *Bulletin No. 10*, United States Bureau of Education, 1917. This bulletin tells of the origin of the present methods of teaching arithmetic.

PARKER, S. C. The History of Modern Elementary Education. Ginn and Company. This is a very good summary of the facts regarding the development of American schools.

CHAPTER III

EDUCATION AS A PUBLIC NECESSITY

The primitive attitude one of neglect. Compulsory education. Compulsion of communities. Later stages of compulsory legislation. American education to 1850. Compulsory attendance. Obstacles to enforcement of compulsory attendance. Newer legislation recognizing complexity of problems of attendance. Supervision a necessary corollary to compulsion. Higher education and public control. Public control adequate only when directed by science. Fiscal problem typical. Exercises and readings.

The Primitive Attitude One of Neglect

One does not have to go far from the door of any educational institution to find people who look on reading and writing—to say nothing of higher forms of education—as luxuries rather than necessities. There is the parent who is willing to take his child out of school for the sake of the wage which the child can earn. There is the negligent parent, often himself illiterate, who is utterly unconcerned about the education of his sons and daughters. Another kind of example appears in the boy or girl who goes out into the trades after a limited schooling and fails to keep up the type of intellectual activity which was cultivated in the school. Many a child who has been taught through years of instruction how to read makes very little use of his training in mature life.

An appeal to the history of civilization reveals the fact that there was a time when the opinion prevailed that education was unnecessary for the common man. The earliest schools were for the aristocracy and for the professional classes. Schools for all the people are of comparatively recent date.

Compulsory Education

In striking contrast with this attitude of neglect and indifference is the fact that to-day there are laws in all the civilized countries of the world compelling children of every social grade to attend school. Society as a whole does not share the slight esteem of reading exhibited by the man who takes his child out of school. Indeed, society has gone so far as to set aside that man's judgment and to assume control of the child to the extent of insisting that the rudiments of an education shall be made universal.

Society still leaves it to the individual to decide whether he is to study higher branches. One may take algebra or not as one elects, but not so with arithmetic. The common interests of our common life dictate that everyone shall be able to count and to make accurate numerical statements. People must know some arithmetic; they must be able to read, or they are a menace to public comfort and safety.

Compulsion of Communities

The full acknowledgment of the fact that education is a public necessity has developed gradually. History shows us the steps by which this fact has been recognized in legislative action. The first step was the adoption of laws requiring communities to provide schools. We may put the matter in terms of contemporary conditions by referring to communities which would to-day be backward in this matter if it were not for state control. Thus there are sparsely settled districts or poor districts which cannot afford good schools, or, indeed, any kind of a school. The state is vitally interested in seeing to it that the untoward conditions in these regions do not deprive the children of an education. In the later years of their lives the children from these districts will surely scatter to other parts of the state. They will be less productive than they would have been if they had been educated. It is much more economical for the state as a whole to take a hand in the training of the children than to have to support even a small number of dependent adults during the unproductive period of later life when the consequences of poor schooling appear.

In some cases the delinquency of a community is due not to economic stress but to shortsighted frugality. Here again the higher authority of the larger community must take control and force the backward group to give the children such training as will bring them to reasonable productivity.

The earliest legislation on this matter is of the type which was quoted in the last chapter, where reference was made to the Connecticut law of 1650. Such legislation was addressed to the community and enjoined on it the obligation to provide schools.

Later Stages of Compulsory Legislation

Such compulsion of the community was followed, but at a much later date, by legislation compelling the child to attend school; and finally the period was reached in the midst of which we live to-day, when the state is taking a hand in the supervision of schools for the purpose of insuring as high and as uniform a grade of education as it can afford.

American Education to 1850

The first period of our national life, during which we were very gradually evolving the conception of a need for public education and were setting up the requirement of schools in every community, extended down to the decade before the Civil War. Professor Cubberley has given a very illuminating description of this period, from which we may quote the following extracts:

> During the early decades of the nineteenth century, schools

and the means of education made little progress. There were among the founders of our states certain far-seeing men who wished for general public education, but it was well along toward the middle of the century before these men represented more than a hopeful minority in most of our states, and in the South little was done until after the Civil War. . . .

To be illiterate was no reproach, and it was possible to follow many pursuits successfully without having received any other education than the education of daily work and experience. A large proportion of the people felt that those who desired an education should pay for it. As the Rhode Island farmer expressed it to Henry Barnard in 1844, it would be as sensible to propose to take his plough away from him to plough his neighbor's field as to take his money to educate his neighbor's child. Others felt that at most free education should be extended only to the children of the poor, and for the rudiments of learning only. Still others felt that all forms of education would be conducted best if turned over to the various religious and educational societies of the time. A system of public instruction maintained by general taxation, such as we to-day enjoy, would not only have been declared unnecessary, but would have been stoutly resisted as well. The best schools, and often the only schools, were private schools supported by the tuition fees of those who could afford to use them, and most of these were more or less directly under church control.

Not until after the beginning of the nineteenth century was education regarded at all as a legitimate public function. . . .

The different humanitarian movements which arose after 1820, and which, among other things, demanded public tax-supported schools for all, had not as yet made themselves felt. The people were poor, and indifferent as to education.

Gradually, and only after great effort, this condition of apathy and indifference was changed to one of active interest, though the change took place but slowly, and differed in point of time in different parts of the country. The Lancastrian system of monitorial instruction (by which a single teacher with the assistance of his best students, called monitors, taught hundreds of pupils), introduced into this country from England about 1806, for the first time made an elementary school training for all seem possible, from a financial point of view. . . .

The idea that free education was a right, and that universal education was a necessity, began to be urged and to find acceptance. The land grants of Congress to the new states for the benefit of common schools greatly stimulated the movement. The published reports of those who had visited Pestalozzi's school in

Switzerland, and had examined the new state school system in Prussia, were extensively read. The moral and economic advantages of schools were set forth at length in resolutions, speeches, pamphlets, magazines, and books.

* * * * *

Just when this change took place cannot be definitely stated. Roughly speaking, it began about 1825 and was accomplished by 1850 in the Northern states. It was a gradual change rather than a sudden one, though rapid advances were at times made. The movement everywhere was greatly stimulated by the educational revival inaugurated by Horace Mann in Massachusetts in 1837. In the Southern states, with one or two exceptions, little was accomplished until after the Civil War and the Reconstruction Period were over. Almost everywhere it took place only after prolonged agitation, and ofttimes only after a bitter struggle. The indifference of legislatures, the unwillingness of taxpayers to assume the burdens of general taxation, the small sense of local responsibility, the satisfaction with existing conditions, the old aristocratic conception of education, the pauper and charity-school idea, and frequently the opposition of denominational and private schools,—all of these had to be met and overcome. The referendum was tried in a number of states, and sometimes more than once; in others, the question of free schools became a vital political issue. . . .

By 1850, the principle of tax-supported schools had been generally accepted in all of the Northern states, and the beginnings of free schools made in some of the Southern states. Six state normal schools had been established, a number of states had provided for State Superintendents of Common Schools and for ex-officio State Boards of Education, and the movement for state control of education had begun. It may be said that it had not become a settled conviction with a majority of the people that the provision of some form of free education was a duty of the state, and that such education contributed in a general way, though just how was not at that time clear, to the moral uplift of the people, to a higher civic virtue, and to increased economic returns to the state. A new conception of free public education as a birthright of the child on the one hand, and as an exercise of the state's inherent right to self-preservation and improvement on the other, had taken the place of the earlier conception of schools as merely a coöperative effort, based on economy, and for the instruction of youth merely in the rudiments of learning.[9]

[9] Ellwood P. Cubberley, "Changing Conceptions of Education," Riverside Educational Monograph, pp. 27-35. Houghton Mifflin Company, 1909.

Compulsory Attendance

The second stage in the development of a public educational system was reached when the states began to see that children must be compelled to go to school. In 1852 Massachusetts passed the first compulsory-education law. In 1864 the District of Columbia followed. In 1867 came Vermont; in 1871, New Hampshire, Michigan, and Washington.[10] From that time on the other states have been enacting such laws. The Southern states, which before the Civil War had practically no public-school system and after the war were economically depressed, were the last to pass compulsory-attendance acts.

Without attempting to deal with the remoter historical development of such legislation, it is possible to show by reference to contemporary reports the difficulties in securing and enforcing such laws. Two quotations from the reports of the Commissioner of Education of the United States indicate the present conditions with regard to compulsory attendance. The report of 1915 makes the following statement:

> The year 1915 was a notable year for the cause of compulsory school attendance. Four States—South Carolina, Florida, Alabama, and Texas—which did not have laws on the subject, enacted laws at the last sessions of their legislatures. This new extension of the compulsory attendance area carries required attendance at school into the section where it has hitherto met the most stubborn resistance; the area now practically includes the entire United States, Georgia and Mississippi alone remaining without laws on the subject.[11]

The report of 1916 supplements this statement as follows:

> Efforts were made to secure the enactment of attendance laws in both of these States [Georgia and Mississippi] in 1916, and in the former the effort was successful. The new law of Georgia, in brief, requires the attendance of every child between 8 and 14 years of age for four months each year. Exemptions from this requirement apply to those who have completed the fourth grade of school work; those upon whom needy members of the family are dependent for support; those whose parents or guardians are unable to provide the necessary books and clothing, unless the same are otherwise provided; those whose services are needed for farm emergencies; those who are mentally or physically incapable; and those who reside more than 3 miles from school. Boards of education of counties and of cities and towns are intrusted with the enforcement of the law in their respective jurisdictions.[12]

Obstacles to Enforcement of Compulsory Attendance

[10] Report of the Commissioner of Education for 1888-1889, p. 471.
[11] Report of the Commissioner of Education for 1915, Vol. I, p. 12.
[12] Report of the Commissioner of Education for 1916, Vol. I, p. 24.

The enactment of laws is only one step in securing attendance. Especially is there difficulty where local authorities are intrusted with the enforcement of the laws. The records of school operations in the Northern states show that compulsory education was not really enforced until in the '80's and later. The sort of difficulty encountered is clearly illustrated by a clipping from the *Statesman*, a daily paper of Austin, Texas, which sets forth the situation late in 1916 under the Texas law, which was then just beginning to be effective.

> The compulsory school attendance law will be effective during the coming year. The compulsory term of the first year of the law's operation will be three months, or 60 school days, and the board of trustees of each school has the authority to specify the months during which attendance shall be compulsory. The Austin City School Board has ruled that the compulsory term shall begin January 1.
>
> The matter of providing truant officers has not yet been dealt with, either by the City School Board or by the County Board of Education. The law provides $2 a day as remuneration to the truant officer for the time actually served by him. The City Superintendent believes that the logical procedure for the city will be to secure the services of the county probation officer, provided it is found practicable for him to take on the additional duties.
>
> The County Board of Education meets next Monday and will probably discuss this matter. It cannot act, however, except on the petition of fifty citizens. In case no such petition is presented, the County Superintendent says that it will devolve on each school principal to report to the County Superintendent those children who are not in school, and she can call on any peace officer to execute the law. It is not thought likely that the probation officer will find it possible to act as truant officer for the county.
>
> The reason why the beginning of the compulsory period was placed so late as January 1 is that many of the children likely to be affected—largely Mexicans and negroes—will be needed in the cotton patch during the fall. Also in the city, many poor boys and girls will be able to earn something during the Christmas holidays. There are serious objections to the plan, however, since the child who enters school so late in the session will be at a serious disadvantage, and the extra attention he will demand of the teacher will work a hardship on the other pupils. Moreover, in the city the school session is divided into two equal periods, the first of which ends only a month after the child is required to begin attendance. This will involve serious difficulties.
>
> The compulsory attendance law applies to children eight to fourteen years of age, with certain exceptions. The compulsory term the second year will be eighty days, the third year 100 days.

> Defective children are exempted; also rural children more than 2½ miles from a school, and on the written statement of a parent that the services of her child of twelve years or more who has reached the fourth grade are needed for the mother's support, such a child may be exempted.

Even a casual reading of this quotation calls attention to the fact that there is the keenest competition between employment and education. The modern industrial system finds children profitable for certain purposes and uses them. If society is to enforce its judgment that these children ought to be in school, that judgment will have to express itself in mandatory terms. The federal government has recently taken a hand in the matter. It is difficult or impossible in some states to get suitable legislation against the exploitation of child labor by unprincipled employers. State legislatures have too often shown themselves subservient to the dictates of such employers. In 1916 the Congress of the United States passed a law restricting child labor in all trades which produce commodities intended for use in interstate commerce. This federal law is another expression of the judgment of civilization that childhood is a period which should be devoted to education.

It is also shown in the Texas quotation that the machinery for keeping account of children is complicated. The ordinary school authorities cannot deal with the matter without adding attendance officers to their staff. These officers must be supplied with adequate information. This in turn calls for a special school census, because the ordinary national enumeration and even the state and city enumerations are not frequent nor complete enough. One of the most progressive of the New England states has recently adopted legislation looking to the creation of a more adequate system of records. This new law is described in the Commissioner's Report of 1916 as follows:

> In order to facilitate the enforcement of its attendance law, Massachusetts provided in 1916 for the registration of minors. City and town school committees are required under the new law to ascertain the name, age, and other essential facts respecting every child between 5 and 7, between 7 and 14, and between 14 and 16 years of age, and respecting minors over 16 years of age who cannot read and write. A card giving these data must be kept for every child or minor. The attendance officer is required to examine these cards and see that children attend school as required by law. Supervisory officers of private schools must within 30 days report the enrollment of children of compulsory attendance age, and when any child withdraws from school must report the same within 10 days.[13]

Newer Legislation recognizing Complexity of Problems of Attendance

Definitions of the period of compulsory attendance are usually based on the

[13] Report of the Commissioner of Education for 1916, Vol. I, p. 25.

number of grades in the elementary school. Laws commonly specify the age of beginning as six and fix the age of fourteen as the upper limit. Sometimes the age of beginning is higher. For example, the 1915 law in South Carolina is thus described by the Commissioner of Education:

> The 1915 act of South Carolina is a local option law. Upon petition of a majority of the qualified electors of a district or "aggregation of districts," the county board of education is required to declare the law in effect in such district or districts, or, on petition of one-fourth of the electors, an election must be held to determine the matter. All children between the ages of 8 and 14 who are physically able and who reside within 2½ miles of school are required to attend for the full term, or at least for four months. Children between the ages of 14 and 16 are required to attend unless lawfully employed or if they can not read and write simple English sentences.[14]

The provisions of this law show how complicated is the social situation with which the community deals in its compulsory laws. The assumption that it is simple to define the necessary schooling for a future citizen is easily refuted by a little consideration.

In the first place, pupils do not go through the elementary schools without interruption; hence the mere specifying of a given age such as fourteen is not enough. Non-promotion, or the removal of the family to another town, or some misfortune such as sickness may delay the pupil so that he reaches the age of fourteen in one of the lower grades. Intelligent legislation is, accordingly, taking this into account. In some states it is required that the child shall finish a certain grade,—usually the sixth,—otherwise he must go to school until he is sixteen. Or, as in South Carolina, he must stay in school until he has acquired the ability to read and write.

In this connection a complication in legislation may be pointed out which is of profound social significance. The definition of adulthood which is given in labor legislation has usually set the age at which a boy may be regularly employed, at sixteen, while the education law of the same state often requires school attendance only up to fourteen. The result is that the youth between fourteen and sixteen has been sadly at sea. He has not had the judgment to stay in school after he was freed by the compulsory-education law, and he has not had the opportunity to enter on regular employment. He has therefore drifted about, working at odd jobs and learning the bad habits of the unproductively employed.

Supervision a Necessary Corollary to Compulsion

Such considerations as these lead to a clear understanding of the reasons why the state is undertaking in increasing degree the supervision of the details of school work. It is not enough that communities should open schools or that pupils should be compelled to attend; the quality of education must be such as to justify the expenditure of public money and the investment of the pupils' time and ener-

[14] Report of the Commissioner of Education for 1915, Vol. I, pp. 12-13.

gy in the business of schooling.

Compulsory education implies obligations both on the side of the pupil and on the side of the community. It would manifestly be inequitable to compel children to go to school if the community failed to provide suitable, safe, and sanitary buildings. Because local wisdom in such matters is often limited, and local judgment biased by considerations of expense, the state has dealt with the matter both through general legislation and through vigorous inspection.

In like fashion it would evidently be indefensible to require pupils to go to school and use inferior textbooks or be instructed by unqualified teachers. Here again the larger community has found it necessary to take a hand. State adoption of textbooks is not uncommon, and state certification of teachers is becoming universal.

More important, perhaps, than anything else is the choice of the subject-matter of instruction. To the ordinary man, as indicated in an earlier chapter, subject-matter seems to choose itself; but it does not. Nor can the local community be expected to know the larger needs of its children. A very striking example of this is furnished by the fact that the federal government has recently set aside vast sums of money for the purpose of subsidizing and directing agricultural and industrial education. The theory back of this action is that even the states, and more certainly cities and towns, are unable to deal with the problems of adequate training for practical life. The largest unit, namely, the whole country, is so much concerned with the efficiency of its citizens in industrial matters that it has undertaken to subsidize and supervise this phase of education.

Such examples make clear the principle under which state laws define the minimum course of study and under which state departments of education are erected to supervise the administration of the course of study. They make clear also the justification for the statement that the control of education ought to be increasingly centralized.

Higher Education and Public Control

There is one aspect of the educational demands of a community which is usually thought of as lying entirely outside the scope of the compulsory-education law. It is ordinarily thought that higher education is a purely individual matter. In the older parts of the country the state has been slow to provide higher schools. Colleges have often been provided for by denominational organizations or by purely private endowments. Even in the field of higher education, however, it is becoming evident that public interests are involved. In medicine, in law, and in training of teachers, the state has been obliged to assume increasingly supervisory powers, and of late the financial provision for such education has been more and more accepted as a public obligation. The result of this evolution is the broader provision out of the public purse for all kinds and all stages of education.

Public Control Adequate only when directed by Science

Enough has been said to show that much is involved in the establishment of a public-school system. The problems which arise in the teaching of pupils are intricate; but when one thinks of education as a public necessity, to be purchased with public funds and to be administered in the interests of the broader community, one sees new justification for the demand that all school problems be managed with wisdom. This demand can be met only when school problems are made subjects of exhaustive scientific study.

Fiscal Problem Typical

The subsequent chapters will take up briefly the problems involved in organizing a school system. The first and most general problem is one of securing funds for the maintenance of the schools. It will be well to reiterate the statement with which the first chapter began. The pupil seldom thinks of costs. The teacher usually overlooks the fact that the community is interested in what schools cost. Yet funds are a prime necessity in organizing a public-school system. We turn, accordingly, to fiscal problems as among the first and most concrete examples of educational problems which must be studied by one who would be intelligent about the school system.

EXERCISES AND READINGS

Whose duty is it to enforce school attendance in the community in which you live? When was the last school census taken? What is the ordinary ratio of school population to the total population? What percentage of children of high-school age are in high school? What percentage of eighth-grade pupils go on to high school? What percentage of high-school graduates go to college?

The ordinary reader will perhaps find it difficult to get answers to these questions. He should make himself a student of the reports of the Commissioner of Education of the United States and of the superintendent of schools in some city which publishes an annual report.

From some school record find out what percentage of enrolled pupils attend school regularly.

If there is a school nurse or a school physician, find out what time in the year is most likely to exhibit small attendance. Verify the finding from the school record.

What substitutes for attendance on public schools are permitted? How many children in the town attend schools other than public schools, and why?

Ayres, L. P. Child Accounting in the Public Schools. Survey Committee of the Cleveland Foundation. (Copies may be secured from the Russell Sage Foundation.) This is one of the volumes of the Cleveland survey and is the only brief statement of the whole matter that there is.

Reports of the Commissioner of Education should be studied as suggested above.

CHAPTER IV

INVESTING PUBLIC MONEY IN A NEW GENERATION

The cost of educating an individual. Total school expenditures in the United States. Cost a determining consideration in school organization. Relation of school expenditures to other public expenses. Urgent demands for economy and efficiency. Expenditures in relation to wealth. Costs of different levels of education. Costs of different subjects of instruction. Costs of classes of different sizes. Salaries. Books and supplies. The meaning of financial organization and educational accounting. Exercises and readings.

The Cost of Educating an Individual

We all know something about how much the family invests in its sons and daughters. The provision made by the father for his children is recognized as an expression of the parent's willingness to give to the second generation as good a start in life as the family can afford. We are less likely to realize the extent to which the community is drawing on its material resources for a similar purpose. The city of Chicago—to choose a single example—gives to each boy or girl who goes through elementary school and high school an aggregate of six hundred and thirty dollars. If a child were notified to go to the city hall when he is eighteen years of age and receive this sum of money, we should recognize what it means for a community to pay for the education of its new generation. We should understand that the children of a city are its wards. When the matter is obscured by the complexities of the social machinery through which this bonus is distributed, we lose sight of the magnitude and directness of public expenditures for education.

The example of Chicago can be pursued even further. The sum stated above is too small, for it is based on the annual expenditures for conducting the schools; it does not include the large outlay for school buildings and for real estate which the city is called upon to make in order to provide rooms in which the education may be given. Nor do the figures cover irregularities. If the pupil does not get through each year's work in regular order, the city is often called upon to provide more than the normal number of years of training.

One further item is to be added to the calculations above given, in the case of those who go to the city normal college. For these teachers-in-training the city pays an additional two hundred and twenty-eight dollars a year, raising the aggregate expended on such a student to nearly eleven hundred dollars.[15] Such students are typical of a vast number of young people who are attending at public expense state normal schools, state universities, and public technical schools. Indeed, even where students attend endowed institutions and pay tuition, the actual cost of their education is commonly borne in very large measure by the community, which in the last analysis is the source of the endowment.

Total School Expenditures in the United States

Another method of presenting the facts is to deal with totals. The figures which represent the expenditure for public education in the United States are so large that the individual who reads them usually passes them over with little comprehension unless he is given some background for comparison. Perhaps this background can be furnished by recalling the statement quoted in the last chapter, where it was pointed out that a century ago there was practically no conception of the principle of free public schools. Schools were supported in large measure by charity or by tuition. Most communities provided only a very short term and collected a rate bill, or personal tuition, from the pupils to supplement the small fund secured from taxation. During the quarter of a century before 1850 there was a widespread movement in the Northern states which gradually secured in the face of much opposition full public support for schools. Rate bills did not disappear entirely until 1871, the last state to abolish them being New Jersey, but at that date the principle of support through general taxation was completely established.

In 1870, as we are told by the Commissioner of Education, the total expenditures for public elementary and secondary schools had reached sixty-three million dollars.[16] Nineteen years later, when the population had increased about 60 per cent, expenditures had more than doubled, reaching one hundred and forty millions. Since that time expenditures have increased by leaps and bounds, far surpassing increases in population, as indicated by the following table:

Table I. Expenditures for Public Elementary and Secondary Schools compared for a period of years, including also a comparison of population for the same periods.

	1889-1890	1899-1900	1909-1910	1914
Population[17]	62,622,250	75,602,515	91,972,266	98,741,324

[15] Average cost per pupil of maintaining elementary schools for 1914-1915 $37.58

Average cost per pupil of maintaining high schools for 1914-1915 $82.36

Average cost per pupil of maintaining Chicago Normal College for 1914-1915 $228.84

Report of the Superintendent of Schools for the Year Ending June 30, 1915, in the Sixty-first Annual Report of the Board of Education of the City of Chicago, p. 196.

[16] Report of the Commissioner of Education for 1916, Vol. II, p. 20.

[17] Ibid. p. 19.

Expenditures[18]	$140,506,715	$214,964,618	$426,250,434	$555,077,146
Expenditure per capita of population	$2.24	$2.84	$4.64	$5.62
Expenditure per pupil in average attendance	$17.23	$20.21	$33.23	$39.04

These gross figures indicate a growth in schools that has never been paralleled in the history of any country. The doubling of expenditures between 1900 and 1910 is due in part to the rapid evolution of high schools. Elementary schools, however, have shared in the development. Teachers are more highly trained than ever before, new courses have been added to the curriculum, and better hygienic conditions have been provided in school buildings. There can be no mistaking the evidence that American communities are willing to support schools in a program of expansion and improvement.

Cost a Determining Consideration in School Organization

An adequate comprehension of the meaning of the statistics of educational costs will make it impossible for the teacher of Latin to sit apart and say that it is not his duty to think of the community. The teacher of science cannot ask for unlimited equipment for laboratory exercises; the teacher of music or arithmetic cannot say that he is interested merely in spiritual and intellectual affairs and that he has no reason to consider material matters. The impressive fact is that a great public trust has been committed to the hands of teachers. The community has erected schoolhouses and taxed itself to the point where school expenditures have come to be looked upon as a serious burden in many a section of the country. It is a professional obligation resting on the teacher, be he of high or low degree, to think of his relation to this matter of public expenditures. The public is likely to become more and more insistent in the demand that public expenditures be absolutely purged of waste of any kind, either the waste that arises from extravagance or the waste that results from inefficiency.

Relation of School Expenditures to Other Public Expenses

There is still another way in which the facts regarding the magnitude of the public investment in education can be formulated. In 1913 the Bureau of Census secured figures to show what proportions of the total funds spent by cities are devoted to various departments, such as general government, police, fire, and so on. For the larger cities it appears that about one quarter of the public revenues go to maintaining schools; in cities of smaller size the fraction is larger, reaching in some cases nearly one half. For purposes of our present study a few examples will suffice. These are given in Table II. Two cases are exhibited in Fig. 4.

[18] Report of the Commissioner of Education for 1916, Vol. II, p. 20.

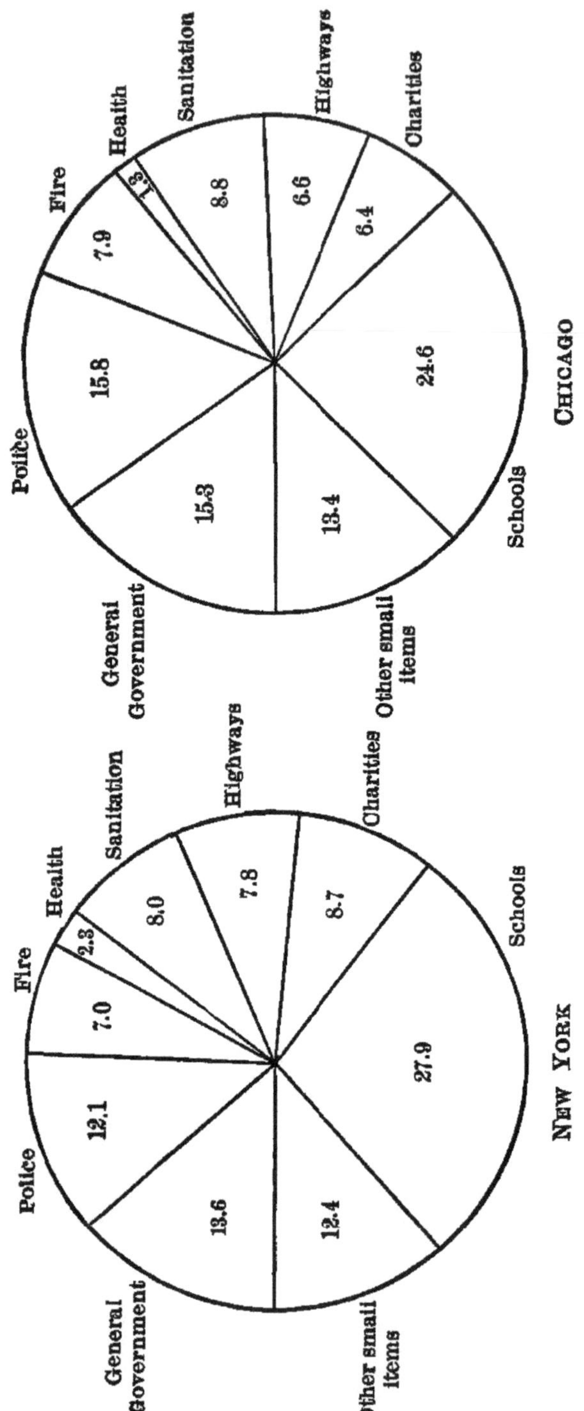

Fig. 4. Proportion of public money spent for public schools and other items

Table II. Per cent of total Governmental cost payments devoted to various City Departments[19]

	General Government	Police	Fire	Health	Sanitation	Highways	Charities	Schools	Other Small Items
New York	13.6	12.1	7.0	2.3	8.0	7.8	8.7	27.9	12.4
Chicago	15.3	15.8	7.9	1.3	8.8	6.6	6.4	24.6	13.4
Philadelphia	13.8	15.0	5.1	1.8	7.1	14.6	10.4	21.6	10.4
St. Louis	12.4	15.5	8.2	1.1	10.2	13.0	6.6	25.3	7.8
Boston	10.8	11.4	8.1	2.9	9.3	10.5	8.3	24.6	14.3
Albany	12.3	13.3	14.1	1.4	7.6	9.3	3.0	27.9	11.1
Dayton	7.6	10.1	9.9	1.5	10.5	18.4	4.1	33.4	4.6
Des Moines	6.1	6.1	15.0	0.8	4.6	9.7	0.3	46.5	10.9
Grand Rapids	9.4	9.4	14.0	3.0	6.8	6.5	1.9	42.3	6.9
Richmond	9.7	10.8	10.6	2.9	12.7	21.6	4.7	21.0	6.1

These figures show why it is that the business man and the taxpayer are addicted to criticisms of school expenditures. It is difficult for the ordinary citizen to get this great expenditure of public money out of the center of his vision. He can, perhaps, be interested by some enthusiast in the introduction of domestic science or civics or some other new course of study; he may even become convinced of the need of improvements in the equipment of school buildings; but sooner or later, when the enthusiast has ceased to speak, the persistent fact that it costs a great share of the revenue of the city to conduct the schools will reassert itself as a dominant item in his thinking.

Urgent Demands for Economy and Efficiency

In not a few cases the problem of financing schools has in recent years become especially acute. Communities are in many cases at the limit now permitted by state laws controlling the levying of taxes. The maintenance of schools even at their present level is very difficult, and all the time there is the urgent push within the system for enlargements and improvements. Other communities which see the rapid increase in school expenditures, even while they are willing to tax themselves more for schools, are asking for clear evidence that school work is being done efficiently.

Such an attitude appears, for example, in a resolution passed by the citizens of Portland, Oregon, at a regular annual meeting of the voters held December 27, 1912:

[19] *Bulletin No. 126,* Table II, United States Bureau of Census, 1913.

> Whereas, the average daily attendance at the public schools of this district has increased from 10,387 in 1902 to 23,712 in 1912, and the annual disbursements have increased during the same period from $420,879.61 to $2,490,477.28; and whereas, it is of the utmost importance that the public schools should be kept at the highest point of efficiency.
>
> It is hereby declared to be the sense of this meeting that a full and complete survey be made of the public school system of this district.[20]

Many other examples could be given of school inquiries which have grown out of the demand for either better administration of finances or more efficient training. In 1910 the Board of Estimate and Apportionment of New York ordered a survey of the schools of that city because the Board did not believe itself to be in possession of adequate information on which to base appropriations for education and because, to use the words of the resolution,

> It is the sense of this Board that efficient and progressive administration of the schools . . . is indispensable to the welfare and progress of the city and that generous appropriations . . . are desirable in so far as assurance and evidence can be given that such appropriations will be expended for purposes and in a manner to promote the efficiency and welfare of the schools and to increase the value and effect of the instruction given therein.[21]

Such quotations show the intimate relation between finance and teaching, between the attitude of the community toward expenditures and the modern demand for a scientifically conducted school system.

Expenditures in Relation to Wealth

Returning to the detailed study of school finance, it may be laid down as a fundamental principle that in general school expenditures are related to the ability of a community to pay taxes. Taking for purposes of illustration the three largest cities, we find that they have different degrees of wealth. New York City has an average wealth of $1765.28 per inhabitant; Chicago has only $1604.20; Philadelphia, $953.65. Evidently the capacity of these cities for supporting schools is very different. The differences in wealth correspond roughly to the varying scale of expenditures for elementary schools in these three cities. New York expends $45.67 per pupil; Chicago, $37.58; and Philadelphia, $32.22. The less wealthy cities commonly spend less on schools.

There is a certain equity in the variation in expenditures above noted. But there are conditions under which the variations in wealth are so great that if expenditure depended on the ability of a community to pay for schools, the children

[20] Quoted in fuller detail on pages 426 et seq. of the "Portland Survey," by Ellwood P. Cubberley. Published by the World Book Company, 1915.

[21] Report of Committee on School Inquiry, p. 61. Published by the city of New York, 1911-1913.

would suffer. In such cases the state must take a share of the costs and must, in the interests of the general community, pay for better schools than the city or district can itself afford.

If one thinks of a mining town, for example, where the population is made up entirely of laborers with large families and where the homes are crowded together in a small area, it will be recognized at once that the ability to support schools is very different from that of a well-to-do manufacturing city or of a sparsely settled, fertile farming region where the children are few and the taxable wealth is comparatively great. In the case of the mining town the state must step in to equalize in some degree the educational opportunities of the children. It is not to the advantage of the state as a whole that the many children of that town should be seriously limited in their schooling, because they will in due time scatter to other communities, and the safety and progress of these other communities require that there shall be adequate educational opportunities in the mining town.

This one example is enough to suggest the problems which arise in the study of support for schools. The sources of these funds and the equitable distribution of state school taxes constitute one of the large problems of public finance and call for careful scientific study. Such questions as the following arise and must be answered: Shall state grants be determined by the pupil enrollment, by the average attendance, by the aggregate attendance, or by the number of teachers employed?

Costs of Different Levels of Education

Turning to details of expenditure, we find a new set of problems. Perhaps the most impressive fact is that there is a wide discrepancy in every city between the average expenditures per pupil in elementary schools and high schools. Again, we may select as typical the facts for the cities referred to in an earlier table. These average figures are less striking than some which could be cited. In Los Angeles, California, the cost per pupil in the high school, at the same date as that for which the figures in Table III were compiled, was $285.67 as contrasted with the cost of $59.41 per elementary pupil.

Table III. Cost per pupil in Elementary Schools and High Schools in selected cities[22]

	Elementary School	High School
New York	$45.67	$105.86
Chicago	37.58	85.15
Philadelphia	32.22	87.10
St. Louis	37.21	113.72
Boston	44.81	82.77

[22] Figures taken from the financial survey of Grand Rapids, Michigan, prepared by Dr. H. O. Rugg and published in the survey of that city published by the Board of Education, 1917, and from the survey of St. Louis by the same investigator.

Albany	35.69	70.56
Dayton	29.85	63.77
Des Moines	33.66	51.17
Grand Rapids	40.45	87.36
Richmond	22.24	56.73

It requires very little consideration to explain why there is a difference between these two types of expenditures. High-school classes are often small, teachers receive higher salaries, and equipment is more expensive. It requires much more consideration to justify the difference. There are some who hold that the elementary school is being sacrificed to the high school. Indeed, there are some people so extreme in their views that they would make all high schools tuition schools. They hold that Boston is in expenditures much less open to criticism than St. Louis. In St. Louis, on the other hand, it is pointed out that a most elaborate scheme of high schools has been organized with a view to providing every high-school student in every section of the city with the broadest possible opportunities. By way of further answer to the critics of the high school, it is asserted that the community gets back in public service from the student who has taken higher courses more than such courses cost. Certain it is, as the figures in Table III show, that cities are making expenditures on a most generous scale for the maintenance of high schools; and the total amount of this expenditure is greater than the table indicates because there are large initial appropriations for school buildings which are not taken into account in these statements of current expenses.

Costs of Different Subjects of Instruction

Pursuing the matter further, we find that there are the widest discrepancies in costs due to differences in the subjects taught, to differences in the number of pupils assembled in class, and to other less conspicuous differences.

In order to bring out the differences between subjects in the same school, Professor Bobbitt has calculated the cost, per thousand student hours, of instruction in twenty-five medium-sized high schools, and presents in Table IV the median[23] cost of each subject.

Table IV. Cost, per thousand student hours, of instruction in High Schools in the various subjects of the curriculum[24]

Subjects	Median Cost
Shopwork	$93
Normal training	92

[23] The median is that figure above which and below which fall half the cases. It is, therefore, a suitable sample of the whole group. It is a better representative figure than the average.

[24] J. F. Bobbitt, "High-School Costs," in the *School Review*, Vol. XXIII, No. 8 (1915), p. 526.

Latin	71
Commercial	69
Modern languages	63
History	62
Household occupations	61
Science	60
Mathematics	59
English	51
Agriculture	48
Music	23

Translating this table into the form of a series of questions which school authorities and communities must face, we may ask: Is it desirable that shopwork be supplied in a school when it costs nearly twice as much as English? Is Latin enough better than modern languages to justify its retention in the program of a school when it costs eight dollars more per unit of instruction?

Like series of facts for the elementary schools can be borrowed from an unpublished study by Mr. G. Lee Fleming of Hibbing, Minnesota, and are reproduced in Table V. Certain selected facts are also exhibited in Fig. 5. The table shows that reading absorbs nearly two thirds of the expenditures of the first grade, while in the third grade the same subject gets a little less than one third of the expenditures, and in the sixth grade about one sixth. Opening exercises require about the same expenditure in all grades. Geography comes into prominence first in the fourth grade. A study of the table will show that financial statements of this type are indexes of academic organization.

Table V. The portion of each thousand dollars spent for instruction in each subject in each of the first six Elementary grades[25]

Subjects	First Grade	Second Grade	Third Grade	Fourth Grade	Fifth Grade	Sixth Grade	Average
Reading	$611	$407	$307	$240	$150	$156	$312
Arithmetic	5	101	176	187	181	190	140
Language	95	110	126	130	178	105	124
Music	86	90	84	67	58	67	75
Spelling	3	92	90	93	80	71	71

[25] G. Lee Fleming, Instructional Costs in the First Six Elementary Grades. Master's Thesis, Department of Education, The University of Chicago, 1916.

Geography	—	—	9	102	124	152	64
Writing	49	68	61	61	52	59	58
Drawing	60	80	55	66	32	42	56
Manual arts	—	—	23	9	60	76	28
Opening exercises	34	21	23	21	24	25	25
Physical culture	11	—	15	14	40	39	20
Folk dancing	11	22	25	—	—	—	10
Hygiene	—	3	6	10	11	13	7
Construction work	28	—	—	—	—	—	5
History	—	—	—	—	10	5	2
Handwork	4	6	—	—	—	—	2
Sense training	3	—	—	—	—	—	1
Total	$1000	$1000	$1000	$1000	$1000	$1000	$1000

Costs of Classes of Different Sizes

A second determinant of costs is the size of the class. One of the simplest ways of reducing expenses is to give a single teacher a large number of pupils to care for. In 1916 the superintendent of schools in St. Louis calculated that the reduction of elementary classes in the schools of that city by an average of one pupil per class would cost the city $65,000 per year. Los Angeles and Indianapolis have small elementary classes, the averages being 23.7 and 24.7 members per class respectively. The cost of elementary instruction is very high, being $59.41 and $50.45 respectively. St. Louis and Chicago have much lower costs, namely, $37.21 and $37.58 respectively. These low costs are secured in a very large measure by grouping children in large classes of 37.6 and 40.3 average membership per class.

Salaries

Teachers' salaries differ in different cities and affect the problems of cost; the number of hours that teachers teach is another cause of variation.

Books and Supplies

Certain cities supply the pupils with books and materials, while other cities require the children to bring their supplies from home. In the long run, the cost falls on the community in either case, but it is differently distributed. In the first case, the taxpayers pay for the supplies as they do for school buildings, each taxpayer contributing according to the assessed value of his property. In the second case, parents pay for supplies according to the number of their children and without regard to their property.

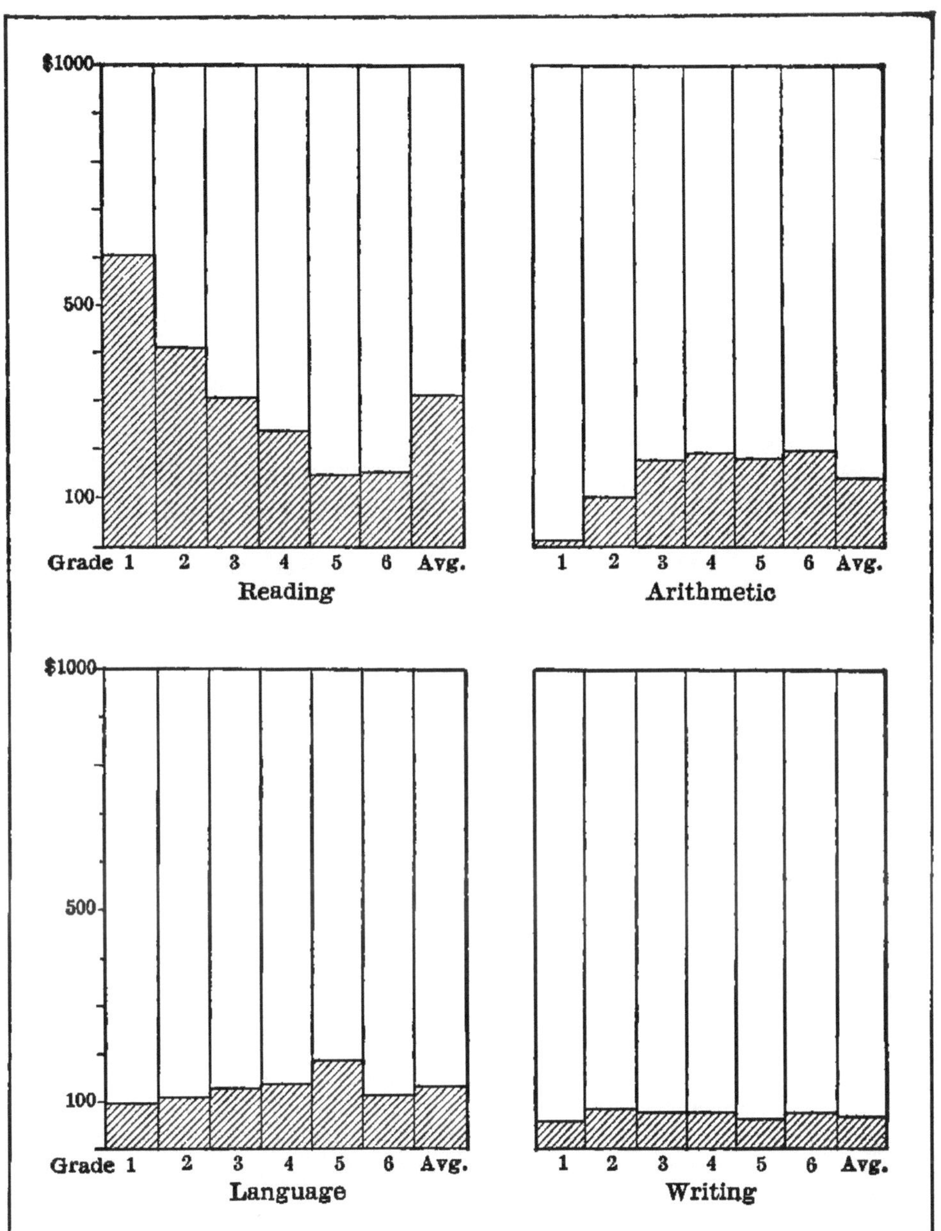

Fig. 5. Distribution in the various grades of each thousand dollars expended for instruction

The relative expenditure in six grades of the schools of Hibbing, Minnesota, for four of the chief school subjects is shown by the height of the columns

In regard to general supplies, there are also differences in policy. Some cities are lavish in furnishing maps and reference books and specimens for nature study, while others are very economical in these respects, sometimes justifying their policy by saying that they put all they can afford to expend into teachers' salaries. The question is thus raised: How far is it legitimate to spend money in providing material equipment, and how far should it be devoted to the payment of high-salaried teachers? Is it well, for example, to ask a teacher of good training in geography to instruct a class without any wall maps? Is it economical to ask a teacher of history to conduct his classes without books of reference? Or, comparing various kinds of material equipment with each other, one may ask whether it is more essential to spend money on well-lighted, well-ventilated rooms that are barren of apparatus or to put up with old buildings and purchase laboratory equipment.

The Meaning of Financial Organization and Educational Accounting

One reason why it is important that questions like those in the foregoing paragraphs be explicitly formulated is that many citizens think of school finance as wholly distinct from school organization. Very often members of the board of education will disclaim any knowledge of the course of study or of the qualifications of teachers and say that it is their sole duty to supervise expenditures. Consideration of the real problems of school finance soon brings to the surface the fact that financial expenditures are merely means to the end of supplying adequate opportunity for all the children who are required by legislation to attend schools. School finance is one aspect of school organization.

In recent years there has been a movement in the direction of better accounting systems which are designed to reveal the needs of the schools and the ways in which these needs are being met. The financial records of progressive school systems, instead of throwing together expenditures in general accounts, are keeping items of supervision distinct from items of teaching. Costs of supplies of various kinds are kept apart. Thus, janitors' supplies are kept separate from crayon and other educational supplies. The cost of coal is used as a means of checking the efficiency of janitors.

The Bureau of Education of the United States has prepared bookkeeping forms, and a number of school systems are keeping uniform records of expenditures. This will greatly facilitate comparisons and scientific studies in the future and will help to make school finance more than a mere haphazard distribution of public money.

EXERCISES AND READINGS

What would it cost to supply all the members of a college class with free textbooks? Would it be equally just to supply a college class with notebooks? with writing paper?

Why is a laboratory fee charged in certain courses? Is a laboratory fee just in a class in physics? in chemistry? in drawing?

In case a boy is going to become a plumber, is the public under any obligation to train him so that he will become an expert? How about a doctor? What steps does the public take to insure efficiency in teachers? in railroad engineers? in mail clerks?

What are the state laws with regard to the amount of tax that may be levied for schools? Are upper limits really necessary?

A certain town is about to build a new schoolhouse. The building will cost in the aggregate about $30,000. If the building is provided with a sightly lawn in front and with an ornamental pattern in the brick, it will cost $400 more than if it is perfectly plain and the yard is made of gravel. If the corridor is made sixteen feet wide rather than twelve, the cost will be $400 greater. Shall the two expenditures be made or not?

Clark, E. Financing the Public Schools. The Survey Committee of the Cleveland Foundation. (Copies may be secured from the Russell Sage Foundation.) This is a volume of the Cleveland survey.

Cubberley, E. P. Public School Administration. Houghton Mifflin Company. This deals with the problems of public-school organization, including the general principles of finance.

Rugg, H. O. Report on the finances of the school system of Grand Rapids in the "School Survey, Grand Rapids, Michigan." Board of Education, Grand Rapids.

Rugg, H. O. Report on the finances of the school system of St. Louis in the "School Survey, St. Louis, Missouri." Board of Education, St. Louis.

CHAPTER V

DELEGATING RESPONSIBILITY FOR CARRYING ON SCHOOLS

Class instruction given over to the teacher. Supervision. Sketch of development of a school system. The community slow to delegate school control. Limits of authority and responsibility not clear. Statement by a public educating association. What is a representative board of education? The functions of a board of education. How a good board gets the work done. Making the machine work smoothly. Report of committee of superintendents. Obsolete administration system. Status of superintendency varies. District control discarded system of school administration. An effective substitute to be discovered. Dangers of this period of adjustment. Organization under scientific principles. Control of school work through tests. A study of the building needs of a city. The errors of democracy. Exercises and readings.

Class Instruction given over to the Teacher

Although the community as a whole recognizes the need of education, and is willing to supply the necessary financial support, it cannot manage directly the details of school operation. The community cannot decide what seven-year-old children shall study. The community cannot decide what ought to be done with a disorderly pupil. It becomes necessary, therefore, for the community to devise some method of picking out suitable representatives who can carry on the schools.

The first task to be thus delegated was that of classroom instruction. One reads in the records of the early town meetings of New England how the whole community participated in the discussion of all financial matters and of many problems connected with the course of study. For example, the site of a schoolhouse, its cost, and its plan have always been subjects of community discussion. Again, the community has often decided whether it wants geography taught or certain branches of mathematics. But when it came to the daily routine of school work, the community employed a teacher and turned the children over to him.

Supervision

The next stage of representative control was reached when the community came to a recognition of the necessity of some kind of intelligent supervision of teachers. Visiting committees were appointed, usually including the clergyman of the town, to look into the work of the classes and report to the town meeting.

So long as communities were small and fairly homogeneous in their social and intellectual characteristics it remained possible to get on with direct town-meeting control of the schools in all except the details of teaching classes and the supervision of teachers. One reads, to be sure, of disagreements at times between the town meeting and the teacher. The visiting committee and the teacher sometimes had a clash, and the supporters of each presented their views with vigor before the whole community. Problems of organization and administration were not lacking even in those simpler days, but the machinery of school management was fairly direct and simple.

Sketch of Development of a School System

How this direct control of schools became impossible with the growth of communities can be illustrated by a single example. In the city of Chicago in its early years the schools were independent of each other. Indeed, in the first years immediately after the incorporation of the town, the schools were private schools to which the taxpayers paid a stipulated sum out of the proceeds of the sale of school lands or out of district levies. The variable character of the teaching which was secured under this plan led to the adoption in 1835 of a partially centralized system of inspection and management. The districts were left independent in all financial matters, but a central board of inspectors was provided which was to unify the schools of the town. This central board was continued after the incorporation of the city, in 1837, but the districts were left independent in financial matters even after that date. The districts voted on the amount to be paid to teachers, on the housing of the schools, and on other matters relating to taxes. There were district committees to care for these local financial matters.

Even though the city government was centralized by the incorporation of 1837, the schools remained distinct. The central board of inspectors adopted certain textbooks, but it appears that the schools paid little attention to this action. How meager was the district provision for schools appears in the fact that it was not until 1845 that the first public-school building was erected.

It is not difficult to imagine the chaos under which such a system suffered. In 1851 the city council took away from the districts the power of hiring teachers and gave it to the central board of inspectors. It also appointed a business manager. The board of inspectors thus gained in power and influence, but they found themselves confronted by educational problems which they could not solve. In 1853 they adopted the plan which was relatively new in American cities, but was coming into vogue, of appointing a superintendent of schools. This officer at once graded the children, organized a uniform course of study, and took steps to equalize instruction in the schools of the city.

The Community Slow to delegate School Control

The historical sketch outlined above gives us a clear insight into the way in which problems of school organization arise. The community must delegate the work of carrying on schools. There is a natural hesitation in intrusting this important work to anyone. As a result, the community is constantly taking a hand, even in these latter days, in all kinds of school discussions. Sometimes the whole city is drawn into a discussion of school matters. Sometimes the individual parent, in his capacity as a citizen, attempts to take into his hands the authority of the community, especially when the way in which the schools are being managed seems to him to be unfavorable to the interests of his children.

Limits of Authority and Responsibility not Clear

The various officials who are created in the process of developing a representative system of school control often find themselves unable to determine the limits of their authority or responsibility. For example, it is almost impossible to determine where the duties of a business manager end and the functions of the superintendent begin. Thus, when it comes to the employment of teachers and the determination of salaries, the question arises whether these matters should be settled on educational grounds or on financial grounds, or on both.

Especially acute is the problem of determining the proper relation of the board of inspectors to the teachers and superintendent. The inspectors, or the board of education as they have come to be called, are chosen as the immediate representatives of the community. They are citizens in whom the community has general confidence, but they are not charged, as was pointed out above, with the daily tasks of teaching. The board must accordingly appoint teachers and a superintendent. These latter are selected because they have training and technical qualifications which the community needs in the schools. The technical officers have in an important sense an independent place in the educational system. It will be remembered that the teacher was the first one to whom the community delegated responsibility for the schools. Not infrequently the community finds its board of representative citizens on one side of a school issue and its technical officers on the other side.

Take a commonplace example. In the development of the course of study it has come to pass that many new subjects have been introduced which cost a great deal. Manual training and domestic science, as was shown in the last chapter, are expensive. Superintendents and teachers are enthusiastic about the educational value of these subjects. Sometimes the board of education has to curtail the expenditures involved because the community does not seem to be prepared to pay the price. If the board is supreme and the superintendent is its servant, how can a campaign of explanation be organized which will show the community what is needed? On the other hand, if the superintendent is at liberty to go directly to the community without the consent or sympathy of the board, complications arise which are not difficult to imagine.

Statement by a Public Education Association

A series of difficulties in the administration of the schools of Chicago brought out from the Public Education Association of that city a statement of the relation between the board of education and the technical officers of the schools which illustrates so clearly the matters discussed in the foregoing paragraphs that it may properly be quoted at length.

WHAT IS A REPRESENTATIVE BOARD OF EDUCATION?

Some people want the school board to be large, so that everyone may be represented. They think that it is desirable that there should be members on the board from every district in the city, every nationality, the various trades, and the various professions.

A board cannot be made into a representative body in this sense. It would never be large enough to include everybody, and it would be unwieldy in action. What is needed is a small board that will be broad in its interests, that will ask many questions covering all sections of the city, and that can act promptly. This board should have laid before it carefully drawn plans touching all the interests of the community.

This small board has to decide general policies and select the people to carry out these policies. It should not operate the schools but should see that they are operated. It should require evidence from the people who operate the schools showing that they are doing it successfully. It should demand and issue reports that are clear and intelligible to the whole community.

THE FUNCTIONS OF A BOARD OF EDUCATION

The functions of the board of education have never been fully understood in American cities because it has been thought of as the means employed by the people to conduct the schools. This is a wrong notion. The people want trained teachers and trained officers to conduct the schools. The people want the board of education to organize the schools so that they shall employ the most expert people who can be secured.

HOW A GOOD BOARD GETS THE WORK DONE

This statement leads to a consideration of the second group of people who have to do with the school organization. The schools could not get on without trained teachers. There was a time when each parent taught his own child. That was in the days when there wasn't much to teach. To-day the parent places his child in the care of a specialist. The parent has come to the specialist because the parent has confidence that the specialist knows how to take care of the children. Teachers are not mere hirelings and nurses, inferior to the children; teachers are trained specialists.

As the system grows more complex there appear several

classes of specialists—some who know how to deal with the pupils, some who know how to provide the children with proper seats and proper ventilation, some who know how to make courses of study, and some who keep the records of the schools.

Furthermore, the school system grows complicated on the material side. Buildings have to be erected and cared for. Land has to be evaluated and cared for. Some people think that all this is an open book to everyone who is in business. The fact is that knowledge of school equipment is just as highly specialized knowledge as knowledge of railroad equipment. A wholesale grocer would not think of himself as competent to estimate the cost of Pullman cars just because he knows about business. The better school systems now have accounting methods in schools which bring out such matters as the cost per unit of teaching in high schools and elementary schools, the standard cost of instruction in different subjects, and the cost of school equipments as related to their sanitary and hygienic fitness.

Every complete school system has its business interests in the hands of competent specialists who know about school costs in detail and in particular.

MAKING THE MACHINE WORK SMOOTHLY

By the time a school system reaches the point where it has all these specialists, it becomes necessary to give much attention to the central planning of a scheme of operation which shall make the whole machine work smoothly. There must be a central office where management is provided. In setting up this central office there has been a great deal of experimenting. Sometimes a teacher has been put in charge; sometimes a board member, in such case the president of the board has taken charge. Some years ago the city of Cleveland tried the experiment of putting a business manager in charge. This business manager appointed the superintendent of instruction. If one goes back into the history of Chicago, he finds that a business manager to take charge of school lands was appointed two years before the superintendent of instruction was appointed.

Gradually out of all the experimenting there has arisen a new type of school officer, a superintendent of schools who is a trained school manager. This manager does not teach; he does not shovel coal into the furnaces in the schools; he does exactly what the head of any great corporation does; he organizes the undertaking. He must know human nature; he must know how to get reports; he must know how to tell the people about the needs of their schools; he must know how to straighten out tangles; and he must know how to judge results. This manager must give his whole time to getting the machinery to work and keeping it in order.

In a large school system the manager's office will be subdivided and there will need to be some further organization to keep it from falling apart. There will be one person in such an office who will know more about heating school buildings and one who will know about the quality of teaching. The more the subdivision the more precautions necessary to hold all parts of the system together.[26]

Report of Committee of Superintendents

Another recent document which throws much light on the problem of the relation between school officers is a report presented to the Department of Superintendence, a division of the National Education Association. This report opens with extracts from a number of letters from superintendents in all parts of the country. The discussion then proceeds as follows:

OBSOLETE ADMINISTRATION SYSTEM

The impression which a careful study of this material [referring to the material upon which the report is based] makes on one's mind is the painful one that most administrative situations are undefined and shifting. Schools are administered, sometimes well, sometimes badly, but in most cases without clear definition of responsibility or authority. Public interests are fortunately protected in most instances, but the machinery is the primitive machinery of the vigilance committee, with now the superintendent, now the board of education, now the city council, now a parents' association, trying to determine what steps shall be taken to promote public welfare.

STATUS OF SUPERINTENDENCY VARIES

In such a situation the accidents of personal influence play an unjustifiable part. Several of the letters from successful superintendents state explicitly or show between the lines that they are entirely in control of the policies of the schools. Some go so far as to say that any effort to define the responsibilities and authority of the superintendent would curtail their influence and would therefore be undesirable. At the other end of the scale are reports which show that the superintendent is shorn of all influence. In many cases he is little more than a clerk, dependent from day to day on the accidents of the board's attitude for the meager authority which he tries to exercise. In some cases he goes to the board meeting only when especially invited. He has teachers sent to him by the board, and he knows nothing about the financial management of the system. Such a superintendent usually recommends

[26] *Bulletin No. 1* of the Public Education Association of Chicago, 1917, pp. 3-5.

the adoption of a state law endowing his office with rights.

The extreme situations referred to above may occur within a single state, showing that there is no such thing as a typical and clearly defined American school administration.

DISTRICT CONTROL DISCARDED SYSTEM OF SCHOOL ADMINISTRATION

The origin of the present situation is not far to seek. American schools were first controlled by the citizens of the district. They met in intimate neighborhood groups and settled the problems relating to their children. Communities were fairly homogeneous, the course of study was simple, school buildings were all about equally unsanitary, and teachers were equally untrained. A majority vote was a democratic and accepted method of carrying the community through these undesirables.

AN EFFECTIVE SUBSTITUTE TO BE DISCOVERED

Within a half century all this has changed. We know to-day that every center in a state is involved in the behavior of each of its communities. Indeed, our generation is witnessing the assumption by the federal government of an influence and authority in education which is without precedent in American history. This is not the place to comment at length on these changes, but one result is absolutely certain—the simple district control of schools is gone. It remains for us to decide what we shall have in its place. What we have to-day is a series of experiments of every variety that can be set up through the exercise of human imagination. Most of these experiments are going on behind closed doors. Most of them involve sooner or later a conflict of authority. Very few of them are understood by the people of the communities in which they exist.

DANGERS OF THIS PERIOD OF ADJUSTMENT

The result is, first, much clumsy administration, even where everybody acts in the spirit of most cordial coöperation. Matters of vital importance to the school are delayed. Secondly, baneful agencies, seeking to profit unjustly, can set up in the school system influences which would have no weight if there were clear and definite responsibility and authority. Thirdly, the people of the community, being uncertain about what is going on, often become restless and critical and unwilling to give adequate support to the schools. Fourthly, the teaching staff sometimes becomes demoralized and relatively inefficient, at times the disorganization goes so far that teachers are actually and openly antagonistic to the board or superintendent, or both.[27]

Organization under Scientific Principles

It is by no means simple to prescribe a remedy for the difficulties which these quotations have described. When a democratic community delegates its unlimited powers to a number of different classes of people, there is sure to be a succession of problems of adjustment. Ultimately all parties will come to recognize the fact that educational problems can be solved only when a full study of the situation is substituted for personal opinion. Every party will have to be ready to acknowledge the supremacy of a thorough scientific statement of the conditions and results of school work.

Fortunately, examples are not far to seek of school administration which is based on scientific study. Two conspicuous examples will serve the purposes of this exposition.

Control of School Work through Tests

In the city of Detroit there has been carried on for the last three years a systematic series of tests in the fundamental school subjects. The teachers-in-training in the city normal school are given courses in tests and in the interpretation of results so that they carry into the school from year to year the type of preparation which makes them intelligent and sympathetic from the first.

At first some unhappy results followed the wholesale measurement of results. Many of the teachers thought that the method was arbitrary and that their work would be misrepresented. Even the good teachers were afraid. They had been accustomed to the purely personal type of supervision based on opinion and answerable, when occasion demanded, by opinion. The teachers who were not sure of the success of their work were violent in their objections. The Board of Education, which at the beginning of the testing was composed of some of the cheapest politicians in the city, led the attack on what they termed a fad and a theory.

Experience has, however, justified in fullest measure supervision by a measurement of results. It has become increasingly clear to all teachers that tests show clearly where the work is strong and where it is weak. Not only so, but the tests help the teacher to determine with precision the exact points where the results need to be improved.

Above and beyond this, however, is the advantage which has come to the schools in their relation to the community. No longer is it necessary for teachers to speak in uncertain terms of their work. If the community will listen, it is possible for the Detroit school officials to make clear by scientific reports based on tests exactly what is going on in every school and in every grade.

The community showed its appreciation of the type of school management which was intelligent enough to base itself on exact studies of results by doing

[27] Report of the Committee on Relation between Boards of Education and Superintendents, in *Journal of the National Education Association*, Vol. I, No. 9 (May, 1917), pp. 967-968.

away absolutely with the corrupt and inefficient board and electing in its place a group of thoroughly representative citizens who are supporting scientific management and developing the schools along lines dictated by such management.

The example of Detroit is by no means the only one which could be cited. An increasing number of cities are revising their courses, training their teachers, and educating the communities by similar methods.

A Study of the Building Needs of a City

One other example must suffice for the present, since the subsequent chapters of this book are devoted to the treatment in outline of the various types of scientific inquiry which ought to govern school organization. This example is borrowed from a report prepared in 1916 by the superintendent of schools of the city of Minneapolis.

In a pamphlet entitled "A Million a Year" there is laid before the citizens of Minneapolis a clear statement, first, of what they had been doing in the way of erecting school buildings for the seven years preceding the report. The report then shows in detail what buildings cost, through a careful analysis of the records for earlier buildings. Then come statements of the uses of schools and the conditions which determine the kind of building which should be put up in each section of the city. Estimates are given in great detail of the needs for five years, and the city is asked to act on the situation as thus described.

The spirit of the study can be clearly seen from the introduction, which is worth repeating in full.

> Why a five-year school building program? The reasons are: that the Board of Education may be able to calculate for some time ahead the financial resources available to meet building needs as these develop; that the numerous children of those sections of the city whose citizenry may not be over-insistent and persistent in their demands for improved and enlarged school accommodations may be as well provided as the children of other sections whose needs, real or fancied, are vigorously and incessantly pushed; in short, that there may be established and carried out a deliberately formulated, comprehensive and consistent policy of providing adequate and equitable building accommodations for all children of the city.
>
> The program, as herein outlined, is the result of nearly a year's study by the Board of Education, by a special committee of the Board, and by the executive officers of the Board.
>
> In making this study and in formulating this program, the Board has invited and has received the suggestions and the coöperation of Parents and Teachers' Associations throughout the city. Two public hearings on the subject were given, to which each of the sixty-two associations was invited to send representatives.

Each association was also invited to submit in writing the needs of the district represented as it saw them.

A generous, indeed an almost unanimous, response was received to both these invitations. The educational policies involved in the program have been discussed by the principals of the schools and by the Educational Council. It has been the effort of the Board throughout to enlist the thoughtful help of those chiefly and most immediately concerned.

The program is published now in order to give still wider publicity to the interests it represents. It is still a tentative program, subject to such modifications as may result from further study by the Board and from suggestions and criticisms that may come from any one interested, whether individual citizen or organization. Such suggestions and criticisms the Board invites.

This program, modified as it may be, will be made the basis of necessary legislation, which is to be the first step in carrying it out. Such legislation, to provide the necessary funds, whether by bond issue or special tax levy, will be sought of the next Legislature.

The people of Minneapolis should understand clearly that the Board of Education has no means whatever of carrying into effect this, or any other, building program, for the Board has no power to raise one cent of money, either by bond issue or through tax levy. The State Legislature only has power to authorize bond issues and tax levies; on the authorization of the State Legislature, only the City Council may sell bonds. On recommendation of the Board of Tax Levy, the Board of Education may levy taxes within the maximum approved.

The Board of Education, representing the people of the city in their educational interests, is formulating this building program. If this program meets the approval of the people, the Board of Education will be pleased to carry it into effect. Before the Board can do this, however, the people, through their representatives in the Legislature, in the Board of Tax Levy, and in the City Council, must provide the necessary funds.[28]

The Errors of Democracy

The funds asked for were voted by the people. It would not be a complete statement of the facts, however, to omit the statement that an unfavorable reaction came in the form of a new board of education which at once began to blockade the kind of policy represented by this study.

American cities proceed slowly to a full realization of the possibilities of a satisfactory school organization. Democracy always masters its problems slowly

[28] A Million a Year, pp. v-vi. Monograph No. 1, published by the Board of Education, Minneapolis, Minnesota, 1916.

and after many slips. The hopeful fact is that more communities are providing agencies for the scientific study of their school problems and are following in their organization the results of such study.

EXERCISES AND READINGS

In most communities there arise, from time to time, demands for new school legislation, or there occur controversies within the board of education or with regard to the superintendent of schools and his authority. As a practical lesson in democratic government the study of the changes that occur at such a time is very informing.

If there is no such exceptionally clear exhibition of the complexity of our public-school government, let the student find out what are the personal and professional characteristics of some board of education.

Would it be better, in some city known to the student, to elect a board or to have it appointed? Is a definition by law of the rights and duties of a superintendent advantageous, or should the superintendent acquire all the power and influence he can get from the board? Should a board of education examine textbooks? Should it determine the scale of salaries to be paid to teachers?

If a class does very poorly in a test in arithmetic, what are some of the different interpretations that can be put on this fact? Is the superintendent responsible, or the teacher, or the home?

Our American cities change teachers and superintendents frequently. What are the elements of cost which enter into such a change?

The best kind of material for reading under this chapter is a superintendent's school report or one of the reports of a survey of a city school system.

Cubberley, E. P., and others. Portland Survey. School Efficiency Series. World Book Company. This is one of the first strong school surveys, and takes up very fully the functions of the different officers of the school system. The parts dealing with administration are largely the work of Professor Cubberley, whose work on administration was referred to under the last chapter.

MacAndrew, W. The Public and its School. World Book Company. A humorous report dealing in an interesting and striking way with a number of administrative problems.

Seventeenth Yearbook of the National Society for the Study of Education. Part II. The Measurement of Educational Products.

Prepared by the National Association of Directors of Educational Research. Public School Publishing Co., Bloomington, Illinois. This report gives a comprehensive survey of the work which is being done by efficiency experts in public-school systems.

CHAPTER VI

THE SCHOOL BUILDING

The building as an evidence of a community's educational views. Contrasts in plans of rural schools. Contrasts in urban elementary schools. A high-school building of the early type. The hygiene of lighting. The hygiene of ventilation and heating. Hygienic equipment. Relation of equipment to the course of study. Modern school construction and costs. The Gary plan for distributing pupils and enlarging the scope of school work. Requirements to be met when the Gary plan is adopted. The construction of consolidated schools. Comparative statistics. Exercises and readings.

The Building as an Evidence of a Community's Educational Views

A study of school buildings furnishes in very concrete form evidence of the new spirit which has come into school organization. The old-fashioned school building was copied from the church. In its externals it often showed its antecedents by the tower and steeple, which sometimes housed the bell and sometimes served merely as an ornament. In its interior there was little or no evidence of careful adaptation of the space to its uses. Small windows, high from the floor and narrow in the space admitting light, were scattered along three sides of the room. Across the fourth side of the room was a raised platform for the teacher. The roof was high and made the space below difficult to heat. A stove was the means of heating; it gave out an excess of heat to the immediate neighborhood and proved inadequate for making the remote corners habitable. The seats were narrow benches, often without backs. In the schools of earlier days these benches ran around the room, the pupils facing the wall, to which was fastened a board that served as a desk on which the pupil might write or lay his book. In later schools the benches were arranged in rows, the desk of one row economically furnishing a back for the bench in front. Add to all this a common drinking cup in a pail of water and sanitary arrangements of the most primitive type, and we have a picture of almost complete disregard for human comfort and hygiene. More than this, we see in such a school building the clearest evidence of a conception of education which was limited to the barest rudiments. There was no provision for varied activities in a school building of the older type. Kitchens in which the girls learn to cook, shops for the boys, laboratories for courses in science, playrooms and libraries, to say nothing of swimming pools and baths, were never thought of, because the course of study was limited strictly to the three R's.

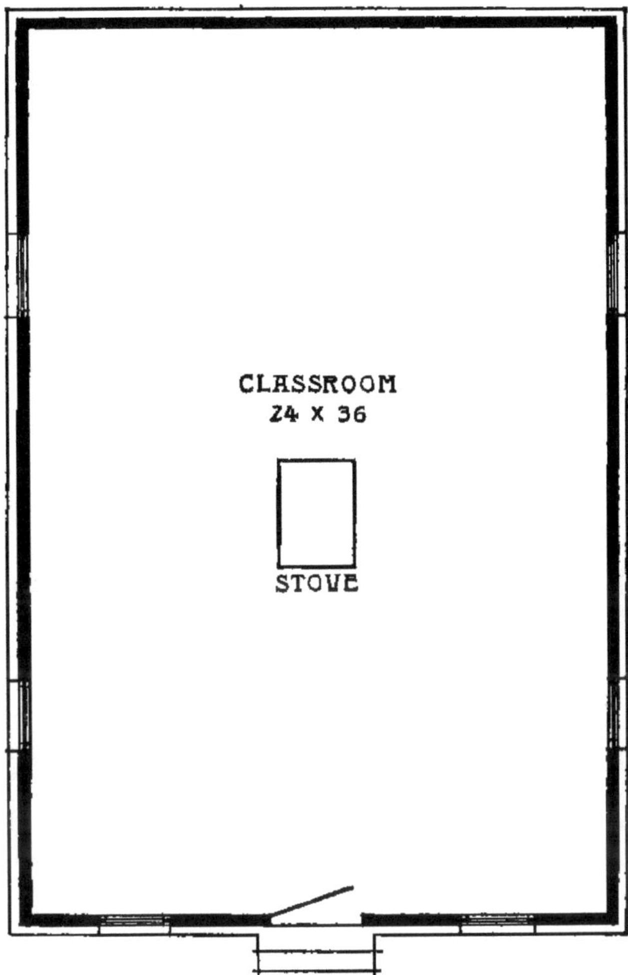

Fig. 6. Floor plan of a typical school building of the old style

The modern school building is the embodiment of a wholly new conception of education. The building is constructed with the utmost deference to the demands of hygiene. The placing of windows, the means of heating and ventilating, the style and arrangement of seats, have all been considered in every possible detail. When the demands of hygiene have been met, the various needs of the school are studied, and the rooms and equipment are arranged with the fullest possible regard for an enriched course of study. The exterior of the building reflects the interest of the community in æsthetics. It is commonly surrounded by an ample playground and often has a garden as well. These changes from the barren buildings of earlier days show that education is thought of as related to the common life of children.

Contrasts in Plans of Rural Schools

A number of concrete contrasts will perhaps serve to give the reader who is likely to be familiar only with modern school equipment some idea of the long road that has been traveled in the evolution of the American school system.

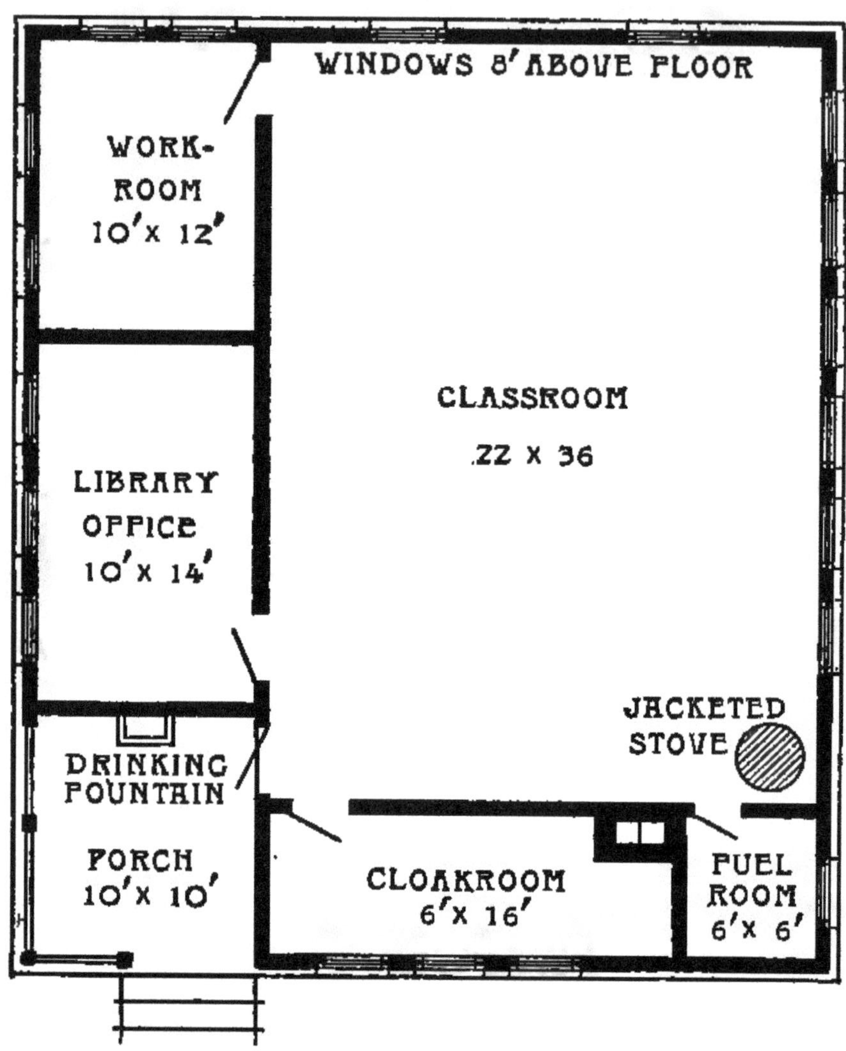

Fig. 7. Floor plan of a well-arranged one-teacher rural school of minimum cost

A ground plan furnished by a bulletin of the Bureau of Education[29] shows (Fig. 6) the old-fashioned one-room school with its small windows and inadequate heating. The light from these windows is badly distributed. The wide wall spaces

[29] Fletcher B. Dressler, "Rural School Houses and Grounds." *Bulletin No. 12,* United States Bureau of Education, 1914.

between windows leave long dark spaces across the room. The fact that there are windows on many sides makes it necessary for someone to face glaring lights on bright days and results in all sorts of cross lights and shadows. The other features of the plan, including the stove, were commented on in an earlier paragraph.

A second ground plan (Fig. 7) shows a well-arranged, simple rural school. The light comes from one side of the room. There is provision for many different activities, and a system of ventilating and heating has been substituted for the stove of former days. The stove is inclosed in a jacket. Into this jacket opens an intake which brings fresh air from outside. A pipe carries the heated air to various parts of the room, insuring its adequate distribution.

The externals of the situation are depicted in Fig. 8.

Fig. 8. An old and a new rural school

Contrasts in Urban Elementary Schools

The evolution is even more impressive when it appears in the many-roomed schoolhouses of a city system. The following paragraphs and figures from the Cleveland survey show how complete has been the transformation of a half century:

> The type of building erected during the 50's is well represented by the Alabama School, although this particular building was not completed until 1861. Several buildings of this general type are still in use in the city. . . . In these early buildings the rooms were large and accommodated enormous numbers of children. Classes ranged from 100 to 200 in each room. There was hardly

a square foot of waste space in these buildings. Originally they contained no corridors, no wardrobes, no toilets, no storerooms, no running water, and no heating plants except stoves.[30] [Figs. 9 A and 9 B.]

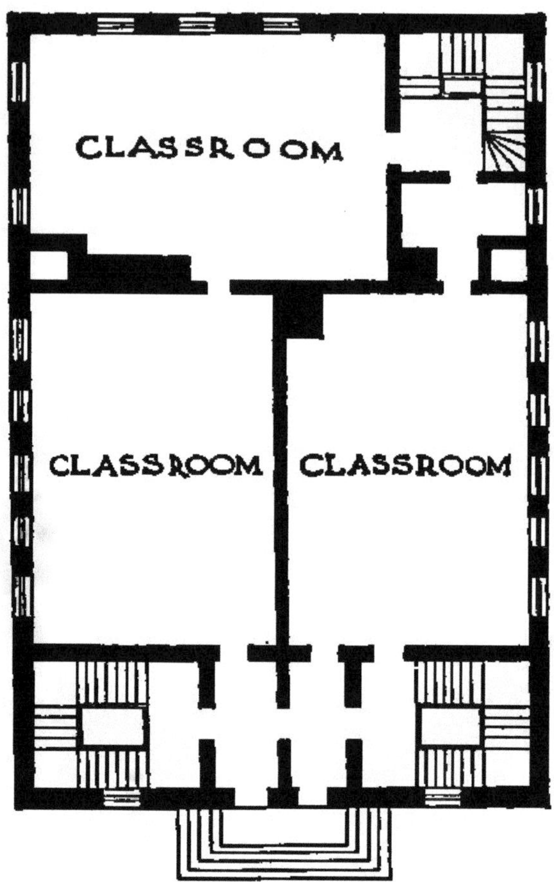

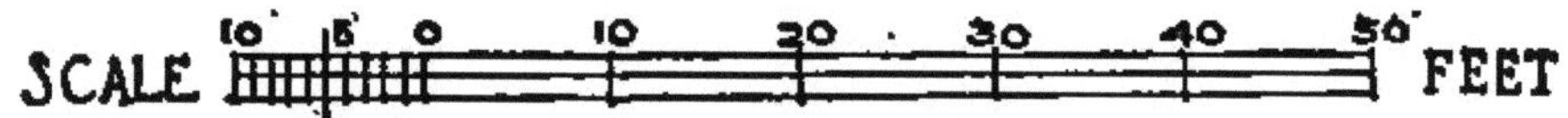

Fig. 9 A. Ground plan of Alabama School

The Empire School, completed in the fall of 1915, represents the most modern type of school architecture. It is entirely fire-proof and so constructed that new wings may be added for future extensions without injuring either the utility or the symmetry of

[30] Leonard P. Ayres and May Ayres, School Buildings and Equipment, p. 23. Cleveland Education Survey. Published by the Survey Committee of the Cleveland Foundation, 1916.

the building. In appearance these newest buildings are great improvements over their immediate predecessors and educationally they are far superior. The windows are banked in sets of five and the masonry is so shaped as to cut off a minimum of light. Auditoriums have slanted floors like theaters, are unobstructed by pillars, and have real stages instead of platforms.

Fig. 9 B. Exterior of Alabama School

Gymnasiums for boys and for girls, swimming pool, playrooms, toilets, shower baths, auditorium, library, shops, and domestic science rooms can all be shut off from the rest of the building so that they can be conveniently used for social and community center purposes. In these schools mouldings are done away with, doors have no paneling, corners of floors and ceilings are smooth and rounded, stairways have solid balustrades, and every endeavor is made to leave dust and dirt no lodging place. Piping for vacuum cleaning, and the most modern heating, ventilating, and regulating apparatus are installed.[31] [Figs. 10 A and 10 B.]

[31] Ibid. p. 35.

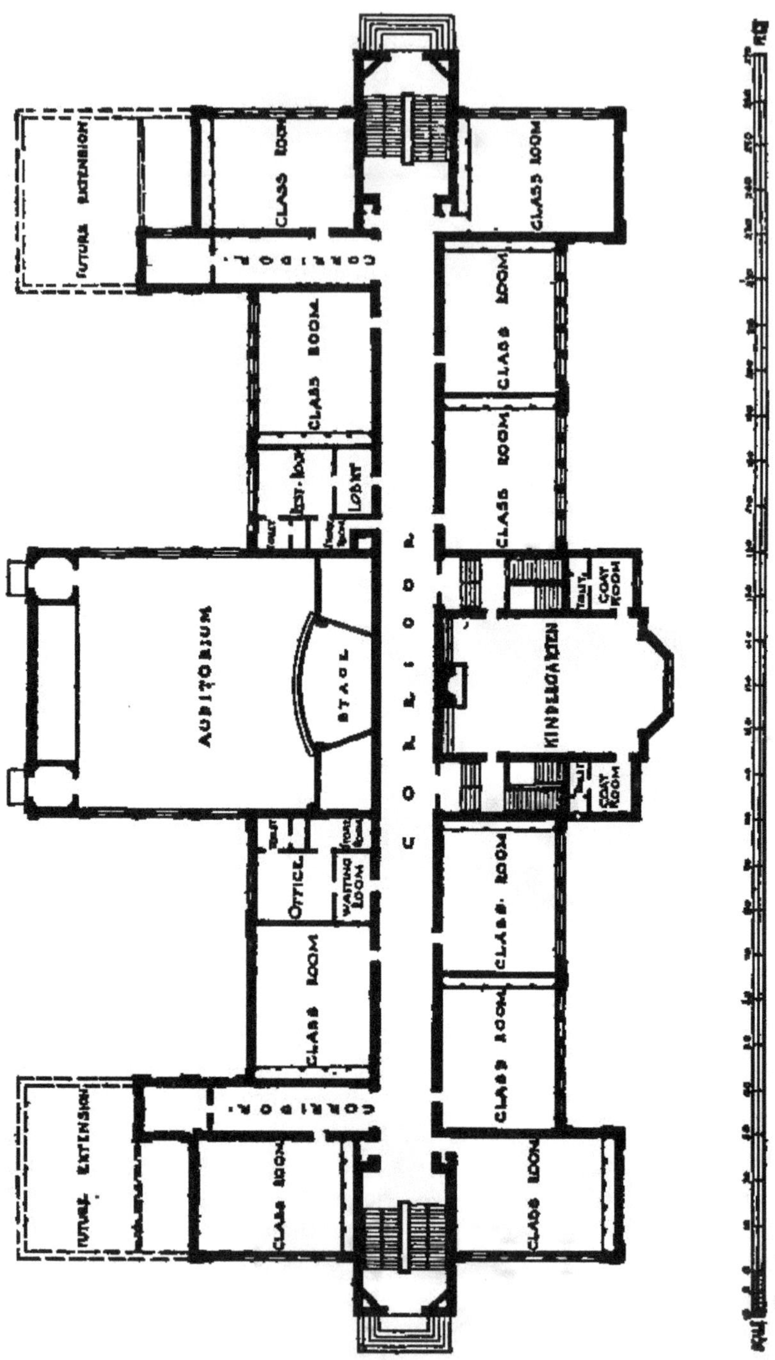

Fig. 10 A. Ground plan of Empire School

Fig. 10 B. Exterior of Empire School

A High-School Building of the Early Type

A similar lesson may be drawn from the study of high-school buildings of successive generations. The following quotation from the Denver survey shows how limited was the earlier conception of the school and its doings.

> The course of study in this school [the East Side High School] was from the first a rigorous, disciplinary course, dominated by literary and classical interests. The issue between science and the classics was clearly drawn even in the early years of the East Side High School's history, but the victory has always been with the literary subjects. . . .
>
> The kind of a course of study which was thought of as necessary in those early days reflected itself in the kind of a building which was erected. The East Side High School building was, in its day, a conspicuous model of high-school architecture. The high ceilings and great corridors and large classrooms showed the generous intention of the citizens of Denver. There were, however, no gymnasium, no lunch room, no shop for manual training, and no special equipments for science courses. In short, the East Side High School stands as a conservative example of a school, strong in its early days, but unable in these days to take on the progressive features of a first-class high school because of physical limitations and because of the hampering traditions which come from

a successful past.[32]

The Hygiene of Lighting

Lest the individual teacher should regard these matters of architecture as very remote from his or her personal interests, let us comment on the evil effects of neglect of some of the hygienic problems which the modern school is designed to solve.

When light is badly distributed, there is a strain on the eyes which results in unfavorable physiological conditions. These unfavorable conditions sometimes take the form of a congestion of the blood vessels in and around the eye, with consequent feelings of discomfort and inability to work. These unfavorable results may appear both in pupils and in the teacher. The conditions are not clearly recognizable through any signs of fatigue which the person affected can readily localize, for we have no sense organ giving direct sensations of fatigue. The result is that the person is unable to do his work, but does not know, unless he has made a special study of the problem, what the difficulty is or how to remedy it. Evidently the problem of lighting cannot be left to natural judgment, and every physical appliance for proper control and distribution of illumination should be provided.

The Hygiene of Ventilation and Heating

In regard to ventilation and heating the situation is much the same as with lighting. Until recently all public buildings were without special provisions for ventilation, it being assumed that enough air would come in through doors and windows. The private dwelling was the model followed in this matter. A dwelling occupied by a few people leaks enough fresh air so that even when all the windows are closed the air is tolerable. When fifty or a hundred people in a public building are crowded into a space that is proportionately much smaller than the space in a dwelling and when, furthermore, through improvements in methods of construction the leakage of fresh air is almost entirely stopped, the situation calls for artificial means of introducing air and distributing it. The situation with regard to fresh air is complicated in all colder climates by the necessity of producing and conserving artificial heat. Modern heating arrangements are capable of maintaining large buildings at a summer temperature even in the coldest weather, but in order to do this at reasonable cost the building must be made as nearly air-tight as possible. The temperatures secured through artificial-heating plants have also brought another evil. The air raised to a high temperature is abnormal in humidity because it is taken from outdoors, where it is cold and the humidity is low, and is raised by heating to a condition where it can absorb a great quantity of moisture. Such air is very dry and takes moisture in an excessive degree from the moist linings of the human respiratory tracts and thus irritates and fatigues the people exposed to the dry air, becoming a serious menace to comfort and even to health. To meet these difficulties it has been necessary to introduce into all public

[32] Report of the School Survey of School District Number One in the City and County of Denver, pp. 134-135. Published by the School Survey Committee, Denver, Colorado, 1916.

buildings artificial ventilating and humidifying systems. Even in one-room rural schools, where the simpler types of architecture must still be adhered to, it is common, as pointed out above, to jacket the stove, thus making it possible to circulate fresh air and to introduce an evaporation reservoir which will render the humidity more nearly normal. Above all it is important that teachers understand that these matters cannot be left to mere chance. Life indoors is artificial at best, and its conditions must be guarded as carefully as possible.

Hygienic Equipment

Not merely has the plan of the building been improved, but the equipment has also been thoroughly worked over. Drinking fountains or individual drinking cups have taken the place of the pail and the common dipper. Toilets have been furnished in a way which makes it possible to keep them clean and wholesome.

The matter of seats may be discussed from both points of view suggested in earlier paragraphs, that is, from the point of view of attention to the health and comfort of pupils and from the point of view of the work which pupils have to do in school. The old uncomfortable benches have given place to comfortable individual seats which, in the best-equipped schools, have been made adjustable so that they fit the individual pupil. Where this complete adjustment to individual size is not provided, at least an approximation is secured by seats of two or three heights in each room. Desks with broad, smooth, sloping tops have been added to make writing and other kinds of school work easy. The most recent improvements have to do with the storage of books and materials. Formerly the pupil's knees were wedged below the storage drawer, or the working top of the desk was inconveniently or unhygienically high. The storage drawer is now being relegated to a position under the chair or to a locker on the side of the room.

Relation of Equipment to the Course of Study

The adaptation of the desk to the pupil's work has been carried to the full limit in the shops and drawing rooms and domestic-science laboratories where work benches and laboratory equipment have been substituted for the conventional seats. That much remains to be accomplished is vividly set forth in the following extract from the writing of one of the most suggestive critics of the present-day school. In the second chapter of "The School and Society" Professor Dewey writes:

> Some few years ago I was looking about the school supply stores in the city, trying to find desks and chairs which seemed thoroughly suitable from all points of view—artistic, hygienic, and educational—to the needs of the children. We had a good deal of difficulty in finding what we needed, and finally one dealer, more intelligent than the rest, made this remark: "I am afraid we have not what you want. You want something at which the children may work; these are all for listening." That tells the story of the traditional education. Just as the biologist can take a bone or two and reconstruct the whole animal, so, if we put before the

> mind's eye the ordinary schoolroom, with its rows of ugly desks placed in geometrical order, crowded together so that there shall be as little moving room as possible, desks almost all of the same size, with just space enough to hold books, pencils and paper, and add a table, some chairs, the bare walls, and possibly a few pictures, we can reconstruct the only educational activity that can possibly go on in such a place. It is all made "for listening"—for simply studying lessons out of a book is only another kind of listening; it marks the dependency of one mind upon another. The attitude of listening means, comparatively speaking, passivity, absorption; that there are certain ready-made materials which are there, which have been prepared by the school superintendent, the board, the teacher, and of which the child is to take in as much as possible in the least possible time.
>
> There is very little place in the traditional schoolroom for the child to work. The workshop, the laboratory, the materials, the tools with which the child may construct, create, and actively inquire, and even the requisite space, have been for the most part lacking. The things that have to do with these processes have not even a definitely recognized place in education. They are what the educational authorities who write editorials in the daily papers generally term "fads" and "frills." A lady told me yesterday that she had been visiting different schools trying to find one where activity on the part of the children preceded the giving of information on the part of the teacher, or where the children had some motive for demanding the information. She visited, she said, twenty-four different schools before she found her first instance.[33]

These paragraphs serve to indicate the close relation between school equipment and the course of study. Since the above criticism was written, general conditions have undergone a radical change. Shops have become common, and there is an increasing emphasis on activities. Correspondingly, there is a change in the conception of the course of study, as we shall see in later chapters.

Modern School Construction and Costs

In the meantime the erection of buildings with shops, auditoriums, laboratories, kitchens, and gymnasiums has given rise to new and urgent problems. First, the cost of these new buildings is great, and many school boards are driven to ask whether the community can afford to erect them. The superintendent of schools of New York City recently reported to the Board of Education of that city that a building program would have to be adopted which would cost the city $40,000,000 in a period of five years. In order to provide buildings many cities have been obliged to issue bonds which will fall, in the years to come, as a financial burden on the

[33] John Dewey, The School and Society, pp. 47-49. The University of Chicago Press, 1907.

generation which is being educated in the buildings.

The urgency of these financial problems is aggravated by the fact that in many school systems the elaborate buildings are not used to the full extent of their capacity. Indeed, it comes to be a most interesting economic and educational problem to inquire what is the capacity of one of these buildings. For example, what does an auditorium represent in the way of actual enlargement of the school plant? Is it merely a place in which the school may come together for a general exercise once a week, or should it be used every day? If it is used for twenty minutes or half an hour every morning, should it be closed during the remainder of the day? As a matter of public economy should it be made available to adults at hours when it is not needed for school purposes, as, for example, in the evening or in the late afternoon?

Such questions as the foregoing multiply with every new addition to the buildings. The old buildings equipped only for study and recitations were economical in the extreme; the new buildings are often lavish.

The Gary Plan for distributing Pupils and enlarging the Scope of School Work

To meet the problems of economy and of adaptation of buildings to educational needs, ingenious ways of rotating classes have been devised. The most conspicuous experiment of this type is that worked out by Superintendent Wirt in Gary, Indiana. Indeed, Superintendent Wirt has advocated the most elaborate extension of the school building and its grounds and a corresponding expansion of the school program. For him the school playground becomes an additional space of great importance in rotating the pupils. Shops and laboratories are to be kept full all day and even in the evening; corridors are to be used as assembly rooms and recreational spaces. He goes so far as to draw the churches and the public library into his plan. With all these available places in which pupils may be instructed, a program is adopted which provides that each room with its special teacher be continuously engaged in some kind of teaching. Pupils are sent from room to room, the theory being that each room shall be kept full at all hours and that each pupil shall get all the different kinds of advantages which the elaborate course of study offers. The reorganization of grade work which is necessary to carry out this program reaches deeper than the addition of new subjects. To make rotation complete, each teacher must be a special teacher and the pupils must move from room to room. Even the lowest grades must be organized under what is known as the departmental plan. Thus, even a second-grade child gets his reading with one teacher and his arithmetic with another.

Requirements to be met when the Gary Plan is adopted

The Gary plan is a very striking example of the relation between the school plant and the school program. In many quarters this relation has not been clearly recognized. For example, some school boards, hearing that twice as many pupils can be accommodated in a Gary building as in an ordinary school building, have instructed the superintendents in their own towns to adopt the Gary plan. The superintendent has to answer: We have an old four-square building which is full in every available corner, there are no shops, and the play space is inadequate.

He often has to go further and question the advisability of departmentalizing the teaching in the lower grades. He is sometimes convinced that a daily program which includes many kinds of activity is distracting and undesirable. The adoption of a new building plan involves the course of study, and the adoption of a new policy with reference to the course of study involves the use of the building. The interesting fact for our immediate purposes is that educational questions that have to do with the content of the course of study and with the methods of teaching are always related to considerations regarding the building.

The Construction of Consolidated Schools

Not only does the school building reflect the internal needs of the school organization which it houses, but there is also a close relation between the school and the distribution of the population in the community. A sparsely settled community invariably used to have a one-room school, because the distances which pupils must travel are such that it is difficult to bring together enough pupils to justify a larger building. The one-room building is likely, however, to offer only the most meager educational opportunities. There is only one teacher. There are no adequate provisions for the pupils who are supposed to be studying, because this one teacher in the one room must be hearing a class recite on some subject at practically every period in the day. The one-room building does not satisfy the progressive community. The device which has been adopted is that of consolidating a number of one-room schools and transporting the pupils through the necessary distances to make possible large schools with separate rooms for pupils of different ages. A consolidated school has facilities which are impossible in a one-room school. These facilities cannot be described without discussing the course of study and also the building and equipment.

The following quotation gives an example of such a discussion:

> In Harrison County, Miss., about 8 miles out from the Gulf and in a typical south Mississippi rural community, may be found the Wool Market consolidated school, the subject of this brief study. Three medium-sized one-teacher schools—Coalville, King, and Oakhead—were brought together two years ago to form this school near the Wool Market post office, on the Biloxi River.
>
> The new house, built by private subscription at a cost of about $2,000, was located within 2 miles of all the children in two of the old districts, while a transportation wagon was used to bring in from 25 to 30 pupils from the Oakhead district, about 3 miles from the new schoolhouse. The territory of the new school covers 27 square miles and now has within its bounds 134 children of legal school age.
>
> Each of the teachers in the abandoned schools, having from 30

to 40 recitations daily to cover the eight grades of the elementary and grammar grades, had no time to do high-school work, and on that account had no high-school pupils. As a result of those conditions the patrons who were able financially to bear the expense sent their children out of the community to school as soon as they were ready for the high school, at an annual cost of from $150 to $200, while the larger number were forced to turn aside to take up life's duties and responsibilities with only the meager training obtained in these little schools. Such conditions obtain in three-fourths of the schools in the South. The Wool Market consolidated school, now serving the same territory, has 23 high-school pupils—16 in the ninth grade, 5 in the tenth grade, and 2 in the eleventh grade—and 20 pupils in the music and expression classes under special teachers.

The aggregate average attendance for the original schools was 60 pupils, according to the records, while the average attendance now in the consolidated school is 110 pupils, with an enrollment of 125. There are only 9 children of school age in the district not in school. In the old schools the number was too small to form an attractive social center and to justify the employment of special teachers, but the new school is fast becoming the center of all social activities of this larger community, employs special teachers in music and expression, and has in the faculty teachers qualified to give instruction in practical agriculture and domestic science. In the interhigh-school contests last spring the Wool Market consolidated school, though only two years old, captured a fair share of the medals in declamation and recitation, while the girls' basketball team claims the county championship.

The school is located on 5 acres of land, which are used for playgrounds, school garden, and practical agricultural demonstration work. Dr. Welch, the community physician, lectures to the school once a week on hygiene and school and home sanitation; and Mr. W. A. Cox, a trustee of the school and a practical farmer and horticulturist, gives the school weekly lectures on agricultural, horticultural, and allied subjects.

After trying the consolidated school two years the patrons and other citizens of the Wool Market community voluntarily levied a tax of $7 per thousand on the property of the district to support the school for an eight or nine months' session.

COMPARATIVE STATISTICS

Cost of the three teachers in old school per month	$128
Aggregate attendance in the three schools	60

Average cost per pupil per month	$2.13
Cost of the three teachers in the elementary and grammar-school grades of the consolidated school per month	$150
Entire cost of the one transportation wagon per month	$50
Average cost per pupil per month in same grades	$2.22
Cost of the four teachers in entire school and of the school wagon per month	$280
Average cost per pupil for the elementary and high school	$2.54

The Wool Market school, with its four teachers and adequate high-school advantages, costs the community only 41 cents per pupil, or a total of $45 per month more than the three little one-teacher schools. To send the 23 high-school pupils out of the community for their high-school education would cost the community at least $1,000 more than this entire school cost the community and county for eight months. Mr. W. A. Cox, referred to above, is authority for the statement that the value of land in the community had increased during the two years as a result of the good school from $10 per acre to $25 per acre.

What has been accomplished in the Wool Market school can be done in almost any community in the South. This and similar instances that might be mentioned lend strength to the contention that adequate school advantages can be provided for the country children in the community near the farm home.[34]

EXERCISES AND READINGS

A new school building with twelve recitation rooms is to be built. Shall the windows of the classrooms open to the north and south or to the east and west? Shall the lockers for coats and hats be in the general corridors or shall there be a cloakroom off each room? How high shall the blackboards be from the floor? How many sides of the room shall be supplied with blackboards? How high shall each step be in the stairways? If the building is designed to accommodate six hundred pupils, what rooms besides the recitation rooms shall be provided? How big should the auditorium be? Should it have a large stage? Shall the toilets be in the basement or on each floor? Is it legitimate to spend money

[34] Communication by W. H. Smith, State Superintendent of Public Instruction, Mississippi. Published as part of the monograph entitled "Consolidation of Rural Schools and Transportation of Pupils at Public Expense," in *Bulletin No. 30*, United States Bureau of Education, 1914 (edited by A. C. Monahan), pp. 82-84.

on a teachers' rest room? Where should the principal's office be?

Is there any difference between the kind of school building to be recommended in San Antonio, Texas, and Minneapolis, Minnesota? What color should the walls of a classroom be? How much playground space should there be around a school building designed for six hundred pupils?

Should school buildings be frame buildings? Should doors open into the building? What is a fire drill, and why is it required?

Report of a Study of Certain Phases of the Public-School System of Boston, Massachusetts, made under the auspices of the Boston Finance Commission, *Document 87* (1916), pp. 185-213. Reprinted by Teachers College.

STRAYER, G. D. Score Card for School Buildings. Teachers College.

TERMAN, L. M. The Building Situation and Medical Inspection. Denver School Survey. Published by the Denver School Survey Committee.

CHAPTER VII

GROUPING PUPILS IN CLASSES

Transition to problems of internal organization. Economy a first motive for grouping. Social influence an important motive. Grouping in the one-room school. Courses of instruction in relation to the problem of grouping. New problems of grouping in large schools. Fundamentally different views on the curriculum. The ungraded class in graded schools. Cases where failures show the urgency of the grading problem. Efforts to adjust instruction to pupils. Readjustments of the curriculum. Problems of grouping in high school. Illegitimate reasons for promoting pupils. Experiments and studies which aim to supply both individual instruction and class instruction. Arrangement of the materials of instruction. Exercises and readings.

Transition to Problems of Internal Organization

The preceding chapters have dealt, for the most part, with aspects of school organization which are external to the classroom and to the operations of instruction. The external organization is set up, however, for the sole purpose of making class work possible. We shall progress, therefore, in our statement of educational problems and principles by turning to the consideration in detail of the organization of the groups to which instruction is given.

The connection of this problem with the one discussed in the last chapter is not difficult to trace. Where a community is small and has few children, a one-room building will serve to house the school. Economy dictates the employment of a single teacher. This one teacher must divide his or her time as best possible in giving instruction to pupils some of whom are very young and others of whom are more mature. On the other hand, where the community is large or where the school is consolidated, a many-room building is required, and the lines of division between groups are drawn in a fashion quite impossible in the one-room school.

Economy a First Motive for Grouping

Some of the simplest motives back of the grouping of pupils into classes are financial. Instruction can be administered economically to a number of pupils when it would be prohibitively expensive to provide a teacher for each learner. Indeed, the demand for large classes in city schools becomes so urgent that it is often necessary to point out the danger of carrying economy so far that it will defeat the purposes of instruction.

Social Influence an Important Motive

On the other hand, it can be shown that even where the motive of economy is not pressing, there are valid educational grounds for grouping pupils into classes. Pupils help each other through their natural social relations. The wholesome rivalry and mutual suggestiveness provided by the class furnish a much better atmosphere for teaching than does the isolation of individual instruction.

Somewhere between the huge class dictated by economy and the small class diminishing to a single individual is the ideal group in point of size for successful teaching.

Grouping in the One-Room School

There are other characteristics than size, however, to be considered in making up proper groups. In order to discover some of these characteristics, it will be well to consider certain concrete types of grouping exhibited in schools.

The type of grouping in the one-room, one-teacher school is in many respects the freest which can be found. The teacher can organize the school with no conflicts in program, because the whole program consists in distributing his own time. The classes can be of any size that the teacher's judgment determines. The reasons for the grouping are purely and simply those which appeal to the teacher.

Under such circumstances what happens? The teacher naturally puts in one group the pupils who are for the first time taking up school work. In other groups he puts those pupils who have approximately the same attainments in each subject. In the classes beyond the first many complications arise. There are some pupils who read well but seem to be deficient in knowledge of number. Other pupils with a taste for arithmetic are very forward in that branch and do only indifferently well in reading and spelling. It is not uncommon in the one-room school for the teacher to regard these differences in ability in particular subjects as adequate reasons for distributing the pupils differently in different subjects. It comes about in the course of time that one and the same pupil will be in the third reading class, in the fourth geography class, and in the fifth or sixth class in arithmetic, while another pupil who has attained to the fifth reader will be lingering behind in the third class in arithmetic.

Courses of Instruction in Relation to the Problem of Grouping

We find ourselves led by the discussion of groupings to a consideration of different levels of difficulty in subjects of instruction and to the rate of progress of each individual in each subject. The teacher in the one-room school has no difficulty in seeing the wisdom of holding together those pupils who have a common grade of knowledge in geography. In like fashion the class in arithmetic must be as homogeneous as possible. There is, however, no recognized demand that a certain section of geography be coupled in the education of any child with any particular section of arithmetic. Pupils are grouped in the one-room school with reference to each subject considered by itself.

New Problems of Grouping in Large Schools

When schools grow to the size where pupils are put into different rooms, as in an eight-room building, a problem arises which was never faced in the one-room school. It is the problem of carrying a group of pupils through all the subjects at the same rate. Thus, when the pupils in an ordinary city school have been grouped together in arithmetic, there are obvious advantages from an administrative point of view in keeping them together in reading and in geography. In ordinary practice the graded school assumes that it is possible to find means of keeping the group together for long periods in all subjects.

This assumption leads to the necessity of asking a kind of question which did not confront the teacher in the one-room school. The kind of question which comes up in the graded school can be illustrated as follows: When a pupil is old enough and intellectually mature enough to study the products and industries of North America in his geography, what phase of arithmetic will be appropriate to hold his attention and stimulate his thinking? When a pupil is old enough to read the history of his own city, what other reading material will insure real effort on his part?

The one-room school escapes these questions for the most part because it is at liberty to allow the pupil to take a different pace in each subject. The one-room school is a place where the subjects of instruction taken in their totality, or the curriculum, as the whole series of subjects may be called, is usually not recognized as important. Each subject has a sequence of its own, but the curriculum as a whole is not thought out. In the graded school the curriculum is one of the matters of major importance. The graded school not only grades pupils; it grades subject-matter of instruction. The importance of this contrast cannot be overemphasized. Many of the problems of the modern school arise at this point.

Fundamentally Different Views on the Curriculum

Let us consider certain cases which will make clear the importance of the contrast. The following extract from the report of the state superintendent of schools in Maine sets forth a definite view on the matters under discussion:

> *More Careful System.* The number of pupils in ungraded schools is shown to be 29,089, a decrease of 1986 from the figures shown for the previous year. It is clear that the work of the schools is becoming more carefully systematized. This fact is further attested by the reduction in the number of schools not using a course of study. In 1904 there were 2323 schools that were reported as following no definite outline of studies. In 1913 this number had dropped to 827 and, as indicated by this report, has now been further reduced to 670. This change, already increasing to no small extent the efficiency of the schools, suggests a promise of the greater advantages that would follow the adoption of a course

> that would in essentials be uniform for the state. While an absolute uniformity that would prevent individual initiative and wise experimentation would retard progress and is not to be desired, there is much to be said in favor of an agreement on established and essential points for all parts of the state school system.[35]

On the other hand, practical efforts are being made in many quarters to overcome the rigidity of the graded system by devising methods of taking the individual out of the group whenever the course of study proves to be inapplicable to his particular needs. In Fond du Lac, Wisconsin, the elementary schools have their programs for the various grades so arranged that language comes for every grade at exactly the same hour in the day; in like fashion, all arithmetic classes are held at the same time, and so with geography and the other subjects. Through this arrangement it is possible for a child who is backward in a single subject to withdraw from the group with which he spends most of the day and to go for the period to another class where he receives a different type of instruction in the subject in which he is behind.

At Gary the schools are so organized that certain teachers in certain rooms teach a particular subject; the general freedom of organization secured in this way is utilized to shift pupils from room to room, thus breaking up the grading system. The possibilities of this arrangement are described in the following quotation:

> If a boy is weak in some particular subject, it is possible to give him double work in that subject. Let us say a 4A boy is weak in arithmetic. It is possible for a time for him to omit some of his special activities and take arithmetic with the 4B class also, thus permitting double time in arithmetic. If he is weak in all of his regular studies it is easy to drop him out of his special activities for a time and permit him to do double work in the regular studies. The special activities are of such a sort that he can return to his classes there without difficulty.[36]

The Ungraded Class in Graded Schools

Another type of experiment is seen in the so-called ungraded class. In many large schools a room is set apart under an especially skillful teacher where pupils who are for any reason out of joint with the curriculum may receive personal attention. Many of these ungraded rooms are so conducted that bright pupils, through a little personal help, are prepared to skip a grade and thus advance more rapidly than the ordinary pupil. Backward children, especially those who are backward in only a single subject, are helped enough to restore them to their classes. Where it is found that pupils are subnormal and permanently unable to keep in line with others of like age, the ungraded class may become a special class. The teacher is then given authority to take all liberty with the subject-matter of instruction and fit it

[35] Report of the State Superintendent of Public Schools of the State of Maine, for the School Year Ending June 30, 1914, p. 21.

[36] John Franklin Bobbitt, "The Elimination of Waste in Education," in *Elementary School Teacher*, Vol. XII (1912), pp. 266-267.

to the needs of the pupils. Sometimes in such special classes reading is practically abandoned and time is devoted to various forms of handwork.

Cases where Failures show the Urgency of the Grading Problem

The foregoing paragraphs have, it is to be hoped, made clear the fact that the grouping of pupils and the organization of the curriculum are closely interrelated problems. The same lesson can be taught by a study of the actual operations of certain school systems which are organized under the graded system.

Fig. 11 shows certain records of failures in the elementary schools of Cleveland for one half of the year 1914. A failure on the part of a child in any school can have no other meaning than this: the child was, at the time of his failure, in the wrong group for his intellectual advantage. There is no effort in such a remark to place the blame for the child's failure. Perhaps the child who fails is indolent. Perhaps the work is too difficult for him. Whatever the reason, failure means that the pupil and the system of grading are out of joint with each other. Hence, when we find pupils failing, we know that the grading system is not working perfectly.

In the figure the diagram at the left shows the percentage of nonpromotions in each grade. About 17 per cent failed in the first grade, about 12 per cent in the second, and so on. It may be well to comment briefly on the high percentage in the first grade. This is due to the fact that some pupils enter school when they are immature. Many pupils lose a great many days of schooling in the first years through contagious diseases, which, as shown by school statistics, are contracted more commonly during the first years than later. The family does not take care of attendance as carefully in the first year as later. The first year supplies the test which in many cases brings evidence of mental deficiency. These and other reasons explain the high percentage of nonpromotions in the first year. The reduced percentage in the second year is explained by the fact that a part of the task of adjusting pupils to the graded system and to the curriculum has been accomplished in the first grade.

The record given in the diagram for the third, fourth, and fifth grades is an impressive exhibition of increasing incoördination between the pupils and the work of the school. So striking is the difficulty in these later grades that we are led to ask for an explanation. This is supplied in part by the diagram in the middle of the figure and by the one at the right. These present the records of failures in two of the most important school subjects.

A record of constantly diminishing failures in reading is exhibited in the middle diagram. This shows that the teachers judge that the pupils improve steadily in reading. There is a satisfactory response to the methods of teaching reading and to the demands of the upper grades. Those pupils who have difficulty in reading in the lower grades are held back or are helped to master the art. The evident fact is that improvement in reading is, according to the record, continuous and satisfactory.

The diagram at the right shows the record in arithmetic. Here is the cause of many of the nonpromotions shown in the diagram at the left. Failures mount up in the middle grades at a rate which shows with manifest clearness that something is radically wrong.

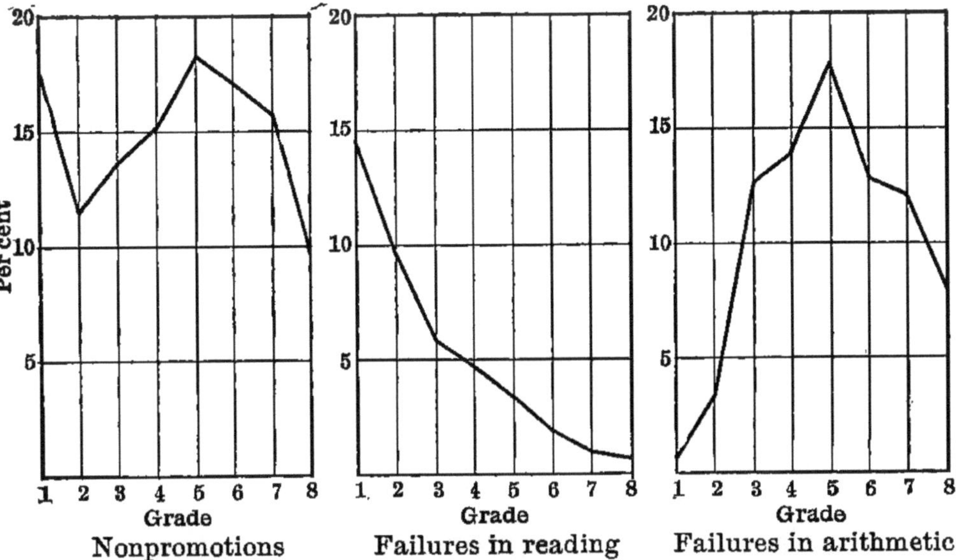

Fig. 11. Record of nonpromotions and failures in Cleveland, 1914

One may venture several remarks in the presence of such records. It does not seem likely that the pupils are stupid, since it is shown that they can read. It is to be noted that they do not have any option about taking arithmetic, nor do they determine what arithmetic they shall study. They are evidently not getting a section of arithmetic in each of the grades which suitably parallels the reading which is administered to them.

Efforts to Adjust Instruction to Pupils

The conditions shown in the figure are paralleled in many school systems. The result is that school officers, seeing the difficulty of doing justice to the pupils, have made radical changes in the grading system in order to meet individual needs. Two extracts from reports by superintendents will show the extent to which school systems will go.

> A study of the performances of the failures in Boise has convinced the entire force that the repeater is generally a quitter, and does about as poor work in his second attempt as in his first trial at the work of a given grade. The stamp of disapproval has been placed upon him. He starts on his second attempt with a grievance against the teacher and the entire institution. The parents as well as the child feel injured, so that the teacher must combat both the antagonism of the home and the hostility of the pupil, who has been trained for failure and not for success, and who becomes either morbidly sensitive or brazenly indifferent. What the laggard would probably do as a repeater is therefore quite

definitely known. If he were permitted to advance, he could hardly do worse and he might do better. It is less expensive and more human to promote him than it is to degrade him. This view of the situation is generally accepted in Boise. The standard for promoting the dull pupil is entirely individual. He is not compelled to do all the work of his present grade before he is permitted to pass to the next. He is even allowed to pass on without manifesting enough ability to justify the hope that he may be able to do the work of the advanced grade. The question is reduced to the one consideration: Would he do better if advanced than he would as a repeater?[37]

Ten years ago no pupil could enter the Newton High School, no matter what his age or educational need, who had not completed satisfactorily all the work of the grammar schools; and a considerable portion—probably one-third to one-half—of all Newton children were then leaving school at fourteen to sixteen years of age with only part of an elementary school education. To-day any boy or girl who needs secondary school instruction—and most boys and girls of high school age, fourteen or fifteen, do need such instruction—may enter some department of the Newton high schools, whether grammar school work has been completed or not; and nearly all—probably from eighty to ninety per cent—of our children are now getting secondary training before leaving school.[38]

Readjustments of the Curriculum

There are other and more fundamental remedies for some of the evils of the graded system. The curriculum can be readjusted. Where any considerable number of pupils fail in a particular subject, it is highly probable that the material of instruction or the method of presentation or both ought to be modified. In some cases pupils ought to be taken out of the regular grades and treated as special cases. The city of Cincinnati was a pioneer in recognizing the need of special curricula for special types of pupils. The whole country has in recent years come to recognize the importance of taking children who are mentally backward or slow out of the grades. Less commonly there is a recognition of the importance of specially arranged courses for the bright pupils.

In the city of St. Louis the curriculum of each grade is administered in units of ten weeks for each section. At the end of each ten weeks a readjustment is possible so that the bright pupils may go forward and the slow pupils may proceed more deliberately. There are at the end of each period of ten weeks a number of promotions which carry individual pupils forward two quarters. The curriculum is so arranged that a rapidly promoted pupil does not omit any essential part of the

[37] Special report of the Boise Public Schools (June, 1915), pp. 17-18.

[38] F. E. Spaulding, The Newton Public Schools, Annual Report of the School Committee, Newton, Massachusetts, Vol. LXXIV (1913), pp. 18-19.

subjects, while the slow pupil has ample opportunity for drill and review.

The grading of the material used in instruction in particular subjects has also been recognized as a problem of the first importance. One of the most thoroughly studied subjects is spelling. Ayres[39] took the thousand words which several investigations had shown to be the most commonly used in ordinary life and tried them out on the pupils of eighty-four cities. As a result of those trials he is able to state that a certain list of words will be spelled with a given percentage of error by pupils of the third grade and with a less percentage of error by pupils of the fourth, fifth, and higher grades. Thus the material of instruction in spelling is graded, not by arbitrarily selecting what the teacher thinks will be appropriate, but by trying out the actual ability of pupils in eighty-four cities.

Problems of Grouping in High School

Thus far the problem of grouping has been discussed from the point of view of the elementary school. The problems of the high school are different in detail, but no less impressive. In the first place, the failures in high-school subjects show the same lack of systematic ordering of the curriculum that was observed in the elementary records cited above. For example, from the survey of the Denver high schools we may borrow a series of percentages showing the failures in various subjects in the five high schools.

Table VI. Percentages of failures in the chief subjects of instruction in the five High Schools of Denver in June, 1915[40]

	East High School	North High School	South High School	West High School	Manual High School
English I	23	15	11	9	31
English II	14	16	10	11	23
English III	16	3	2	15	20
English IV	3	1	2	8	13
Mathematics I	23	24	26	28	50
Mathematics II	17	21	28	20	19
Commercial arithmetic	46	16	33	—	—
Elementary science	13	9	14	21	7
Botany	21	14	14	14	24
Physics	10	15	18	17	34

[39] Leonard P. Ayres, A Measuring Scale for Ability in Spelling. The Russell Sage Foundation, 1915.

[40] The Work of the Schools. Part II of the Report of the School Survey of Denver, p. 158. Published by the School Survey Committee, Denver, Colorado, 1916.

Chemistry	0	4	14	6	20
Physiography	11	15	12	—	—
History					
Ancient	12	17	11	10	15
English	12	17	7	5	—
Medieval and modern	12	9	8	8	13
American	—	7	—	—	—
Latin I	22	16	10	29	40
Latin II	14	20	14	11	18
German I	20	15	24	5	19
German II	19	2	3	0	0

Table VI is worthy of careful study. Let us compare English I and II, which are required of all students, with Mathematics I and II, which are also required. In almost every case the percentage of failures in mathematics is greater. This goes to show either that the grading in mathematics is more exacting or that the students are less well qualified to carry the courses. The exception to the rule that mathematics shows more failures than English, which appears in the second year of the Manual High School, suggests that possibly the students in that school see the importance of mathematics as a professional course. The difficulty with this explanation is the enormous mortality in that school in the first-year course in mathematics. Perhaps the pupils who are likely to fail are dropped during the first year.

While the failures in mathematics are uniformly higher than in English, the policy of the different schools is strikingly different. In the East High School the two subjects are about alike, while in the West High School the failures in mathematics are relatively very high.

Such contrasts become more impressive if we draw the records in Latin into consideration. In the West High School, Latin in the first year is like mathematics, while in the South High School it is like English. Elementary science also shows wide divergences in practice.

A number of startling facts appear if the table is made a subject of careful study. What these facts mean is not difficult to set forth. The subjects now included in the curriculum of the high school are only imperfectly adjusted to the abilities of the students. The community has a right to question instruction which results in failure on the part of one student out of four. It certainly must be aroused at the lack of coördination between schools within a single system which show differences as marked as those exhibited in Table VI.

Other problems in the grading of high-school students and the subject-matter in which they are given instruction grow out of the laxity which has crept into the administration of the elective system. Thus, if we consider certain subjects which are open to students of different classes, such as the first course in Spanish or French or the course in ancient history, we find that senior students are allowed to enter the same class as freshmen because the organization of separate divisions would be too expensive. The result is either a reduction of the requirement in class work to the level of the more immature student or undue effort to bring the lower student to a reasonable understanding of the subject.

Illegitimate Reasons for promoting Pupils

The problems which have been pointed out will perhaps be seen most vividly if some types of promotion are cited which are likely to interfere with instruction.

Sometimes the school allows a pupil to move up a grade or class, although it is known that he has not done the work below, because the parents of the child have influence and it does not seem safe to antagonize them.

Sometimes the pressure of numbers in the lower grades or classes is so great that the teacher sends a pupil on in order to make room for the younger pupils, even when it is evident that the pupil will not be able to carry the higher work.

Sometimes the teacher in a given grade is anxious to unload the backward or disorderly and therefore incompetent pupil on someone else, and since the open road is into the next higher grade, the child is sent on.

Promotion is sometimes controlled by the calendar. Because the date for closing the schools has arrived, and the long vacation is at hand, pupils are declared to have completed the work whether they have or not.

Sometimes it is more or less explicitly argued that the backward pupil is larger than the other children of like intellectual attainments and he should therefore be sent to the upper-grade room where the seats are larger.

When such reasons for promotion are deliberately set down in black and white, they are evidently not legitimate reasons. Many a pupil has, however, been dealt with on exactly such grounds.

Experiments and Studies which aim to supply both Individual Instruction and Class Instruction

The indefensible reasons given above for advancing pupils ought to make anyone who expects to become a teacher the more ready to turn to the careful study of the problem. It is undoubtedly a social and financial necessity that pupils be grouped in classes. It is equally necessary for purposes of administration that the groups have some kind of permanency and some degree of internal uniformity. It is certainly legitimate that the individual's needs be asserted to the extent of freeing him from absolute subordination to the interests of the group.

Such a statement of the case would seem to dictate a double type of instruction which will recognize more than does the present rigid class system the need of individual freedom and the value of class solidarity.

Many experiments have been tried in the effort to solve this problem. The Batavia system, so called, puts two teachers into a room, one to supervise individual work and one to teach groups. There are various systems of individual promotion which advance a pupil whenever he is ready.

Recently Principal Allen[41] of the high school of Springfield, Illinois, has developed a system of supervised study in which the students put themselves through certain prepared exercises and in this part of their work receive individual help and are allowed to progress at their own individual rate. Later the class meets for recitation as a group. The recitation group is made to depend for its composition on the rate at which students complete the individual exercises. The class is accordingly readjusted frequently, and in order to provide time for individual work the length of its meetings is somewhat less than the conventional high-school period.

The instructional plan thus arranged requires certain readjustments of the program and certain divisions of labor among the teachers which differ from the ordinary. But, above all, it calls for the separation of those aspects of the subjects of instruction which are suitable for individual work from those aspects which are suited to class exercises.

Arrangement of the Materials of Instruction

We are constantly brought back by our discussions of the organization of classes to a consideration of the curriculum. The materials of instruction are capable of advantageous and economical use only when they are adapted to pupils. Our next problem, therefore, is to consider some of the general principles which underlie the organization of the general curriculum and of particular subjects.

EXERCISES AND READINGS

What are some of the limitations in the training of a child who gets his education from a private tutor rather than as a member of a class? Show that the most satisfactory size for a class depends in large measure on the subject of instruction. In certain subjects, such as typewriting and bookkeeping, instruction often becomes almost purely individual instruction. Observe such a class and describe the method of instruction.

If terminology is employed in a strict way, a "course" refers to a series of lessons in a single subject, a "curriculum" to a coherent group of courses. What devices are adopted in high schools to compel students to think of curricula rather than courses? What are the advantages and what are the evils of the elective system?

What is the highest percentage of failures which ought to be tolerated in a class? What conditions affect your answer to the

[41] For a fuller discussion of this experiment, see pp. 180-181.

foregoing question? Is a "stiff" course the best course? What class in high school has the "stiffest" requirements?

Dealing with the illegitimate methods of promotion enumerated in the closing paragraphs of the chapter, describe some thoroughly practical method of handling each situation without making the mistake indicated.

HOLMES, W. H. School Organization and the Individual Child. The Davis Press, Worcester, Massachusetts. Contains a list of references on the subject.

CHAPTER VIII

THE TRADITIONAL CURRICULUM AND ITS REORGANIZATION

Importance of a study of the curriculum. The specialized curriculum of higher schools. Problems of generalizing a specialized curriculum. Traditional character of mathematics courses in high schools. Suggestions of new subjects. Present-day social demands. Traditional neglect of industrial education on the part of the public. The demand for revision of the curriculum. Summary. Exercises and readings.

Importance of a Study of the Curriculum

The last chapter failed of its purpose if it did not concentrate the attention of the reader on the school curriculum. The organized body of materials of instruction constitutes one of the most important factors which enter into the life of the school system. Along with the board of education, with the grading system, and with the staff of teachers and supervisory officers stands the curriculum as a kind of dominating personality always exercising a leading influence in the determination of every educational policy. It will be the business of this chapter to open the discussion of the curriculum by commenting on the history of courses of study and by pointing out some of the changes which recent years have wrought.

The Specialized Curriculum of Higher Schools

If one goes back to the beginnings of any school system, it will always be found that the original courses of study grow directly out of the intellectual ideals of the times. For example, if one goes back to the beginnings of medieval universities, he finds that these institutions grew up because there was an interest in certain well-defined bodies of ideas. At Bologna one Irnerius had made himself acquainted with the laws of the northern Italian cities, and students came from all Europe to hear him expound these laws. The course of study was directly related to a specific demand.

A professional theological curriculum was organized at the time of the founding of the early American universities. Harvard was at first a school for the training of clergymen. At that time there was no demand for lawyers trained in the New World. The law came from England, and from the same source came the lawyers. Medicine had hardly developed into a profession. Preaching and listening to sermons were, on the other hand, among the most absorbing occupations of the colonists, and Harvard was established to provide those who could preach. The courses of study were arranged according to the traditions of the single profession towards which the graduates were aiming.

Problems of Generalizing a Specialized Curriculum

We may pursue this example further as typical of the complications which ultimately grow up around any course of study. The original purpose of Harvard was expanded with the passing years. A demand arose for lawyers and doctors; in the effort to meet this demand the institution was divided into separate schools. Still later students came to college seeking a general training not leading to any profession. Through all these changes in the demands of the student body the original courses of study have persistently battled their way down to the present. No clearer evidence can be found than this, that courses of study once created become vital factors in all the later life of the school. The college courses of study were in the first place the product of a particular professional demand. While satisfying this particular demand they became strong enough so that at a later period they have often dominated educational policies.

It is too flippant a remark to say that the classical education of the clerical period became the fashion and that later generations were afraid to be out of fashion, but something of this sort is what really happened. The traditions of a generation are hard to break. The father who took Greek as a part of his education hesitates to see his son enter upon life without the same equipment. Courses of study thus come to have an intellectual sanction which it is extraordinarily difficult to break down.

Traditional Character of Mathematics Courses in High Schools

Another example of no less impressive a type can be drawn from the high-school curriculum of the present time. There is hardly a tradition of high schools which is more fixed than that of requiring algebra in the first year and geometry later. This practice persists even though it is a well-known fact that in many schools failures in high-school algebra are more numerous than in any other high-school course. Also, there is a clear recognition of the fact that by being required of all students in the first year algebra is in effect made the prerequisite of admission to the courses in science and literature which are open only to students who have reached the later years of the high school. The question which the student of education must raise is this: How did algebra secure this position of commanding importance, and how does it hold this position when experience shows that so many students cannot take it with success? The answer to these questions throws a strong light on the nature of the curriculum.

Mathematics in general gained a preëminent position in the educational scheme of the Western World as far back as the fifth century before Christ, in the days of Pythagoras. The branches of mathematics which were chiefly cultivated in those days were geometry and arithmetic. Geometry flourished as an experimental science, and arithmetic consisted in the most elaborate speculations about prime numbers and the properties of odd and even numbers. After these sciences had reached a certain maturity they were transferred to the University of Alexandria, where, in the third century before Christ, Euclid formulated the principles of geometry into the logical form which has persisted to our own time. If one asks why the same service was not rendered for arithmetic at the University of Alexandria, the answer is to be found in the fact that the Greeks had no adequate method of expressing number. They used a system of letters even more clumsy than the system employed by the Romans after them. If one needs further demonstration of the reason why arithmetic did not develop in the classical world, let him try to multiply DCCLXXVII by XCIX. Arithmetic was very little cultivated, therefore, while geometry was put into perfect logical form. Since arithmetic was so little developed in the ancient world, algebra never succeeded in getting a real start.

Geometry, thus launched as a systematized branch of learning superior to arithmetic, has held its place through all generations. In the medieval institutions the perfect logical form of geometry was fully recognized. Geometry was used to sharpen the logic of many a mind. Arithmetic developed only so far as it was needed for the practical purposes of daily life.

In due time there came into Europe oriental scholars who brought with them that marvelous invention—the Arabic numerals. They brought also the science of algebra with its profound abstractions. The Arabic numerals soon superseded the clumsy Roman numerals, and the common man found that he could easily deal with the practical matters of life by means of this number system which rendered all calculations simple. With arithmetic of the new type came algebra. The scientists of Europe found that the algebraic methods opened up possibilities of mathematical reasoning which were of the first importance to science. Algebra and arithmetic flourished. But did these two newcomers in any degree disturb the position of geometry? Not at all. Algebra may be as abstract as any subject in the curriculum, but its historical relations were from the first with arithmetic, while geometry was related to logic and the higher subjects. Geometry has continued since 300 B.C. to be a higher course. The situation in the high schools of to-day is in no sense due to a careful study of the degree of abstraction involved in geometry and algebra. It is in no sense a recognition of the fact that geometry was the first of the two subjects to develop. The present situation can be understood only by recognizing the strength of tradition and the persistence of a practice when once it gets itself established.

The situation is the more impressive because even a superficial study of the intellectual needs of pupils shows that there ought to be instruction in the lower grades in the discrimination of forms and designs. One does not master the forms even of common things until his attention has been turned to them again and again. The consequences to the curriculum of the elevation of geometry to the upper school are far-reaching in a negative as well as in a positive way. Space study has been kept out of the lower schools because the only orthodox form of space study is the geometry of the higher schools. Space study ought to have a place in the curriculum of every grade.

In the case of algebra, on the other hand, tradition has operated to keep the subject in the lower classes of the high school. That it would be better to change this situation appears in the fact that textbooks in algebra have in recent years been made much easier in the effort to fit the subject to pupils' needs, in the fact that some high schools have made it elective, and in the fact that some high schools have rearranged the whole subject-matter of mathematics, breaking up the historical lines of division.

Suggestions of New Subjects

Other evidences that the curriculum is in need of radical reform appear when one notes that schools are curiously blind in the subjects which they omit. A recent writer has pointed out in a very interesting way the weakness of the ordinary school in its failure to give children any training in the use of money. A quotation from his introductory chapter will show the force of his criticism.

> Most people if suddenly asked, "What financial training did you have as a child?" would probably say, "None." If asked, "What financial training are you giving your own children?" many parents would give the same answer. All parents, however, do incidentally give lessons in finance and a few give definite instruction with regard to money.
>
> The teacher, if thus questioned, would usually say something about arithmetic or perhaps refer to some system of money-saving that is being operated by the school. Much has really been done that educates children financially, but probably not one person in ten has ever seriously studied the problem of the need of financial training of children and of how that need at each age may best be met.
>
> A moment's reflection tells one that many adults do not know how to spend their money wisely and that still fewer know how to keep it safely or invest it successfully. Every day we see people spending money in ways that bring little satisfaction. Others are tortured by the fear of losing what they have, while still others are investing in schemes that promise much and yield little or nothing.
>
> Charity workers are especially impressed with the inability of poor people to spend wisely the little money they get. One woman whose family was in a starving condition spent all of the dollar that was given her for canned lobster, and another in a similar situation had a picture taken.
>
> Rich sons and daughters often spend the money accumulated by their fathers in even more foolish ways. In general it is only the common people who have had much experience in saving and spending money, who spend it wisely and many of these have paid a high price for their knowledge. If carefully planned

financial training were given, the number spending wisely would doubtless be greatly increased.[42]

Present-Day Social Demands

Other suggestions are being made these days for a change in the course of study. Sometimes the suggestions take the form of social movements. Such social movements often come in the form of violent criticisms of existing practices. These criticisms will be understood only when it is recognized that back of them there is often a social pressure which has not been understood and is now finding voice in a demand that requires immediate attention. It will be well for us to seek some examples of this type in order that we may come to understand that the school system is answerable at all times not merely to earlier social ideals which were incorporated into courses of study but also to the new ideals which arise with the later developments of community life.

An example of the type we are seeking appears in a study which was made in 1913 in the city of Minneapolis. The following extracts from an article published on March 10 in the *Morning Tribune* of that city state the case fully:

> A year ago a group of men and women interested in the welfare of boys and girls, and somewhat acquainted with conditions that confront them upon their entrance into industrial life, decided that it was time to make a survey of the city. There had been much talk of training for the trades in the public schools, and apparently there was reasonable ground for this advocacy. . . .
>
> Was there a real demand, or was this a new educational fad sweeping across the country, to be lost in the great abyss of educational nostrums, along with vertical writing and basketry? That was to be determined.
>
> Educators are usually learned men; but this world generally does not ascribe to them an abundance of sound sense. These learned men have charge of the greatest plant in the world—our schools. A half million employees are at work at an annual expense to the nation of $450,000,000. The product of this institution should be manhood and womanhood, efficient to take its place in the world of workers, and firmly established in habits of right thinking and noble action. Yet who is accounted efficient for the work of to-day?
>
> Certainly not the armorer, no matter how skilled—for what need have we of him? Possibly not the bootmaker; for the best and latest in boots come from big factories. And so rapidly do industries change that confusion awaits the man still using methods of ten years ago. No system of education can be efficient until the conditions of life to which pupils go are thoroughly known. No

[42] Edwin A. Kirkpatrick, The Use of Money, pp. 1-2. The Bobbs-Merrill Company, 1915.

> manufacturer would think of setting his machines to make "whatnots" or muzzle-loading guns; they were all right in their day but that day is now yesterday. The first thing for the man of business is to know what the market demands. And the managers of the schools must explore their market to know what is demanded of the education factory. That is the reason for this survey.
>
> The commission was made up of persons well known in the city and representative of differing interests. . . .
>
> Ten months were spent in gathering the information, and a month in studying it and getting it into shape for presentation. The tables have been arranged in the following order: First, a set of three tables, showing the sources of the material studied, by school, by age, by grade, and by nationality, and the causes of retardation; second, a table showing upon whom the responsibility should be placed for the child's leaving school; third, four tables setting forth the reasons for leaving school, and the economic status of the family; fourth, a table indicating the education of the children after leaving the public school; and fifth, five tables showing the industrial history of each child, his wages, the number of jobs, the kind of work, and his advancement.
>
> In the discussion comparisons are frequently made with similar reports from other cities, and following these are the conclusions reached by the committee and recommendations for further work.

It will not be possible to give in detail all the results thus obtained. It must suffice to repeat here the figures which summarize the table of causes for leaving school. The percentages of pupils leaving for each cause are given with the statement of the cause.

Ill health	5.7 per cent
Had to go to work	35.5 per cent
Child's desire to earn money	8.2 per cent
Kept vacation work	2.6 per cent
Disliked or not interested in school	29.6 per cent
Trouble with teacher	3.1 per cent
Failure to pass	1.1 per cent
Further public school not worth while	14.2 per cent

The number of pupils who leave because they do not like school or do not believe it worth while is disturbingly large. That there should be so pronounced an adverse judgment on the part of pupils is perhaps to be explained in a measure by their immaturity and restlessness; but part of the school's problem is to meet this immaturity and restlessness and to train the pupils with full regard to all that goes to make up their individual tastes and abilities.

It is especially important that a careful study be made of all available recommendations for improving the situation. We turn, therefore, to some of the leading recommendations of the Minneapolis commission:

> That as rapidly as would be economical, the schools be organized on the "six-three-and-three" plan, beginning differentiated courses in the B seventh grade. These courses should follow three broad lines: (1) Leading toward the academic courses in high schools. (2) Toward the commercial courses, or directly to business. (3) Toward manual training in high school, or directly to manufacturing and mechanical pursuits.
>
> That preparation for the trades can be best and most economically closely related to working conditions, while the necessary skill shall be gained in actual work under the usual commercial conditions.
>
> That the membership of the Thomas Arnold school be enlarged to include all boys who have reached the age of fifteen and have not yet reached the seventh grade. And that a similar school be organized for girls.
>
> That a department of vocational guidance be organized.
>
> That, as an adjunct to the board of education, an advisory commission of 15 members, composed of employees, employers and educators, be established, whose duty it shall be to report changes in the demands of business and industry, and to advise modifications of the course of study to meet these new demands.
>
> That a law should be enacted, making it mandatory that a boy shall be either in school or at work up to his eighteenth year, and that the department of vocational guidance be charged with the duty of enforcing such a provision.

This report has been reproduced at length because it furnishes a concrete example of the kind of demand which is being made on many sides for a complete remaking of the curriculum. The comments about school officers are also typical of much that is being laid at the door of the present-day pedagogue. Better than any theoretical answer to these critics is a careful study of the whole problem of reorganizing the curriculum.

Traditional Neglect of Industrial Education on the Part of the Public

The reasonableness of the demand that the schools prepare boys and girls for their work in the world raises at once the question: Why have the schools ever neglected this need? The answer to this question is supplied in part by the remoter history of schools which was touched on in an earlier chapter and in the early paragraphs of this chapter. European and American schools first dealt with professional and theological problems and have accordingly always had a strong leaning toward the literary subjects.

The early history of the American educational system throws light on this particular matter in a way which will help the reader to understand the present situation with regard to industrial education and traditional education.

At the same time that the New England colonies were passing laws establishing schools where children were to learn to read the Bible, they provided in such laws as the following for training in industrial lines. The Connecticut law of 1650 provides that "all parents and masters do breed and bring up their children and apprentices in some honest lawful labor, or employment, either in husbandry or some other trade profitable for themselves and the commonwealth, if they will not nor cannot train them up in learning, to fit them for higher employments, and if any of the selectmen, after admonition by them given to such masters of families, shall find them still negligent of their duty, . . . the said selectmen, with the help of two magistrates, shall take such children or apprentices from them, and place them with some masters for years, boys until they come to be twenty-one, and girls to eighteen years of age complete."

The conception of responsibility which lies back of this law is wholly different from that expressed in the legislation providing for reading-schools. A public officer was put in charge of reading. He was stimulated to carry on his work by the rewards which he received in the way of compensation for his services. The control of industrial education by the public was very slight. We can imagine some selectman whose attention was by chance drawn to a neglected child, debating with himself the wisdom of setting in motion the magistrates and his fellow selectmen in enforcing this somewhat vague law. The fact is that the law was not enforced. It became a dead letter, and public attention to vocational education has no history in this country until recent years, when the pressure of industrial competition has forced its recognition.

In the early days of the nation's life the absence of any definite plan for public vocational education of young people was not a serious matter. Industrial life was relatively simple, and the family lived close to its sources of supplies. The family was able to take care of the children's preparation for industrial life without aid or interference from the state. But social and industrial conditions have changed. With the development of factories, of elaborate systems of transportation, and of urban life it is no longer possible for the family to train the children, and the demand begins to be urgently felt that some agency give adequate preparation for the practical later life of the children, and that more especially where families are not well-to-do.

For a long period after this demand was felt the school went on with its specialized task, and the public was complacent to see the school neglect vocational training. The specialized task of the school, as thought of in those days, was to teach reading and the other subjects which naturally attached themselves to the literary tendencies that grew up in a reading-school. Private institutions, such as business colleges, sprang up as agencies for satisfying the demand for special vocational training. These were tuition schools and secured their students in many cases by criticizing the public school as incompetent and wasteful. In some cases employers, realizing the necessity of training their workers, made it a part of their industrial organization to teach certain branches of the trades. In other cases, a boy going into an occupation which had no regular training-school, either in a private institution or in the industrial plant, got his training as best he could by accepting a low wage and blundering along until he learned his trade. Even to-day the private training of young people for industry is conducted on a scale that shows how new is the idea that the public school is responsible in any degree for such training.

The Demand for Revision of the Curriculum

The historical sketch given above illustrates, as do the earlier examples presented in this chapter, the natural conservatism of the school curriculum on the one hand and the inevitableness of an expansion of the school on the other. Historically, the common school had no duties in the direction of vocational training. But we are beginning to realize that it is not profitable to try to throw off responsibility. To-day the school must cope with an urgent social problem. The curriculum was and is literary in its major content. The problem of the future is to expand it so that it shall combine with its literary content a new and productive body of vocational training.

SUMMARY

Our study of the curriculum has established, first, the important fact that courses of study are real factors to be dealt with in any school situation; second, the motives which give rise to particular forms of instruction are superseded in the course of school history by new social needs. Nevertheless, the curriculum tends to persist, and often because of its conservatism becomes a menace to progress. Suggestions for innovations come through the insights of individuals or through the formulation of social demands. Whatever the source of suggestions for change, the student of education will find his problem in the fact that the curriculum is undergoing change as is every other phase of modern life. How to understand the changes that are imminent and how to direct them into productive channels is a major problem of the science of education.

EXERCISES AND READINGS

Find new subjects other than those mentioned in the text which have been introduced into either the high-school curriculum or into the curriculum of the grades. Within the older courses find some new topics which have been introduced. New subjects in general are not looked on as entirely respectable. Why is this? What should be done to make them respectable?

Why does training for vocation seem less respectable than

conventional school work? What is to be done to meet this situation?

Do people in general know what changes ought to be made in the curriculum? Note that the Minneapolis study found difficulties. For these it had clear scientific evidence. Did it have equally clear grounds for its recommendations? Should it have had? How could it secure evidence of this latter type?

Relating this discussion to the first paragraphs of Chapter I, let us inquire what steps with regard to informing the community are necessary to the success of a new program of studies.

Whose duty is it to plan new courses—that of the board of education, the superintendent, or the teacher who is a specialist in some subject?

Bobbitt, J. F. What the Schools Teach and Might Teach. Published by the Survey Committee of the Cleveland Foundation. (Copies may be secured from the Russell Sage Foundation.)

Koos, L. V. The Administration of Secondary-School Units. Supplementary Educational Monograph No. 3, Vol. I, of the *School Review* and the *Elementary School Journal*. The University of Chicago Press. Contains a summary of the practices of the approved schools of the North Central Association.

Minimum Essentials in Elementary-School Subjects. Fourteenth Yearbook of the National Society for the Study of Education, Part I, 1915. Public School Publishing Company, Bloomington, Illinois. This is an effort to bring together a statement of the essential requirements for the elementary curriculum.

Report of the Committee of Ten on Secondary Education. National Education Association. American Book Company. The most important report ever prepared in relation to the organization and courses of study of the high school. Its appearance marked the beginnings of the present era of high-school expansion.

CHAPTER IX

SPECIALIZED EDUCATION VERSUS GENERAL EDUCATION

Present-day wavering between specialized and general training. The theory of separate schools for different classes of people. Statement of principles. Public demand for a new curriculum. Commercial courses in high schools. Agricultural high schools. Part-time courses. Various types of trade schools. The Manhattan Trade School, New York City. Practical applications as parts of academic courses. Studies of social activities. Exercises and readings.

Present-Day Wavering between Specialized and General Training

Because there is an urgent social demand for the reorganization of the curriculum and because the principles which should underlie a sound curriculum are as yet not clear, there is much running back and forth in the educational world and much controversy that at times grows very bitter and even personal. Experiments are set up and lauded or assailed. Optimists are hopeful that out of this experimentation will come much good. Pessimists see in it the failure of a democratic educational system.

The recent controversies have revived the ancient dispute between a general education which makes the "all-round man" and specialized education which serves some particular purpose. This controversy can be illustrated by two kinds of examples. First, let us listen to those who are interested in higher education for the classes of students who are going to high school and college. Later we shall find that there is another level at which the same kind of controversy is going forward.

The following statements and counter-statements illustrate the extent to which the dispute is carried:

> I suggest, that, in the first place, a man educated in the modern sense, has mastered the fundamental tools of knowledge: he can read and write; he can spell the words he is in the habit of using; he can express himself clearly orally or in writing; he can figure correctly and with moderate facility within the limits of practical need; he knows something about the globe on which he lives. So far there is no difference between a man educated in the modern sense and a man educated in any other sense.

There is, however, a marked divergence at the next step. The education which we are criticizing is overwhelmingly formal and traditional. If objection is made to this or that study on the ground that it is useless or unsuitable, the answer comes that it "trains the mind" or has been valued for centuries. "Training the mind" in the sense in which the claim is thus made for algebra or ancient languages is an assumption none too well founded; traditional esteem is an insufficient offset to present and future uselessness. A man educated in the modern sense will forego the somewhat doubtful mental discipline received from formal studies; he will be contentedly ignorant of things for learning which no better reason than tradition can be assigned. Instead, his education will be obtained from studies that serve real purposes. Its content, spirit and aim will be realistic and genuine, not formal or traditional. Thus, the man educated in the modern sense will be trained to know, to care about and to understand the world he lives in, both the physical world and the social world. A firm grasp of the physical world means the capacity to note and to interpret phenomena; a firm grasp of the social world means a comprehension of and sympathy with current industry, current science and current politics. The extent to which the history and literature of the past are utilized depends, not on what we call the historic value of this or that performance or classic, but on its actual pertinency to genuine need, interest or capacity. In any case, the object in view would be to give children the knowledge they need, and to develop in them the power to handle themselves in our own world. Neither historic nor what are called purely cultural claims would alone be regarded as compelling.

Even the progressive curricula of the present time are far from accepting the principle above formulated. For, though they include things that serve purposes, their eliminations are altogether too timid. They have occasionally dropped, occasionally curtailed, what experience shows to be either unnecessary or hopelessly unsuitable. But they retain the bulk of the traditional course of study, and present it in traditional fashion, because an overwhelming case has not—so it is judged—yet been made against it. If, however, the standpoint which I have urged were adopted, the curriculum would contain only what can be shown to serve a purpose. The burden of proof would be on the subject, not on those who stand ready to eliminate it. If the subject serves a purpose, it is eligible to the curriculum; otherwise not. I need not stop at this juncture to show that "serving a purpose," "useful," "genuine," "realistic," and other descriptive terms are not synonymous with "utilitarian," "materialistic," "commercial," etc., for intellectual and spiritual purposes are genuine and valid, precisely as are physical, physiological, and industrial purposes.[43]

The answer in florid and perfervid terms offered by a champion of the classics is as follows:

> I have left myself only a few words to sum up and define the main issue raised by the so-called modernist reform of education. It is not the place of physical science in our civilization and in our universities: that is secure. It is not the opportunity of industrial or vocational training for the masses: we all welcome that. It is not the conversion of the American high school into the old Latin-verse-writing English public school: nobody ever proposed that. It is not the prescription of a universal requirement of Greek or the maintenance of a disproportionate predominance of Latin in our high schools and colleges: there is not the slightest danger of that. It is the survival or the total suppression, in the comparatively small class of educated leaders who graduate from high schools and colleges, of the very conception of linguistic, literary, and critical discipline; of culture, taste, and standards; of the historic sense itself; of some trained faculty of appreciation and enjoyment of our rich heritage from the civilized past; of some counterbalancing familiarity with the actual evolution of the human man, to soften the rigidities of physical science, and to check and control by the touchstones of humor and common sense the *a priori* deductions of pseudo-science from conjectural reconstructions of the evolution of the physical and animal man.
>
> It is in vain that they rejoin that they too care for these things, and merely repudiate our exclusive definitions of them. That is, in the main, only oratorical precaution and the tactics of debate, as, if space permitted, I could show by hundreds of citations from their books. The things which, for lack of better names, we try to suggest by culture, discipline, taste, standards, criticism, and the historic sense, they hate. Or, if you prefer, they are completely insensitive to them and wish to impose their own insensibility upon the coming generation. They are genuinely skeptical of intellectual discriminations which they do not perceive, and æsthetic values which they do not feel. They are fiercely resentful of what they deem the supercilious arrogance of those who possess or strive for some far-off touch or faint tincture of the culture and discipline which they denounce as shibboleths, taboos, and the arbitrary conventions of pedants.
>
> From their own point of view it is natural that they should deprecate with sullen jealousy the inoculation of the adolescent mind with standards and tastes that would render it immune to what one of them has commended in print as the "science" of

[43] Abraham Flexner, A Modern School, pp. 8-9. Published by the General Education Board, New York City, 1916.

Elsie Clews Parsons. The purpose, or, at any rate, the tendency of their policies is to stamp out and eradicate these things and inculcate exclusively their own tastes and ideals by controlling American education with the political efficiency of Prussian autocracy and in the fanatical intolerance of the French anticlericalists. Greek and Latin have become mere symbols and pretexts. They are as contemptuous of Dante, Shakespeare, Milton, Racine, Burke, John Stuart Mill, Tennyson, Alexander Hamilton, or Lowell, as of Homer, Sophocles, Virgil, or Horace. They will wipe the slate clean of everything that antedates Darwin's *Descent of Man*, Mr. Wells's *Research Magnificent*, and the familiar pathos of James Whitcomb Riley's vernacular verse.

These are the policies that mask as compassion for the child bored by literature which, they say, it cannot be expected to appreciate and understand, or behind the postulate that we should develop æsthetic and literary sensibilities only by means of the literature that expresses the spirit of modern science, not that which preserves in amber the husks of the dead past.[44]

The Theory of Separate Schools for Different Classes of People

Both writers above quoted are speaking of those learners who are to have large opportunities of higher education. What is to happen to the common masses, to whom the last writer grants the "opportunity of industrial or vocational training," is still in doubt. There are, however, disputants who are trying to settle this question also. To illustrate we may borrow from a pamphlet issued by a great commercial organization in its campaign for legislation which should transform the school system of the city of Chicago and the state of Illinois.

STATEMENT OF PRINCIPLES

Definition: Vocational education includes all forms of specialized education, the controlling purposes of which are to fit for useful occupations, whether in agriculture, commerce, industry or the household arts.

1. State aid is necessary to stimulate and encourage communities to carry on work in vocational education, but local communities should be permitted to initiate and should partly maintain such courses or schools.

2. The vocational schools should not compete or interfere with the present public school system, but should supplement it by providing practical instruction in vocational lines for youth between fourteen and eighteen who have left the present schools. To guard against any competition with the public schools as now

[44] Paul Shorey, "The Assault on Humanism," *Atlantic Monthly*, July, 1917.

> organized, a special tax should be levied for the support of vocational schools, which, with the State grant for their support, should not be taken from the funds now provided by law for the support of the public school system.
>
> 3. The proper expenditure of State moneys for vocational schools should be fully safeguarded, while at the same time the initiative in adapting measures to local conditions should be left with the local authorities. To secure these ends the general management and approval of these courses and schools should be left to a State commission, while the local initiative and direct control should be exercised by a local board composed of employers, skilled employees and local superintendents of schools.
>
> 4. An efficient system of vocational education requires different methods of administration, different courses of study, different qualifications of teachers, different equipment, different ways of meeting the needs of pupils and much greater flexibility in adapting means to ends than is possible under the ordinary system of public school administration. For these reasons these schools should be under a separate board of control, whether carried on in a separate building or under the same roof with a general school, so that they may be free to realize their dominant purpose of fitting for useful employment.[45]

If the last two quotations are stripped of their decorations, they reveal a demand for a distinct class system of education. Broad education is for the few. Specialized education is another matter,—let it be developed for the masses.

Public Demand for a New Curriculum

It is interesting to note that the masses, so far as they can express themselves, are asking for a change in the traditional curriculum and are likely to get it. The masses are expressing their demands through the courses sought by their children.

Our problem will perhaps be clearer if we turn from the writings of those who discuss these matters to the changes which are actually going on in the schools of the country.

Commercial Courses in High Schools

High schools in all parts of the country are giving commercial courses in increasing degree. The first type of industrial education to be extensively cultivated in the United States was commercial education. This consisted in training for clerical positions and was carried on for the most part in private "business colleges." The reason for the early demand for this particular kind of training is to be sought in the fact that America has for years been a country devoted on a vast scale to exporting raw materials. Commercial training, which has to do with the shipping

[45] Vocational Schools for Illinois, pp. 1-2. Published by the Commercial Club of Chicago.

of goods, was accordingly the first to grow here. The extent of the demand for commercial training is vividly set forth in a report of the City Club of Chicago published in 1912, which contains the following chart:

There are at least	There are only
19,000 STUDENTS	**17,781 STUDENTS**
in	in all
Private Commercial Schools and 800 in Private Industrial Schools	Public High Schools
in Chicago, and at least	in Chicago and only
$1,485,000	**$1,114,526**
is paid for	is expended for
TUITION	**MAINTENANCE**

Fig. 12 Enrollment in Private Vocational Schools and in Public High Schools of Chicago[46]

The high schools of the country entered into competition with the private commercial schools, and for some years the competition has been running high. The private schools solicit and get a large patronage on the ground that they do not teach anything that is useless. They give short, compact courses fitted to pupils' needs. The high schools point out that the short courses leave the stenographer with a meager vocabulary and the clerk with no outlook on life.

The public schools are gradually pulling ahead of their competitors because they are employing a higher grade of teachers than formerly and are doing the work in a fashion which is technically more complete. In the meantime the commercial courses are becoming more "respectable" and are being taken by a better grade of students. The effect of the election of commercial courses by a better grade of students is such as to modify the whole program of the school in the direction of more attention to the needs and practices of business life.

Agricultural High Schools

A second type of vocational course appears in the high schools of rural communities where much attention is being devoted to agriculture. Indeed, the increase in the number of high schools in the country in recent years has been very largely due to the fact that rural communities have taken an interest in carrying the training of pupils beyond the rudimentary subjects of the elementary curriculum.

This movement relates itself to the development of a department of agriculture in the Federal government and to the generous subsidy through that depart-

[46] A Report on Vocational Training in Chicago and in Other Cities, p. 38. Published by the City Club of Chicago, 1912.

ment for agricultural experiments in centers of education in all the states. Three years ago a large Federal subsidy was set aside for the further promotion of agricultural demonstrations and schools, and the recently enacted Federal legislation for industrial education includes provision for more agriculture.

Part-Time Courses

A third movement which has recently attracted a great deal of attention and favorable comment was started in the engineering school of the University of Cincinnati and is known as the part-time plan. Classes are organized in such a way that their members spend one week or one month in the shop of some manufacturing plant and the next period in school. A second group alternates in the reverse order, so that the shop and the school are at all times engaged in regular work. Where this plan is well organized, there is a special school officer, called a correlator, who sees to it that there is some direct connection between the shop work and the courses taken up in the schools.

The part-time plan aims to supply that mixture of practical opportunity and training in science, mathematics, and the academic subjects which will lead to both vocational efficiency and a general education.

Various Types of Trade Schools

Fourth, there are all kinds of schools for young people in the trades. Some of these hold their sessions at night, when the working day is over, and others are organized to take the young worker out of the shop or store for a limited number of hours during the working day. In the matter of instruction some give only special training intended to make the worker more skillful; others give general courses in civics, or history, or even in literary subjects.

Some of these schools for workers are organized by the corporations which employ the workers. Thus, telephone companies and dry-goods stores find that it is economical to train their employees. Some of the schools are conducted by the school system and are provided with pupils either through the voluntary demand on the part of learners or through the operation of state laws or municipal ordinances compelling children to attend such schools until they are of a certain age.

Fifth, trade training is provided not merely for those in the trades but also for those who are preparing to enter them. Trade schools are sometimes supported out of the public purse, sometimes by private endowments. The method of instruction is that of requiring the learner to go through a definite series of exercises which will give him skill in the trade. The strictly technical training is usually supplemented by some "general" training.

The following quotation gives a brief summary by one specialist in vocational education of the writings of another specialist in the same field:

THE MANHATTAN TRADE SCHOOL, NEW YORK CITY

This trade school for girls is now a part of the public-school system of New York City. Its early history as a privately supported institution is of absorbing interest, and has been tersely written by Mrs. Mary Schenck Woolman, in her book entitled "The Making of a Trade School." In this volume she gives an interesting account of the first experiment in the United States to deal in an adequate way with the problem of furnishing vocational training and guidance to children destined to enter industrial life, otherwise wholly unprepared, at the earliest possible age.

The aim of the school is frankly stated to be the giving of help to the youngest wage earners, but its ideals are of considerable breadth. They are to demonstrate to the community what education is needed for "the lowest rank of women workers" in order that a girl may become self-supporting and adaptable, "understand her relation to her employer, to her fellow workers, and to her product," and value health and moral and intellectual development.

The necessity for this effort was found in the unfortunate social and economic conditions, and especially in the lack of opportunity for progressive work. "After several years spent in the market" the girl was found to be little better off than on her entrance into industrial life.

After investigation, trades were selected in which are used the sewing machine (foot and electric power), the paint brush, paste brush, and needle. In organizing instruction all unnecessary waste was eliminated; short, intensive courses were planned to give knowledge and skill in the technical aspects of the selected trade, and to develop mental alertness on the part of the worker. It has been observed that "the academic dullness which is shown at entrance comes frequently from lack of motive in former studies." The fundamental importance of health and the value of trade art as a help to progress are given special emphasis.

The supreme value of the school's trade-order business, as an educational asset, is shown in the following quotation:

> It provides the student with adequate experience on classes of material used in the best workrooms; these girls could not purchase such materials and the school could not afford to buy them for practice. The ordinary conditions in both the wholesale and the custom trade are thus made a fundamental part of instruction. Reality of this kind helps the supervisor to judge the product from its trade value, and the teaching from the kind of workers turned out. Through the business relation the student quickly feels the necessity of good finish, rapid work, and responsibility to deliver on time. The businesslike

> appearance of the shop at work on the orders, and the experience trade has had with the product, have increased the confidence of employers of labor in the ability of the school to train practical workers for the trades. . . . The business organization and management required in the adequate conduct of a large order department can itself be utilized for educational purposes.

A chapter devoted to representative problems makes an illuminating analysis of the difficulties which must be met and solved by those organizing schools for workers in the lower grades of industry. While the instruction must be direct and specific, some preliminary general training is needed, and work intended to awaken vocational interests should also be provided. Mrs. Woolman believes that all this might and should be given in the public elementary school. Other difficulties are the keeping of the school organization flexible and sensitive to ever-changing trade conditions, and in "close contact with industrial and social organizations of workers in settlements, clubs, societies, and unions, that all phases of the wage earner's life—pleasures, aims, and needs—may be appreciated." There is the difficulty of securing suitable teachers, and of working in harmony with the ideals of organized labor.[47]

Practical Applications as Parts of Academic Courses

The effect of these experiments in vocational education is clearly discernible in the traditional courses. Reading books are beginning to include extracts which deal with practical matters. Mathematics textbooks are presenting more than ever before practical problems drawn from commercial, trade, and agricultural life. Science, both in elementary and advanced forms, is turning to practical applications. In short, there is going on a kind of intellectual compromise which will eventually make training in skill an accepted part of a general training.

General training has until recently been so proud of itself that it has not willingly accepted association with courses designed to cultivate skill. The result is that the common man has gained the impression that there is a wide gulf fixed between general education and practical life. One hopeful symptom of the present situation is that discussions of general education are becoming very much more democratic. To be sure, there are examples of the proud exclusiveness of former days still to be found in the writings of those who do not understand the reach of modern reforms in the curriculum, but these cases are likely to become fewer as the years pass. In the meantime the practical world is making long strides in the direction of an appreciation of the value of a general education. The shop mechanic should read. He should be independent in his cultivation of contact with the most recent movements in his trade. The teacher who teaches reading is coming

[47] Frank M. Leavitt, Examples of Industrial Education, pp. 149-151. Ginn and Company, 1912.

to recognize this as clearly as does the employer, and very shortly the idea that reading is an artificial somewhat, cultivated exclusively for purely intellectual reasons, will give way to the broader view that even the artisan gains in efficiency by reading.

When that time comes there will be no room for the theory that there should be a different school for the tradesman and the professional class. There will be differentiation within the courses. There will be an elective opportunity for each pupil which will adapt the curriculum to his special needs, but there will be no industrial school on the other side of the street, with a separate course, a different kind of teacher, and a different governing board. Such a cleavage of social interests would be disastrous to the academic subjects quite as much as to the practical subjects. Academic life cannot bury itself in the past; it must make its contribution to the activities of the present.

Studies of Social Activities

Nowhere is the future more clearly forecast than in the new lessons which are being introduced into both the elementary schools and the high schools for the purpose of teaching social organization. Under the title "community civics" or "lessons in community and national life" the social sciences are beginning to offer to the lower schools an exposition of the life of the people who make up society. These courses, like all new applicants for admission to the crowded curriculum, are finding some difficulty in making their way into the school. In spite of these handicaps the movement toward the introduction of social studies into the general school is now sufficiently under way to be described as one of the most hopeful innovations in the curriculum.

EXERCISES AND READINGS

What would be the effect on a community of putting different social classes of children into different schools? Is this done in any degree? Is the principle involved in such a suggestion different in its essentials from the elective system?

What classes of students elect commercial courses? If a school were set up which taught exclusively commercial courses, would the attitude of teachers and students toward their work be better than in a school which gives general academic courses also?

Should agriculture be taught in city high schools? It is sometimes argued that the country school should have a course of study different from that given in the city school. Does the argument touch spelling? arithmetic? drawing?

The part-time experiment has failed in a number of cases where the correlator is not appointed. Can you see why?

At what age should trade training begin? Connect this discussion with the earlier discussions of (*a*) compulsory education and (*b*) costs.

Is reading a practical subject? Is science a natural and desirable part of a trade course? The Federal government has appropriated money for trade training. Can any part of this money reasonably be spent in teaching arithmetic? history? literature?

FARRINGTON, F. E. Commercial Education in Germany. The Macmillan Company. A book dealing with one phase of the matter.

ROMAN, F. W. The Industrial and Commercial Schools of the United States and Germany. G. P. Putnam's Sons. An interesting comparison of the provisions made in Germany for trade education with various American efforts in the same direction.

Eleventh Yearbook of the National Society for the Study of Education. Part I, 1912, Industrial Education. Public School Publishing Company, Bloomington, Illinois.

Eleventh Yearbook of the National Society for the Study of Education. Part II, 1912, Agricultural Education in Secondary Schools. Public School Publishing Company, Bloomington, Illinois.

Lessons in Community and National Life. Published in 24 numbers (October, 1917, to May, 1918) by the United States Bureau of Education.

CHAPTER X

EXTENSION OF SCHOOL ACTIVITIES

A general social movement. Credit for home activities. Bulletin for teachers: home credits. Relation of home work to traditional school work. After-school classes and vacation classes. Continuation classes for adults. Demonstrations as means of economic and social improvement. Entertainment as part of the educational program. Associations aimed directly at the improvement of schools. Correspondence schools. Principles required to systematize educational activities. Exercises and readings.

A General Social Movement

It would be a mistake to treat the innovations in the course of study which were discussed in the last chapter as concessions to a narrow demand for mere gain through the better training of workmen. To be sure, there are some who would be willing to curtail the educational opportunity of the common people in order to insure that type of contentment which is supposed to dwell in the mind untrained in higher ideas. But these are fortunately not likely to succeed in their plans. The movement for a better industrial training is part of a larger movement for a broader social and economic life for all. The important fact about the whole movement is that changes within the school parallel a general effort to deal with all the problems of modern life as problems of popular education.

No exhaustive study of educational extension can be undertaken in the short compass of a single chapter. Indeed, there is hardly more than space to enumerate the types of activity which enter into this movement. Confining ourselves, then, to this very modest effort, the following outline will serve as a rough classification of the major phases of the school-extension movement.

First, there are activities of pupils which lie outside the school but are systematized and promoted through the supervision of the school. Second, there are organized efforts to supplement and enlarge school work by adding to the opportunities offered to pupils out of school hours or during vacations. Third, there are continuation courses offered in the schools for adults who have been limited in their educational opportunities. Fourth, there are various forms of educational propaganda through which communities are to be brought to a more satisfactory economic or social status. Fifth, there are legitimate and refined forms of entertainment, some intellectual and some purely social, which are provided at public expense either in the school building or in other meeting places. Some of these social activities are directed toward the cultivation of a direct interest in the schools; some have no special relation to schools. Sixth, there is at present a great movement for the spread of education through correspondence schools.

Following this outline, concrete examples of each type of activity may be briefly described.

Credit for Home Activities

First, the extension of school supervision is illustrated by the fact that in a township high school the girls who are taking cooking are required to do each day a certain amount of laboratory work in the kitchen at home. This is reported by the parents, and the cooking teacher visits the homes from time to time to inspect the work. Again, in many agricultural schools home gardening is required as a part of the course. Sometimes a school officer is employed to keep up the supervision of this home work during the vacation period. Another series of examples under this heading is to be found in those systems where miscellaneous home activities are credited by the school on the report of parents. The following quotation taken from Superintendent Alderman's book on home credits shows how far the matter has been carried in some quarters:

Below is the Spokane County plan.

BULLETIN FOR TEACHERS: HOME CREDITS

> The following are the rules and reward offered for home work. This work is to be done during the school week. No one is compelled to enter this contest, and the pupil may drop out at any time.
>
> All work must be voluntary on the part of the pupil. Parents are requested not to sign papers for pupils if the work is not voluntarily and cheerfully done.
>
> The rewards for this work are:
>
> One half-holiday each month to the child who has earned one hundred or more home credits, and has not been absent or tardy for the month; also 5 per cent will be added to his final examination. The pupil who earns one hundred or more credits each month but fails in perfect attendance will have the 5 per cent added to his final examination.
>
> In addition, the board of directors may offer a prize to the pupil in each grade who shall have the greatest amount of home credits, and shall be neither absent nor tardy during the term, or from the adoption of these rules.

List of Home Credits

Personal cleanliness	2	Retiring before 9 o'clock	1
Cleaning teeth	1	Feeding and watering chickens	1
Cleaning finger nails	1	Feeding and watering horses	1
Practicing music lesson	2	Feeding and watering cows	1
Dressing baby	1	Feeding and watering hogs	1
Washing dishes	1	Gathering eggs	1
Sweeping floor	1	Cleaning chicken house	1
Making bed	1	Going for mail	1
Preparing meal	2	Picking apples	2
Making a cake	1	Picking potatoes	2
Making biscuits	1	Bringing in wood for to-day	1
Churning	2	Splitting wood for to-day	1
Scrubbing floor	2	Bringing in water for to-day	1
Dusting	1	Grooming horse	1
Blacking stove	1	Milking cow	1
Darning stockings	1	Working in field	2
Delivering papers	2	Going for milk	1

E. G. McFarland,
County Superintendent of Schools.

The following statement is made by Superintendent McFarland as to the effect home credits had on attendance in 1913-1914:

> We attribute the increase in our attendance this year in the schools of Spokane County, outside the city of Spokane, largely to the Home Credit System and our certificates for perfect attendance. While the enrollment was 108 less than last year, yet our attendance was 16,712 days more. At the present rate of 16 cents per day, the pupils earned for the county, from the State appropriation, nearly $2700 more than last year. With the same enrollment as last year the increase of apportionment would have reached approximately $6000.
>
> The credit slip for the school week provides for a daily record of "chores or work done" from Monday to Friday inclusive. It does not contain a stated list of duties; the blanks are to be filled in by the child. The list of home credits is furnished each district, but the teacher uses her judgment in allowing credit for any chore peculiar to her locality.[48]

In Greeley, Colorado, the high school gives credits for courses taken in the

[48] L. R. Alderman, School Credit for Home Work, pp. 89-91. Houghton Mifflin Company, 1915.

Sunday schools. The teachers, under this plan, must be approved by the school authorities and the work must be graded. In many schools credit is given for music taken at home. Sometimes the results of this instruction are examined, sometimes not. In the latter cases teachers are sometimes approved by the school and their work then accepted without further question.

Relation of Home Work to Traditional School Work

All these examples make it clear that the school organization is being used to systematize activities which without school credits are carried on very irregularly. The supervision of the school is undoubtedly of advantage to the activities. Is the draft made on the supervisory energy of the school legitimate? The answer to this question is, in some cases, undoubtedly no. Thus, if the school is not supplied by the public with supervisory energy beyond that commonly devoted to the routine of ordinary school work, it is difficult to manage without distraction some of these new kinds of credits. Again, if outside activities are allowed to take the place of regular school courses, the dangers become even more apparent. The advocates of the home credit system assert that the drawbacks are slight and offer examples to show that there is no conflict, but rather help for the school work.

> A boy in one of the Portland, Oregon, schools had trouble with his spelling, getting a mark of only 4½ on a scale of 10. Soon after home credits were put into use by his teacher he came to her and anxiously inquired if he could help out his spelling grade with a good home record. The teacher graciously assured him that he could. The boy brought in each week one of the very best home record slips, and in some mysterious manner his spelling improved as his hours of work increased. He does not need his home record to help out his spelling grade now, for last month he received more than a passing mark, 7½, in his weak subject. The knowledge that there was help at hand relieved his nervousness, and gave him confidence.[49]

After-School Classes and Vacation Classes

The second type of extension to be noted is that which adds to the regular school work by giving supervised opportunity outside the ordinary curriculum.

One example is that of a high school which tried the experiment of requiring manual training. The students grumbled a good deal about the course because it was so different from their other work. The course was abandoned. In its place was opened a voluntary class after school hours to which only students who secured a high grade in their regular work were admitted. There was a larger demand for the course than the shop could satisfy.

Vacation schools are often supported by groups of citizens interested in providing for pupils who have to remain in the city during vacation and have no

[49] L. R. Alderman, School Credit for Home Work, pp. 32-33. Houghton Mifflin Company, 1915.

suitable employment or recreation to keep them off the streets. So valuable is this addition to school work that it is very often taken over by the school system.

A great deal of school gardening is being encouraged by finding vacant lots or providing land in unsettled districts. School supervision sometimes cannot be extended to cover this work. This movement has been evolved during the recent campaign for food cultivation and conservation into a general social movement.

Athletics are sometimes organized under school supervision; sometimes only advisory help is furnished by the schools. The playground is opened to pupils after school hours or a special playground is provided. The matter of supervised play is important enough to justify a full discussion in a later chapter.

Some schools are providing moving-picture exhibitions out of hours for the pupils. The experiment has been successfully carried out by charging enough for such entertainments to pay their cost, the school thus furnishing only the place and the organization.

All these examples show that there is an unused margin of time and energy which pupils will use somewhere. Especially in cities it becomes a serious problem to insure wholesome conditions for the use of this surplus. If the pupils need further opportunities and the schools can provide them, it is certainly legitimate to carry out such plans. To be really educational all these activities need supervision. Supervision, of course, means either more expenditure of money to secure additional supervisors or an increased demand on the energies of present school officers. The present provision for instruction and supervision is seldom excessive. Expansion, therefore, ought to be faced as a new demand.

Continuation Classes for Adults

Continuation courses for adults are intended to carry on the schooling of people who for some reason or other have found it necessary to stop ordinary school work. In many cases continuation classes are conducted at night in what is commonly known as night school. Here there are two types of courses, one designed to give training in the conventional academic subjects, the other to give greater efficiency in the practical occupational life of the student. As an example of general courses not connected with industries we may cite the special courses for immigrants which have of late been matters of an especially urgent campaign by the Bureau of Education, as indicated in the following paragraphs from a paper by Mr. Wheaton, the specialist on immigration in the bureau:

> Education, however, is the most potent force toward inculcating American ideals and impulses. The English language and a knowledge of the civic forces of the country are indispensable to the alien in adjusting himself to America. Through our common speech comes understanding. Without it the pages of our newspapers are meaningless and ordinary matters of business with Americans must be transacted through the medium of an interpreter. Only by overcoming inability to speak English, by eliminating illiteracy among aliens, and by instilling the ideals,

> attitudes, and habits of thought of America, can we hope to make real American citizens of the strangers within our gates. . . .
>
> The education of children of immigrants in the day schools has always been considered a primary and essential function of the school system. But the training of adults in English and civics has not been generally so considered. Evening schools, through which only can adults be reached effectively, have usually been regarded merely as adjuncts to the day-school system, and hence are maintained when funds can be spared or eked out. Adequate facilities for the adult are rarely organized and maintained as an organic part of the educational system with a specific appropriation and unified supervision. In fact, education of immigrants has been left too largely to the well-intentioned but sporadic interest and effort of private organizations and individuals. The provision of public facilities may, therefore, be treated at present and for some time to come as a legitimate extension activity for educational systems.
>
> It is with this latter conception in mind that the United States Bureau of Education has for a considerable period been actively engaged in promoting the extension of facilities for the education of immigrants over the compulsory attendance age. Authority to undertake this extensive program is derived from the organic act creating the bureau in 1867 and from various acts of Congress making appropriations for the purpose of promoting industrial and vocational training, the elimination of illiteracy, and the cause of education generally.[50]

The industrial phase of continuation education was noted in the discussions of the last chapter. It remains only to add that the industrial courses for adults have done much to make available for mature workers the kind of training which the school is now beginning to give to children.

Continuation classes are often provided by organizations outside of the schools, such as the Christian associations for young men and women, and labor unions, and through private endowment.

Demonstrations as Means of Economic and Social Improvement

The fourth type of educational activity may be described as educational propaganda. The Federal government, especially through its Department of Agriculture, has promoted scientific farming where there was no initial impulse on the part of farmers to go to school. This work was supported, especially in the Southern States, by the General Education Board. It sometimes took the form of an appeal to the boys and girls as well as to adults. A typical case is set forth in the first

[50] H. H. Wheaton, "The United States Bureau of Education and the Immigrant." *The Annals of the American Academy of Political and Social Science,* Vol. LXVII, No. 156 (September, 1916), pp. 273-274.

report of the General Education Board.

A club consists essentially of a group of boys varying in number from twenty-five to one hundred, and ranging in age from ten to eighteen. Corn and cotton are both cultivated, but corn is preferred: first, because the South needs more corn; secondly, because corn lends itself better to study and selection. As a rule, each member works a plot of one acre. The county superintendent of education is usually in charge. . . .

Driving through Macon County, Alabama, not long ago, two strangers observed, in a large field of ordinary corn, a patch standing out like a miniature skyscraper. They dismounted to interview the owner. A Negro boy approached.

"Is this your corn?"

"Yes, sir."

"How did you come to grow it?"

"One of Dr. Knapp's men showed me, sir."

"Why did you plant it so far apart in the rows?"

"Because, sir, most all that grows comes from the sunshine and the air."

"When did you plow?"

"Last fall, sir."

"Why?"

"To make plant food during the winter."

"Where did you get your fertilizer?"

"From the bottom, sir."

"How many times did you cultivate?"

"Six times, sir."

"Why?"

"Because there's water down next to the clay, and when I don't plow the sun draws it all away."

"When did you put in the cowpeas?"

"After the last plowing, sir."

"What did you do that for?"

"Because the cowpeas get out of the air nitrogen, and put back in the ground about as much as the corn takes out."

How many valuable lessons had this remote Negro lad learned from doing one job right! But this is not the end of the story. His double crop was worth $52. From his pocket he pulled a dirty little pass-book, the entries in which showed what the crop had cost. Reckoning his own time at ten cents an hour and his father's mule at a dollar a day, he netted a profit of $30 to the acre. His younger sister, it appeared, had had an equally profitable quarter of an acre in cotton. Three years later both were students at Tuskegee, paying for their education with the money earned as club workers.[51]

Equally impressive examples could be supplied of transformations in homes brought about by demonstrations in cooking, house decoration, and costume design given by teachers of domestic science and household art.

Entertainment as Part of the Educational Program

The problem of providing proper entertainment for people in the city and proper places for the coming together of social groups in country and city communities is one of the serious problems of modern life. The church serves less than it used to the purposes of a meeting place for the community. The schools have been called on to help solve this problem. The extent to which the demand exists is illustrated by the following quotation from the Cleveland survey[52]:

> According to the custodians' reports the total after-class lettings of school accommodations during 1914-15 numbered 3,469. Of these, 462 were for mothers' club meetings, class dances, pupil society meetings, pay entertainments, bazaars, or some other kind of purely school function and 3,007 were lettings to outside organizations. A large part of the latter consisted of clubs or Sunday-school classes connected with some 27 different churches which, along with two dozen or more specifically named athletic societies, sought the use of school gymnasiums and showers for basketball and similar indoor games. The varied character of the bodies which hired the auditoriums, club and classrooms can best be discovered from a perusal of the following partial but representative list.

GROUPS USING SCHOOL ACCOMMODATIONS

Twentieth Ward Improvement Association	D. A. R. Clubs
East End Chamber of Commerce	G. A. R. Post
East End Neighborhood Club	Normal Alumni
Women's Suffrage Political League	Alumni Club
Municipal School League	Sanitation Club
Spanish War Veterans	Civic League

[51] The General Education Board: An Account of its Activities, 1902-1914, pp. 58, 61-62. New York City, 1915.

[52] Clarence Arthur Perry, Educational Extension, pp. 82-85. Cleveland Education Survey. Published by the Survey Committee of the Cleveland Foundation, 1916.

Ladies' Relief Corps
Knights of Pythias Lodge
Public School Association
Garment Workers' Union
Warner Civic Association
Social Center Club
Teachers' and Mothers' Club
Western Reserve Dental Club
Thespian Dramatic Club
South End Choral Society
Mendelssohn Choir
Boys' Glee Club
Boy Scouts
Boy Cadets
Camp Fire Girls
Y. W. C. A.
Mothers' Club
Anti-Fly Campaign
Boys' Chef Club
Patrons' Club
Social Club
German Club
Latin Club
Syrian Club

These names show concretely what a wide range of Cleveland's social elements are nowadays seeking the kind of facilities which a modern school edifice possesses. In the majority of cases these groups were obliged to pay custodians' fees ranging from 30 cents to $5.00 an evening depending on the size of the quarters used. That fact attests the genuineness of this demand and its vigor is further evidenced by the rapid growth in volume which, as shown in the following table, has practically doubled during the past two years.

GROWTH OF AFTER-SCHOOL USE OF SCHOOL FACILITIES BY NEIGHBORHOOD ORGANIZATIONS

	1913-1914	1914-1915	Per Cent Increase
Organizations using buildings	298	596	100
Total lettings	1,932	3,007	56
Fees paid to custodians by organizations	$1,729.91	$2,813.55	62
Aggregate attendance	120,511	276,253	129

Associations aimed directly at the Improvement of Schools

A social organization which is of special importance to the schools is the parent-teachers' association, which is coming to be a common adjunct of every school. Such an association often helps the school to secure equipment which it needs, and furnishes a useful avenue for the dissemination of ideas with regard to school policies. Sometimes the school officer finds that the proper relation of the association to school administration needs definition. He then falls back with satisfaction on the words of a recent writer in the *Atlantic*:

> Running a school or a class is a technical or expert job. It cannot as a rule be done by an untrained person; and untrained people, seeking to break in, are likely to do more harm than good. The

school situation, indeed, resembles the situation in medicine fifty years ago. The practice of medicine at that time was atrocious; but it had to be improved, and it was improved by doctors, not by laymen. I shall not spare the schools; but schools must be improved by schoolmen—and they will be.

We have then reached this point. Intelligent parents wish to have a say in the education of their children. But schools must be conducted by trained persons. The training of these persons is, however, largely antiquated. Are we not deadlocked?

I think not. Parents cannot tell teachers what to do or how to do it. But what they can do is to ask questions. They can, like the man from Missouri, require "to be shown." At first blush, this may not look like very much. But if my readers will bear with me for a moment, perhaps they will see that the right and the duty of asking "to be shown," of asking persistently and continuously "Why?" "Why?" gives parents all the leverage they need or can use in making over the education of their children.

Our schools could not be perfect. I won't even stop to argue that they can all at a bound make themselves much better than they are. Parents cannot possibly make many practicable suggestions by way of improving them. But just because we all know so little, just because schoolmasters are so hampered by tradition and organization, just because parents are so helpless in making practicable suggestions, for these very reasons the complacent following of traditions is the most inexcusable of attitudes. The schools which are now too conventional, too complacent, too free from deep-seated and unhappy doubts, should be tentative, inquiring, investigating, skeptical in their point of view. They will be assisted in becoming tentative, inquiring, skeptical, and experimental if parents will, year after year, make them tell *why*, make them show *why*. For when people are called on to show why, they begin to look into what they are doing, and out of this critical scrutiny will come doubt, invention, and finally something living in place of something long since dead.[53]

Correspondence Schools

This discussion has not included, as perhaps it should, university extension, libraries, rural-community organization, and other agencies. It must, however, make reference to one popular movement which has grown in recent years to proportions that are literally vast. The correspondence schools of this country do an enormous amount of more or less valuable teaching. The qualifying phrase "more or less valuable" is justified by the fact that many of the correspondence schools are purely commercial enterprises and provide a very low grade of courses. The

[53] Abraham Flexner, "Parents and Schools." *The Atlantic Monthly* (July, 1916), pp. 26-27.

number of such schools, however, shows the demand for education, the evidence in this case being the stronger when we recognize that in many cases the quality of instruction is not such as to encourage the student.

Principles required to systematize Educational Activities

The list of activities which carry education far beyond the limits of the traditional curriculum could be extended. A complete list would include newspapers and magazines with their lessons on health, on food and economic problems. It would include the churches and many social organizations. The purposes of the present exposition have, however, been adequately served if the reader has been impressed by the popular demand for a broad educational program.

EXERCISES AND READINGS

Complications sometimes arise in the matter of credits, not from the fact that they are given within a certain institution but rather from the fact that a second institution to which students go cannot deal with the credits. Suppose that a certain high school gives credit for gardening. Should the college accept the credit toward admission? Is it legitimate to substitute Sunday-school courses for senior English?

What would you want to know about a music teacher before crediting her pupils with a high-school credit in music? How would you find out how much work the music pupil had done? If you think an examination a good method, would you give credit for typewriting to a boy who learned to write outside of school and could pass an examination?

The distinction between an education and school credits is sometimes painfully evident. Describe cases in which the effort to get credits interferes with school work.

When a community is very enthusiastic about social centers, it often asks the board of education to open the schools at night. Should the board charge a fee or give the use of the building without charge? In case the board does not have money enough to furnish the children with playground apparatus, should it give the use of buildings free?

Perry, C. A. Wider Use of the School Plant. Russell Sage Foundation. This book treats in a comprehensive way of all the different types of outside activity carried on in schools.

The Annals of the American Academy of Political and Social Science, September, 1916, Vol. 67, No. 156. Concord, New Hampshire. The number is given over to a symposium in which a number of authors give an account of the outside activities which have in recent years been attached to the school.

CHAPTER XI

PRINCIPLES INFLUENCING THE ORGANIZATION OF THE CURRICULUM

Necessity of practical decisions in spite of confusion. The doctrine of discipline. The doctrine of natural education in the form of the doctrine of freedom. Concentration and interest. Popular attitude toward discipline. Examples of discipline and freedom. Natural education and recognition of individual differences. Natural education as training for life. Training in the methods of knowledge and general training. Examples of views on formal training. Prominence of curriculum in determining quality of instruction. Bases for judging curriculum and syllabi. Formal discipline and transfer of training. Relation of subjects to maturity of pupils. Summary. Exercises and readings.

Necessity of Practical Decisions in Spite of Confusion

With the expansions in education that have been reviewed in foregoing chapters, there has come a certain confusion and uncertainty of practice which sometimes tends to lower the standards of work in the school.

Consider a concrete case. A small city can afford to offer only a limited number of courses in its high school. Shall the choice fall on Latin or typewriting? Among the sciences shall botany or chemistry be provided? Botany would relate itself well to agriculture, and chemistry would be a basis for domestic science. Sometimes in the effort to meet both demands, weak courses are tolerated, and teachers are either overloaded because they are called on to carry heavy programs or are inadequately compensated in the effort to provide a sufficient number to do all the work demanded.

Nor is it the school alone which is confronted with the necessity of choosing; the individual student must elect. There is a high school in a small city in Illinois, as shown by the last report of the North Central Association of Colleges and Secondary Schools, which enrolled in 1915 four hundred and sixty-one students. This school offered twenty-three units in academic subjects and twelve units in vocational subjects. If each pupil took five units a year, which would be a very heavy program, he would be able to complete in four years only twenty units, or fifteen less than the school offers. Another high school in the same state with an enrollment of five hundred and thirty-two students offers an aggregate of forty-four units.

Finally, there are choices to be made within these choices, because after the decision has been reached that botany is to be taught, the teacher must select from the abundant material within this science that which seems most productive. The student, also, gives more attention to one subject than to the others which he is pursuing, thus exhibiting another kind of selection.

Choices have to be made, and every choice has back of it some prejudice or some clearly thought-out principle or some experience collected by the teacher or pupil through contact with earlier educational problems. Our business in this course is, first, to become aware of the chief reasons for the choices actually made in schools, and, second, to take up some of the evidences which justify one or the other of these reasons. The present chapter will be devoted to a brief statement of the principles most commonly urged as the basis of choice.

The Doctrine of Discipline

The historical reason for training children which has come down to us from the religious traditions of the Middle Ages, and more directly from the austere beliefs and practices of the Puritans, is the supposed demand for a curbing of the naturally perverse tendencies of children, for a disciplining of nature into a higher form of morality. This reason has in more recent times been phrased in new terms. The mind, it is said, must be made strong through struggle with difficulties as the athlete becomes skillful and muscular through training. If the training seems for the time being monotonous and overvigorous, well and good; the end justifies the effort. This is the doctrine of discipline.

The Doctrine of Natural Education in the Form of the Doctrine of Freedom

Against the notion of discipline there has been matched, especially in the last century, the opposing notion that all good qualities are natural and will express themselves freely if the artificial restraints of life are removed. Rousseau, in his famous attack on social conventions, pointed out the truth that the child is naturally an eager learner. Biology reinforced Rousseau's teachings with the doctrines of natural selection and the survival of the fittest, meaning by the fittest those able to take on complete adaptation to the present environment. The belief that nature is a safe guide has led to the doctrine of freedom for the child in all matters of intellectual development.

Concentration and Interest

The antithesis between discipline and freedom, between training which aims to transform the child's nature and training which gives the child's nature opportunity to express itself without restraint, can be illustrated as follows. On the one side it is said that children have no power of concentration of attention. They are flighty and erratic. They must be made to think steadily in order to train their minds for hard mental work. On the other side it is asserted that when a child's interest is aroused through an appeal to his natural tastes he will exert his mind to the limit of its powers, and this is all that can advantageously be required.

Popular Attitude toward Discipline

When the antithesis between discipline and natural interests is presented to the present-day world, it must be said that there is a widespread disposition to set aside discipline as arbitrary and puritanical. Our generation is in favor of natural development. Perhaps it would be truer to use the past tense in the last statement because the social attitude toward discipline has been profoundly affected by the war. Never in the history of this country has the lesson been clearer than it is at the present that social coöperation means the training of the individual to make some sacrifices. The American school has carried the elective system and its concessions to individuals to an extreme which is likely to be limited somewhat in the future by a recognition of social obligations.

Examples of Discipline and Freedom

It may be well to illustrate this abstract discussion of discipline and freedom with concrete examples. One of the most emphatic pronouncements in favor of the doctrine of freedom is that of Madam Montessori, an Italian physician whose system of education has been much heralded in this country as a substitute for the kindergarten. According to this writer's views the pupil should have perfect freedom. The contrast with the kindergarten is described as follows by one of the observers of the two institutions:

> A contrast between the Montessori school and the kindergarten of the more formal and traditional type may serve to give a clearer picture of the Montessori procedure, and consequently of the Montessori conception of liberty as it appears in practice. The most evident difference is seen in the function of the teacher. The kindergartner is clearly the center and arbiter of the activity in the room. The Montessori directress seems, on the contrary, to be at one side. The kindergartner contemplates at each moment the whole of her group; the directress is talking usually to one alone—possibly to two or three. The kindergarten children are engaged in some sort of directed group activity; each Montessori child is an isolated worker, though one or more comrades may look on and suggest. The arrangement of the room shows the same contrast. The kindergarten has a circle about which all may gather, and tables for group activity. The Montessori room is fitted, preferably, with individual tables, arranged as the children will. (In the writer's observation, there has been little deviation, however, from arrangement in formal rows.) Montessori provides long periods, say of two or more hours, while the kindergarten period rarely goes beyond a half-hour. During the period assigned for that purpose practically all of the Montessori apparatus is available for any child (except for the very youngest or the newest comers),

> and the child makes his choice freely. The kindergartner, on the other hand, decides very nicely what specific apparatus shall be used during any one period. The Montessori child abides by his choice as long as he wishes, and changes as often as he likes; he may even do nothing if he prefers. The child in the traditional kindergarten uses the same apparatus throughout the period, and is frequently led or directed by the teacher as to what he shall do. At other times he may be at liberty to build or represent at will whatever may be suggested by the "gift" set for the period. The Montessori child, each at his own chosen task, works, as stated, in relative isolation, his nearest neighbors possibly looking on.[54]

At the other end of the educational system we find the example of "stiff" courses in college designed to "weed out" the slothful and incompetent. The "stiff" course is required mathematics, or a foreign language, or a course in English composition. Opposition to stiff courses expresses itself in the demand for an undiluted elective system in which the student may take whatever serves his purposes.

Natural Education and Recognition of Individual Differences

The advocacy of a natural education takes a different turn when it drops the word "freedom" and emphasizes the fact that individuals differ radically in their native capacities. Some pupils have an aptitude for one kind of work, others for other types. The school is to-day committed to a recognition of these differences and to a study of their meaning. There is a movement known as the vocational-guidance movement which is making progress in the direction of the discovery of methods for finding out what studies can properly be undertaken by students in view of their varying natural endowments. The individual's natural bent being discovered, his educational training can be directed to the highest possible cultivation of his powers. Nature is thus recognized but is not made the dominant fact. The vocational end is the controlling factor in the situation. The attainment of this end may require the most rigid disciplining of one's powers. The direction of this disciplining is dictated by nature, but not the particular steps of education. As a result of such a discussion it begins to appear that there is no fundamental reason for the abandonment of the idea of discipline even if there is a complete recognition of natural individual differences.

In concrete cases the opposition to the doctrine of discipline may, however, be acute. The pupil may say that he has absolutely no natural capacity for algebra or spelling. The teacher may answer that these are universal requirements and that there is no escape from these necessary studies because of individual differences. In such a dispute, tradition, on the one hand, and the wider opportunities of the modern curriculum, on the other hand, are likely to be arrayed against each other. Algebra as the conservative subject is likely to defend the view that discipline is necessary, whereas manual training and domestic science are likely to emphasize the natural attractiveness of the practical training which they offer. Thus it has

[54] William Heard Kilpatrick, The Montessori System Examined, pp. 14-15. Riverside Educational Monograph. Houghton Mifflin Company, 1914.

come to pass that certain subjects, especially the older subjects in the curriculum, have come to be regarded as the defenders of the doctrine of discipline, while the newer subjects have often been regarded as opposed by their very character to the doctrine.

Natural Education as Training for Life

Still another turn is given to the discussion by an emphasis on the social demands of later life. As society is constituted, individual differences are sure to play a large part in determining success or failure. Furthermore, society as constituted in its commercial organizations accepts without hesitation the principle of division of labor. Why should not the school be like society? Why should not the school be a miniature world with all the different types of life that will later become real to the pupils? Practical needs thus come into the foreground.

Training in the Methods of Knowledge and General Training

Two views are sometimes offered in opposition to the doctrine of a strictly practical training. First, it is said that the pupil in order to prepare for later life must pass through certain forms of training which are preliminary, intended to set up his mental machinery before it begins to produce anything. Otherwise expressed, it is said that the pupil must get the tools of knowledge before he tries to take part in real life.

Second, it is said that there is no possibility in the complex society of the modern world of foreseeing just what will be the practical needs of pupils when they grow to adult life. It will therefore be better, it is argued, to aim at a broad flexible training which can in due time be turned into any channel that circumstances may dictate.

Examples of Views on Formal Training

The dispute which is introduced by these opposing statements is one of the bitterest in modern educational writings. Let us borrow two quotations which will present the case in detail. Frank M. McMurry has given in his report on the schools of New York City a striking example of the advocacy of direct and constant attention to social needs. In giving the quotation from this author it is possible to include incidentally his description of an earlier view of the curriculum which emphasizes general training or methods of thought rather than special content.

> **PROMINENCE OF CURRICULUM IN DETERMINING QUALITY OF INSTRUCTION**
>
> Thirty years ago the belief was often expressed that it made little difference *what* one studied, but all the difference in the world *with whom* one studied. That belief made almost any curriculum acceptable, and directed attention to the personality of the teacher and to *method* as the principal factors determining the effectiveness of instruction.

That belief, however, has been greatly modified. While no one will deny the importance of the teacher's personality, most persons will admit that the proper expression of personality and skill in method are both greatly dependent upon the subject matter of the curriculum. Carefully selected subject matter is prerequisite to skill in method of presentation. Without a good curriculum there is bound to be great waste.

BASES FOR JUDGING CURRICULUM AND SYLLABI

1. By Relation of Subject Matter to Children's Purposes

In harmony with the previous discussion of standards for judging the quality of instruction, as a whole, the quality of the curriculum in particular is to be determined partly by its tendency to influence the tastes, purposes, and hopes of children. Any curriculum for the elementary school should have its content selected from among those experiences of mankind that have seemed most valuable. That is to be presupposed. But this selection can be indifferent to the tendencies, interests, and capacities of children in general, and of certain ages in particular, and aim only at present storage of facts and ideas that may count in a dim future, i.e., in adult life. Or it may be made with constant reference to the abilities, tastes, and needs of children at the present time. In the former case, motive on the part of children is overlooked; in the latter case, the extent of provision for it is accepted as one of the standards by which the curriculum is to be judged. We represent the latter point of view.[55]

The group of thinkers to whom McMurry refers with disfavor as absorbed in methods rather than content has never been more ably represented than by President Hadley, extracts from whose statement are as follows:

Greek is an intellectual game where the umpires know the rules better than they know the rules in the game of French, for instance, or history, or botany. A man's rating in an examination on any one of these last three subjects is largely the result of accident unless the examiner is quite unusually skillful. A man's rating in Greek, on the other hand, means something. There never were intellectual competitions keener than the classical competitions at Oxford in the days when the best men in England wanted their sons to learn that particular game.

Unfortunately, a large number of the strongest men, both in England and in the United States, have decided that this game takes more time than it is worth. Personally, I believe that this change of mind is in many respects a misfortune; that in trying to get more practical results in the way of knowledge or culture

[55] Frank M. McMurry, Report on Educational Aspects of the Public School System of the City of New York, 1911-1912, Part II, p. 265.

a great many American college boys have lost the training which the Greek would have given them and gained nothing of equal value in its place. . . .

It was a mistake for the advocates of the old curriculum to think that all the students required the same treatment. It is, I believe, an equal mistake for the advocates of the elective system to think that each student requires a different treatment. For while there is a very large number of subjects of interest to study, and an almost infinite variety of occupations which the students are going to follow afterwards, there is a comparatively small number of types of mind with which we have to deal. If we can have four or five honor courses, something like those of the English universities, where the studies are grouped and the examinations arranged to meet the needs of these different types, we can, I think, realize the chief advantages of the elective system or the group system without subjecting ourselves to their evils. I am confident that we can secure a degree of collective intellectual interest which is now absent from most of our colleges, and can establish competitions which will be recognized not only in college but in the world as places where the best men can show what is in them.

It may be objected that any such arrangement would render it difficult for a boy to study the particular things that he was going to use in after life. I regard this as its cardinal advantage. The ideal college education seems to me to be one where a student learns things that he is not going to use in after life, by methods that he is going to use. The former element gives the breadth, the latter element gives the training.[56]

Formal Discipline and Transfer of Training

The controversy here illustrated has led to the development of a number of technical phrases. The doctrine that emphasizes form or method as opposed to content is known as the doctrine of formal discipline. The advocates of this doctrine defend the view that training gained in one field will transfer to other fields of activity. Stated in these terms the doctrine is referred to as that of the transfer of training.

The doctrine of transfer of training is capable of experimental and statistical verification or refutation. A vast body of evidence has been collected in recent years. The conclusions to be drawn from this evidence are clear. There are certain general habits, such as concentration of attention and power of arranging and expressing ideas, which carry over from one field of experience to another. The transfer of training is facilitated if the original training is given in such a form that it lends itself readily to application in new spheres of thought. So important is the development of general habits that it is entirely legitimate to proceed at every

[56] Report of the President of Yale University, 1908-1909. Published by the University, New Haven, 1909.

stage of education slowly enough to give to each subject its relations through a variety of possible applications. It is recognized as impossible to give in the schools direct special training for all possible lines of activity upon which the pupil is to enter. Some effort must be expended in cultivating what may properly be called the applying attitude of mind. Once the applying attitude is aroused in any individual, the transfer of training will be likely to go on through individual recognition of the advantages of application.

Relation of Subjects to Maturity of Pupils

The quotation from McMurry given some pages back suggests another aspect of this whole matter which has been a subject of much dispute. When should certain kinds of training be introduced into the curriculum? A quotation will help to make the problem clear.

> So far as high-school instruction is concerned, the most important practical question raised in the present discussion is whether the ability to learn a foreign vocabulary varies with age. It is almost universally claimed that a student must begin a language when young in order to learn it effectively and economically. In opposition to this theory, we shall maintain, as in the case of motor skill, that a foreign vocabulary can be learned just as economically at the later end of the period from six to eighteen years of age as at any other part of it. As the basis for this contention we have some very closely related evidence from experimental psychology, in the work done upon facility in memorizing at different ages.[57]

If the statement here quoted is accepted, it still remains an open question whether the pronunciation of a foreign language is worth acquiring and whether pronunciation is to be sought as an important element of the study, for if it is, there is little doubt that young children acquire it more easily and more accurately than do older persons.

The example is introduced not for the purpose of attempting a settlement of the question but for the purpose of showing that the organization of the curriculum raises questions which are now answered for the most part on the basis of mere prejudice, but should be answered in the light of a body of broad, scientific evidence. Certainly the problem of the distribution of a pupil's studies through the various periods of his mental development is one of the most important of these problems.

SUMMARY

> The doctrine of discipline holds that it is desirable by training to transform in some measure the natural tendencies of the child's mind.

---

[57] Samuel Chester Parker, Methods of Teaching in High Schools, pp. 318-319. Ginn and Company, 1915.

The general doctrine of natural education emphasizes the importance of following the lines of natural development in education. Often this doctrine is so formulated as to be opposed to the doctrine of discipline.

When dealing with the intellectual side of the pupil's nature the doctrine of discipline takes the form of a demand for cultivation of concentration. Natural education asserts the right of the child to his personal interests and is liberal in making concessions to these interests.

The form of the doctrine of natural education most directly opposed to the doctrine of discipline is the doctrine of freedom. According to this view the pupil should be left to follow his natural impulses.

Another form of the doctrine of natural education recognizes the differences between individuals as important considerations in governing their training.

Training for practical life is a very common basis for the organization of the curriculum and has been amply illustrated in earlier chapters.

Training in the methods or tools of knowledge is in some measure opposed to the demand for practical training.

Training of general intelligence is advocated because it gives the student greater freedom in adjusting his career to the circumstances of later life.

Training in the forms of knowledge, or formal training, sometimes called formal discipline, is practically synonymous with training of general intelligence.

The doctrine of transfer of training is one formulation of the doctrine of formal discipline. Evidence is abundant that transfer takes place. Its degree and the methods of securing it are subjects of vigorous investigation.

The adaptation of training to the maturity of pupils is one of the most important requirements in arranging a curriculum. In a later chapter this will be discussed under the title "Periodicity in the Pupil's Development."

EXERCISES AND READINGS

The arguments for and against disciplinary subjects should be followed in detail. Thus, why so much arithmetic in the lower school? Is it necessary to have as much as we do in the upper grades, even admitting its value in the lower grades? Are students of higher mathematics practical men?

A child brought up in an indulgent home is sometimes pointed out as a horrible example of a child brought up with unlimited freedom. Is the example just? What are the different meanings which may attach to the term "freedom"?

What does maturity on the part of a pupil mean? What are the marks of increasing maturity? Can maturity be produced by deliberately adopted school methods?

What elements of one's own education can be traced to the demand on the part of some teacher or parent for discipline? Was the demand when put into actual operation in the school successful in producing general improvement in one's ability?

Classify subjects in the curriculum as designed to satisfy different aims. How many different aims can be distinguished as appealing to men of ordinary experience in their efforts to secure an education? Booker Washington used to say that he found many people desiring an education in order that they might escape from hard work. Is this a common desire? Is it legitimate? Is it harder to earn one's living by composing music or by keeping books? Why do men want an education?

Heck, W. H. Mental Discipline and Educational Values. John Lane Company. A summary of the arguments for and against formal discipline with a very strong bias against.

Judd, C. H. Psychology of High-School Subjects. Ginn and Company. Especially the chapter which deals with formal discipline, with an affirmative statement of what such discipline means.

McMurry, C. A. Conflicting Principles in Teaching. Houghton Mifflin Company. An interesting and balanced summary of the general principles discussed in this chapter and other principles of like type.

CHAPTER XII

INDIVIDUAL DIFFERENCES

Adaptation of curriculum to individual pupils. Low grades of intelligence. Differentiated courses. Tests of general intelligence. Exceptionally bright pupils. Sex differences. Differences in industrial opportunity for the sexes and corresponding demands for training. Household arts as extras. Demand for new courses for girls. Individual differences which appear during training. Democratic recognition of individual differences. Exercises and readings.

Adaptation of Curriculum to Individual Pupils

A number of times in the last few chapters the discussion has been brought to the point of recognizing the importance of individual differences. The teacher cannot determine merely from a knowledge of history what history is suitable for a given type of pupils. In the elective system of the high school and of the college there is a liberal recognition of the principle that instruction must be adapted to individuals, both in content and method. The present chapter will be given over to a treatment of some of the individual differences among pupils which are of dominant significance in formulating the curriculum.

Low Grades of Intelligence

The most striking example of individual deviation from the average grade of intelligence is to be found in the cases of those unfortunates who continue throughout life to be deficient because they have underdeveloped nervous systems. As a result of heredity or pathological conditions in early childhood a certain number of persons, conservatively estimated as two in every thousand, are permanently subnormal. These cases vary in degree. The lowest grade defectives, known as idiots, are defined in the Report of the British Royal Commission on the Feeble-minded as persons "so deeply defective in mind from birth or from early age that they are unable to guard themselves against common physical dangers." The less defective are classed as imbeciles, feeble-minded, and morons, each class representing a further approach toward normality.

The lower grades of defectives are so dependent on the care of others that they do not reach the school at all, but the higher grades either escape detection until they try to learn reading and arithmetic or through the persistence of parents are brought to school in the hope that their defectiveness may be temporary. Some of the highest grades succeed in learning enough so that they pass out of the first grade. They do not master reading, but they learn to repeat the words sufficiently to deceive the teacher with the appearance of having recognized the printed symbols.

Differentiated Courses

As soon as a defective child is discovered, it is advantageous for him and for the other pupils in the school that he be given some form of special training. In most cases it is more than useless to try to give him the ordinary school courses. He cannot learn to read well enough to enable him to get information from books. He can, on the other hand, acquire some of the simple arts of self-support. It would be better for all concerned to give up the effort to teach such a child reading.

The major objection to a program of this type is that it is sometimes extremely difficult and, in the early years, often quite impossible to decide whether the child is really defective or is merely slow in development. Some children come to their normal powers slowly, but ultimately reach a level of intellectual and physical efficiency so high that they are not to be classed with the defectives. One hesitates, therefore, to give up the teaching of reading in the case of a particular child until all possibility of his development is past. It is better to err on the side of too great training than to despair at too early a date.

Tests of General Intelligence

In the effort to discover defectives various systems of tests have been devised. The general assumption back of all these systems is that a defective child is one whose mental development has prematurely ceased. For example, a twelve-year-old child may be behind in his development to such an extent that he has a mind like a four-year-old. If, now, it can be determined what mental powers are possessed by an ordinary four-year-old and if the defective can be shown to possess the same powers, and no more, it is possible to adapt instruction to his real intellectual needs. Technical students of the problem have accordingly drawn the distinction between physiological age and mental age. In the example cited above the physiological age is twelve; the mental age, four.

A system of tests of this kind has another use. If a child is put through the tests at intervals of a year, it can be ascertained whether he is improving or standing still. In this way some of the uncertainties as to the permanence or temporary character of his deficiencies can be removed.

Tests of the type under discussion are called tests of general intelligence. An example taken from one of the most widely used systems, namely, the Binet-Simon series, will serve to show what the tests are and how they are used. The special form of the test here quoted is that worked out by Professor Terman. His exposition of one of the fifth-year tests is as follows:

> *Materials.* It is necessary to have two weights, identical in shape, size, and appearance, weighing respectively 3 and 15

grams. If manufactured weights are not at hand, it is easy to make satisfactory substitutes by taking stiff cardboard pill-boxes, about 1¼ inches in diameter, and filling them with cotton and shot to the desired weight. The shot must be embedded in the center of the cotton so as to prevent rattling. After the box has been loaded to the exact weight, the lid should be glued on firmly. If one does not have access to laboratory scales, it is always possible to secure the help of a druggist in the rather delicate task of weighing the boxes accurately. A set of pill-box weights will last through hundreds of tests, if handled carefully, but they will not stand rough usage. The manufactured blocks are more durable, and so more satisfactory in the long run. If the weights are not at hand, the alternative test may be substituted.

Procedure. Place the 3-and 15-gram weights on the table before the child some two or three inches apart. Say: *"You see these blocks. They look just alike, but one of them is heavy and one is light. Try them and tell me which one is heavier."* If the child does not respond, repeat the instructions, saying this time, *"Tell me which one is the heaviest."* (Many American children have heard only the superlative form of the adjective used in the comparison of two objects.)

Sometimes the child merely points to one of the boxes or picks up one at random and hands it to the examiner, thinking he is asked to *guess* which is heaviest. We then say: *"No, that is not the way. You must take the boxes in your hands and try them, like this"* (illustrating by lifting with one hand, first one box and then the other, a few inches from the table). Most children of 5 years are then able to make the comparison correctly. Very young subjects, however, or older ones who are retarded, sometimes adopt the rather questionable method of lifting both weights in the same hand at once. This is always an unfavorable sign, especially if one of the blocks is placed in the hand on top of the other block.

After the first trial the weights are shuffled and again presented for comparison as before, *this time with the positions reversed*. The third trial follows with the blocks in the same position as in the first trial. Some children have a tendency to stereotyped behavior, which in this test shows itself by choosing always the block on a certain side. Hence the necessity of alternating the positions. Reserve commendation until all three trials have been given.

Scoring. The test is passed if *two of the three* comparisons are correct. If there is reason to suspect that the successful responses were due to lucky guesses, the test should be entirely repeated.

Remarks. This test is decidedly more difficult than that of comparing lines. It is doubtful, however, if we can regard the difference as one due primarily to the relative difficulty of visual discrimination and muscular discrimination. In fact, the test with weights hardly taxes sensory discrimination at all when used with children of 5-year intelligence. Success depends, in the first place, on the ability to understand the instructions; and in the second place, on the power to hold the instructions in mind long enough to guide the process of making the comparison. The test presupposes, in elementary form, a power which is operative in all the higher independent processes of thought, the power to neglect the manifold distractions of irrelevant sensations and ideas and to drive direct toward a goal. Here the goal is furnished by the instruction, "Try them and see which is heavier." This must be held firmly enough in mind to control the steps necessary for making the comparison. Ideas of piling the blocks on top of one another, throwing them, etc., must be inhibited. Sometimes the low-grade imbecile starts off in a very promising way, then apparently forgets the instructions (loses sight of the goal), and begins to play with the boxes in a random way. His mental processes are not consecutive, stable, or controlled. He is blown about at the mercy of every gust of momentary interest.

There is very general agreement in the assignment of this test to year V.[58]

Exceptionally Bright Pupils

Thus far the discussion has been of inferior individuals. There are likewise individuals who are superior to the average. Schools have ordinarily taken little account of these. They do not constitute urgent problems in the same sense as defectives. The supernormal child can get his lessons, if he will, so that the teacher will never have to bother with him. A moment's thought on the matter, however, will convince anyone that society has more to gain from a proper system of training supernormal children than from special provisions for the subnormal. Since defense is of the most vital importance, we may say that society had at the outset to defend itself against the harm that might be done by subnormals. But defense having been provided in adequate degree, attention should turn to the possibilities of great benefit which may be expected from special training of the unusually bright.

Various devices have been suggested for the treatment of the supernormal. In general, the principles underlying these suggestions are the same as the principles for the treatment of subnormals. Separate the unusually bright and give them a type of training which will best develop their personal powers.

In a school system which has only a few special cases of the one type or the other it is extremely difficult to follow the suggestion of special training for special levels of ability. The matter must be left in such cases to the ingenuity of the teacher. The bright pupil should be given extra work and, so far as possible, special

[58] Lewis M. Terman, The Measurement of Intelligence, pp. 161-163. Houghton Mifflin Company, 1916.

attention. The dull child should be allowed to do some useful handwork. Where the system is larger, special rapid classes—express classes, as they have sometimes been called—should be organized for the bright pupils, while slowly moving classes are provided for the backward pupils.

Sex Differences

Leaving the degrees of intelligence, we turn to a distinction which is of an entirely different type—the difference between boys and girls.

It is difficult to disentangle this problem from a mass of social considerations which attach to it. Women and girls have grown up under a social system that has assumed on their part fundamentally different tastes and interests from those of men and boys. The social system has sometimes expressed itself in terms which imply inferiority of women as compared with men. It is natural, therefore, that at a period when women and girls are taking a new place in the social scheme, there should be at first a good deal of attention given to the demonstration that women are not inferior to men. The simplest demonstration can, of course, be given by putting girls into the same classes with boys and requiring of them the same intellectual tasks. For some years past the experiment has been under way. Girls have shown themselves not only quite as competent intellectually as boys but in some respects superior.

During the period of experimentation, however, there has persisted a difference in tastes and interests; and the demand for a special training for girls was never louder than to-day when the proof that girls are quite as competent as boys seems to be incontrovertible.

The reasons for this demand are connected in part with the later practical uses to which girls expect to put their training and in part with the fact that girls give attention to certain groups of facts which boys neglect, while boys, on the other hand, have their special spheres of interest.

For example, boys are always brought up to interest themselves in mechanical appliances. When a boy comes to study natural science, therefore, it is easily possible to introduce the subject by examples of a mechanical type. Parents do not give girls mechanical toys, society assumes that girls will not engage in occupations which call for a knowledge of machinery, consequently they do not readily take up courses in physics which begin with mechanics.

The present situation, then, is something like this: girls are proved to be equal to boys in school ability, but continue with the full sanction of society to have tastes and interests different from those of boys.

Differences in Industrial Opportunity for the Sexes and Corresponding Demands for Training

The contrast in industrial demands which the school must meet in dealing with boys and girls who are preparing for clerical positions is shown in the following summary of conclusions reached by the Cleveland survey:

> Training for boys and girls should be different in content and in emphasis.
>
> The usual course of study in commercial schools is suitable for girls and unsuitable for boys.
>
> A girl needs, chiefly, specific training in some one line of work. She has a choice among stenography, bookkeeping and machine operating.
>
> A boy needs, chiefly, general education, putting emphasis on writing, figuring, and spelling; general information; and the development of certain qualities and standards.
>
> * * * * *
>
> Boys' training looks forward to both clerical work and business administration; but as clerical work is a preparation for business and is likely to occupy the first few years of wage-earning, training should aim especially to meet the needs of clerical positions.
>
> Clerical positions for boys cover a variety of work which cannot be definitely anticipated and cannot therefore be specifically trained for. But certain fundamental needs are common to all.
>
> Most of the specialized training for boys should be given in night continuation classes.
>
> Girl stenographers need a full high school course for its educational value and for maturity. Girls going into other clerical positions can qualify with a year or two less of education; but immaturity in any case puts them at a disadvantage.
>
> Boys' training, for those who cannot remain in school, should be compressed into fewer than four years. Immaturity in the case of boys is not a great disadvantage.[59]

To many readers not prepared by a full consideration of the facts the above conclusions may seem untenable. A brief section of the argument will therefore be important in carrying conviction. This argument is presented in the following quotation:

> If we wish to generalize broadly about the work of boys and girls we can say with truth that the majority of boys begin as messengers or office boys and subsequently become clerks or do bookkeeping work. As men they remain in these latter positions or, in at least an equal number of cases, pass on into the productive or administrative end of business. The majority of girls, first and last, are stenographers or to a less extent, assistants in bookkeeping

[59] Bertha M. Stevens, Boys and Girls in Commercial Work, pp. 179-180. Cleveland Education Survey. Published by the Survey Committee of the Cleveland Foundation, Cleveland, Ohio, 1916.

or clerical work. There are of course boy stenographers and girl clerks, and there are women in general administrative work; but that these are a minority this report has several ways of showing.

Boys' work may be expected to take on the characteristics of the business that employs them; girls' work remains in essentials unchanged even in totally changed surroundings. For example, a boy who is clerk in a wholesale house will have work very unlike that of the boy who is clerk in a bank; but girl stenographers in both businesses will have an experience that is practically the same.

Boys' work, within limits, is progressive; girls' work in its general type—with individual exceptions—is static. Boys as a rule cannot stay at the same kind of work and advance; girls as a rule stay at the same kind of work whether or not they advance. Boys in any position are expected to be qualifying themselves for the "job ahead," but for girls that is not the case. Boys may expect to make a readjustment with every step in advancement. Each new position brings them to a new situation and into a new relation to the business. Girls receive salary advancement for increasingly responsible work, but any change in work is likely to be so gradual as to be almost imperceptible if they remain in the same place of employment. If they change to another place those who are stenographers have a slight readjustment to make in getting accustomed to new terms and to the peculiarities of the new persons who dictate to them. Bookkeeping assistants may encounter different systems, but their part of the work will be so directed and planned that it cannot be said to necessitate difficult adaptation on their part. The work of clerical assistants is so simple and so nearly mechanical that the question of adjustment does not enter. These girl workers do not find that change of position or firm brings them necessarily into a new relation to the business.

Even moderate success is denied to a boy if he has not adaptability and the capacity to grasp business ideas and methods; but a comparatively high degree of success could be attained by a girl who possessed neither of these qualifications. A boy, however, who has no specific training which he can apply directly and definitely in work would be far more likely to obtain a good opening and promotion than a girl without it would be.

The range of a boy's possible future in commercial occupations is as wide as the field of business. He cannot at first be trained specifically as a girl can be because he does not know what business will do with him or what he wants to do with business. The girl's choice is limited by custom. She can prepare herself definitely for stenography, bookkeeping, or machine operating and be sure that she is preparing for just the opportunity—and the whole opportunity—that business offers to her. Her very limitation of opportunity makes preliminary choice and training definitely possible things.[60]

Household Arts as Extras

There is another respect in which the present-day training of girls differs from that of boys. Girls are being trained in the science of home-making. Where a girl intends to take up some vocation in the business world, her desire for courses in the household arts complicates the situation very seriously. The boy who is going into business wants a general education plus some business training. The girl wants all that the boy has plus household arts.

Demand for New Courses for Girls

The demand for the complete education of girls gives rise to many unsolved problems. For example, shall physics as at present taught be required as an introduction to cooking, or shall the cooking course be made to carry all the physics that the girl needs? The course in physics, be it remembered, contains many an example that is drawn from the boy's sphere of interests in mechanics and does not appeal at all to the girl's interests.

Or one may ask a similar question about economics. Shall the girl be given a special course in marketing in which examples are drawn from the daily activities of home life, or shall she wait until she can take the conventional course in political economy where the problems are often those of international trade and banking?

It would be impossible to secure anything like unanimity for any answer to these questions. The uncertainty in regard to the correct answer calls attention to the opportunity which is offered to the intelligent women of the teaching profession to solve a problem which is new and complicated, but all the more important because there are no guideposts to mark the way.

Individual Differences which appear during Training

The individual differences discussed up to this point may be described as native differences. In addition, there are differences which appear in the course of training. These, in turn, divide into two classes. There are differences which seem to result from varying degrees of mastery of the subjects taken in school, and there are differences in taste and outlook which arise as the pupils mature to the point where they begin to exhibit personal ambitions.

Recent studies of attainments of pupils in school subjects show how striking are the differences among individuals. For example, it is shown in the Cleveland survey that in the fifth grade of one and the same school there are pupils who read orally only 7, 8, or 9 lines in a minute, while others read orally 19 or 20 lines. In silent reading the variations are even greater, covering rates from as low as 4 lines

[60] Bertha M. Stevens, Boys and Girls in Commercial Work, pp. 14-16. Cleveland Education Survey. Published by the Survey Committee of the Cleveland Foundation, Cleveland, Ohio, 1916.

a minute to as high as 40 lines.[61] What is true of reading is true in equal degree of all the other subjects. The facts are graphically shown in Fig. 13.

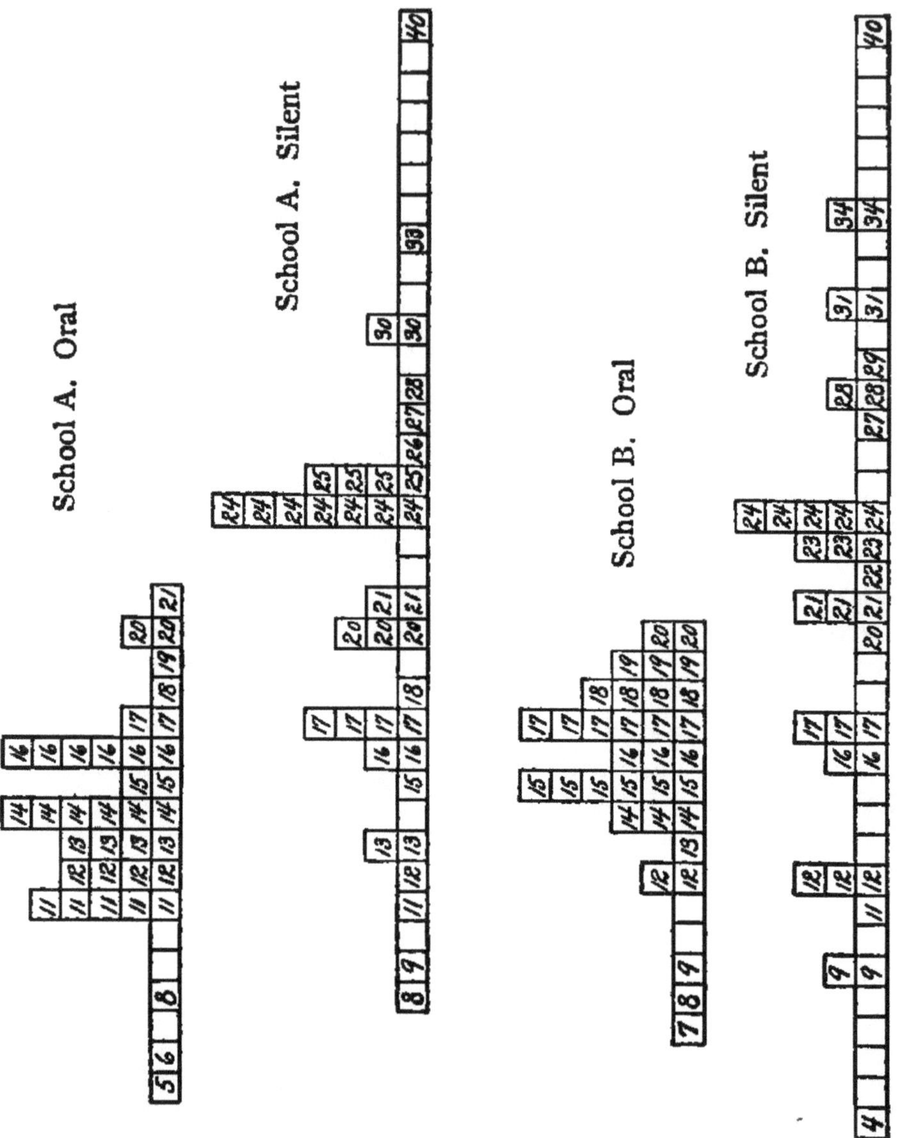

Fig. 13. Individual differences in the number of lines read in a minute by pupils in the fifth grades of two schools

Each small square with a number represents an individual; the number indicates the lines which he was able to read in a selected passage in one minute

[61] Measuring the Work of the Public Schools, pp. 131-133. Cleveland Education Survey. Published by the Survey Committee of the Cleveland Foundation, Cleveland, Ohio, 1916.

The type of individual difference which develops when pupils begin to look forward to their places in the practical world is of great significance in organizing school work. School experience in this matter is clearly reflected in the following resolution adopted in 1915 by the Department of Superintendence of the National Education Association:

> Resolved, That we note with approval the increasing tendency to establish, beginning with the seventh grade, differentiated courses of study aimed more effectively to prepare the child for his probable future activities. We believe that as a result of these modifications a more satisfactory type of instruction will be developed and that a genuine economy of time will result.[62]

The differentiation of the curriculum here demanded is required in order to keep in school those pupils who have reached the point where any simple uniform curriculum would fail to furnish the variety which they require to meet their developing tastes and their demands for special training.

Democratic Recognition of Individual Differences

The differentiation of the courses for individual pupils was at one time thought to be contrary to the democratic principle that all pupils must be treated alike. We are coming to see that a democracy has need of many kinds of people and that the truest expression of the principle of equal treatment is through liberal provision for individual differences.

EXERCISES AND READINGS

> Evidently low grades of intelligence are most likely to be found in the lower grades. Is the elimination of low-grade children from the regular classes advantageous to them? It is sometimes argued that they gain from association with the bright children.
>
> With regard to the bright children, it is pointed out that they may be pushed along too rapidly. How can this danger be avoided?
>
> Are the elections of courses made by students in high school indicative of sex differences? What tendencies in economic life can be noted as bringing men and women to the same levels of occupation? Are these tendencies likely to change the conclusions reached in this chapter?
>
> What types of school work are adjusted, even in the present school program, to the individual characteristics of pupils? How is the discussion to be related to the chapter dealing with the grouping of pupils? Is the argument of this chapter in favor of individual tutoring? How far should it be insisted that all the

[62] Proceedings of the National Education Association for 1915, p. 256. Published by the Secretary of the Association, Ann Arbor, Michigan, 1915.

members of a class be kept together for a year in their attainments in arithmetic? in Latin? in English literature? in typewriting? in laboratory physics?

How far down in the elementary school can individual election of courses be organized with profit to the pupils? Could a medical school or an engineering course be organized on the elective plan?

Galton, Francis. Inquiries into Human Faculty and its Development. E. P. Dutton and Company. One of the earliest studies of individual differences in mental characteristics, with special emphasis on differences in mental imagery.

Thorndike, E. L. Educational Psychology (especially Vol. III). Teachers College.

Thorndike, E. L. Measurements of Twins. Science Press. A study of the degree to which individuals are alike.

CHAPTER XIII

PERIODICITY IN THE PUPIL'S DEVELOPMENT

Recognition of periodicity in present organization. The meaning of infancy. The period before entering school. The primary period one of social imitation. The period of individualism. Early adolescence as a period of social consciousness. The new school adapted to adolescence. Later adolescence a period of specialization. The reorganized school system. Exercises and readings.

Recognition of Periodicity in Present Organization

Both the school curriculum and the general organization of the school program in such matters as the length of class periods and the forms of order required, reflect the fact that the pupil passes through distinct periods or epochs in his physical and intellectual development. Each of these epochs requires that a certain type of subject-matter be used for instruction and that a certain type of school discipline be administered. There is a progressive maturing of the pupil and a corresponding broadening and deepening of the education which can be given him. The general outline of this maturing process will be reviewed in this chapter.

The Meaning of Infancy

Before examining the changes which take place during school life, it will be instructive to review the general matter which has been discussed by John Fiske under the title "The Meaning of Infancy."[63] Writing from the point of view of the student of evolution, Fiske calls attention to the fact that the period of infancy has gradually lengthened with the increase in complexity of animal forms. The lowest animals have practically no period of infancy. They begin their independent lives with all of the capacities of the adult. For example, when a unicellular animal is produced, it results from a division of the parent cell into two equal parts. Each part immediately takes up an independent life, and it may be said that adulthood begins at birth. Further up the scale the parent organism provides protection and food, and the infant requires a longer period of time to arrive at adulthood.

This lengthening of infancy is paralleled by an increase in complexity of the animal form itself. The highest stages of complexity are reached in man, and here we find also the longest period of infancy. The human infant is helpless for years, and the care which parents must give to it includes not only the provision of food

---

[63] John Fiske, The Meaning of Infancy. Houghton Mifflin Company, 1909.

and protection but also the gradual training of the child to assume the responsibilities of an independent life.

When viewed by the evolutionist, infancy and even childhood thus appear to be the clearest evidences of the need of educational care. Indeed, childhood may be described as a period of preparation or of gradual maturing of the powers until the individual can carry on his independent personal activities.

The Period before entering School

Just as the period of childhood taken as a whole has a clearly definable character and purpose in the economy of life, so each epoch within this period can be set off from the others as serving a distinct purpose in the child's development. This is especially clear with regard to the years that precede school. In all civilized countries there is practical agreement that regular schooling shall begin with the normal child in the sixth year. To be sure, there are special institutions like the kindergarten, which receive children at an earlier age, but these institutions aim to serve in a somewhat more systematic way the same purposes that under other circumstances are served by home training.

What is the character of the education given in the home or the kindergarten preliminary to the work of the primary school? The answer to this question can be given negatively by saying it is not of a type which belongs to a public institution. When the pupil comes to primary school he must be reasonably prepared to live with people who are comparative strangers. This implies that he must have a sufficient command of language to make his wants known and to understand what others want him to do. He must be somewhat independent of maternal care, and must be ready to be initiated into a social world where his individuality will be recognized as somewhat detached from that of everyone else. Put in positive terms, the pre-school training may be described as training in language and in personal independence of a very elementary type.

This statement can be applied to the kindergarten, where the purposes of the pre-school training have been brought to fairly clear consciousness. The kindergarten gives the child much opportunity to play with things that are given to him. He must learn to distinguish objects for himself; he must learn to handle them with enough skill so that he becomes an independent individual. Second, he must play with other children, learning through games that social life consists of a give and take which marks him off from others and yet makes him responsible to the group. The social training of the kindergarten is a preparation for life in an institution where the pupil will have to recognize the reciprocal duties of life in a large group. Third, the chief instrument of social life, and the most important means of effective contact with the group, is speech. The kindergarten child, through songs and stories, learns words and sentences and cultivates the power to which home-training also contributes—the power of independent oral communication.

The kindergarten does in an energetic and systematic way what the home does incidentally, for in any home, however meager its resources, the child learns in five years something of his mother tongue and something of the demands of group living. The pre-school period is an important epoch in education as well as in physical growth. We recognize the physical fact that the child must cultivate strength enough to run around independently and to use his hands in holding what he needs. So it is also in the sphere of his mental life; he must be able to take care of himself.

The Primary Period One of Social Imitation

At five or six years of age the pupil comes to the primary school. His experience is very limited; his senses are open to the impressions of color and sound and touch, and he eagerly or timidly mixes in the social group which is often to him bewilderingly large and strange. The key to the understanding of this period is to be found in the simple psychological principle that out of all the bewildering mass of childish experience it is persons who attract the child's most vivid attention. The experiences of childhood are to be thought of not as meager but as confusing in their abundance. The world is so full of a number of things that one hardly knows where to turn. In the mass of this experience one turns to some person and follows in a docile way the lead of that person. The first grade is a place where children do what others do. First-graders are a flock of sheep. The teacher can lead them into almost anything because they are eager to do whatever they see others do.

Sometimes this period is described as a period when children are absorbed in sense impressions. This statement is true if it means that colors and sounds constitute the content of experience. It is false if it is meant to teach that little children are absorbed in the study of objects. The sounds and colors which hold the attention of primary children are those which attach to people. A little child will give up a plaything which he has in hand for a less attractive plaything in the hands of someone else. Primary children are social creatures first, last, and all the time.

This description of the primary child's mental attitudes gives us the formula for the organization of the primary course of study. There is an eager desire on the part of the first-grader to write his name. He does not need any artificial stimulation to undertake writing. Other people write; that is enough for him. He is eager to be initiated. Other people look into books; he must do the same. The period is not a period for nature study in any analytical scientific sense. It is a period for social companionships. The primary child likes animals as playthings; he is not interested in studying their structure. Show an animal to a little child and let him ask the questions that are in his mind, and social questions are the only ones which will come. "Where can I get one?" "Will it bite me?"

The judgment of the race has been right; this is the period for the teaching of reading and writing. The oral language which the pupil acquires in the pre-school period is the basis on which the primary work must be erected. The first reading lessons are lessons in the association of known oral symbols with those complicated social devices, the printed symbols. The ability to live in society which the pupil brings to the first grade must be extended through the mastery of language in its written and printed forms.

The utter absorption of the child of this age in society rather than in material things is attested by his credulity for fairy tales which are full of people but are grotesquely impossible in their description of material facts. In his eager desire to illustrate every story he hears, the child produces drawings which have very little merit as representations of things but are often expressive of action in the highest degree. A child of this age is keen in his observation of people but neglectful of things.

The Period of Individualism

The primary attitude of mind lasts about three years. In the normal child nine years of age is a turning point. By this time he has learned to read fairly independently. He can write and can solve simple problems in arithmetic. He has control of some of the simpler objects about him. He has imitated his elders until he has habits of his own. Now comes a change. Sometimes the change is sudden and violent. The pupil who has been laboriously writing from copy throws the example of his copy book to the winds and composes a note to one of his friends in a rapid, scrawling hand. The child has become an independent master of writing for his own private purposes. So it is with his other activities. Even in social matters he asserts his independence by refusing to follow the dictates of the teacher. School discipline suddenly comes to be a serious problem.

The change here described reflects itself in a fact of administration which is of frequent recurrence. Pupils fail of promotion in the fourth or fifth grade much more commonly than in the second, third, or sixth. In other words, there is here, just after the primary grades, a period of violent readjustment.

The readjustment which comes at this point can be described by saying that the pupil is entering on a period of self-recognition. The primary child is an imitator absorbed in social examples. The intermediate child is an individualist. He is aware of his own powers and ambitions. The boys of this period have been described as young barbarians. They are disregardful of the rights of others. They step on the little children; they refuse to be friends with the girls. They are ambitious to leave school and do something to assert their independence.

The school has dealt with this period with much less intelligence than it has exhibited in the primary years. In general, the intermediate grades have followed in subject-matter and in methods too closely the example of the successful primary grades. The result appears in the fact that the migration out of elementary schools is very common in the fifth and sixth grades. The intermediate grades have been described as periods of drill. If there is one kind of work that is not appropriate here, it is routine drill. There ought to be a new and thoroughgoing study of the needs of this period and the introduction of a type of instruction which will meet the needs of children who are vividly aware of themselves and of their personal relations to the world.

That a change is coming about in the methods of dealing with pupils in these years is shown by the fact that the elementary school is setting apart the fourth, fifth, and sixth grades as the years in which the strictly elementary work is to be completed. Much that was postponed to the seventh and eighth grades under the older form of organization will doubtless be brought down into the intermediate grades. The children will no longer be drilled in the forms of the social arts while waiting for the enlarged opportunities of the upper grades, but will be introduced at once to experiences with the objects of the physical world. They will be encouraged to see things and handle them for themselves.

Early Adolescence as a Period of Social Consciousness

The close of this period of individualism is marked by physical and mental changes of a very definite and significant type. From twelve years on the child begins to realize anew the social world about him. Physical changes are going on within him that stimulate this type of thought. The literature of education has emphasized the fact that at this period there is a maturing of the sex organs and an accompanying development of feelings and interests in the opposite sex. There has been doubtless an overemphasis on the sexual characteristics of this period. The fact is that a profound general physical and mental change is going forward.

On the physical side the organism which has been accumulating powers through its mastery of the fundamental processes of life is now ready for its last large development. We shall understand the meaning of this statement only when we realize that the organism has to cultivate a whole series of internal habits in order that it may be internally harmonious. The little child is easily disturbed, for example, in his digestion. This means that the habits of digestion are not established. The immature nervous organism of the pupil needs training to bring it to the point where digestion will go forward without interruption or distraction. The same is true of circulation and respiration. The organism has to learn to live. The school period is a period of mastery of these internal processes quite as much as a period of intellectual training.

At about twelve years of age the inner coördination is reaching its consummation. If one were to select for discussion the most significant physical fact that marks this period, one would lay stress on the development of the heart. This organ grows rapidly in size and strength. Its more vigorous action raises the blood pressure throughout the body. Organs which have been slow in their development now grow rapidly. The whole life of the individual is intensified. It is not alone the sex organs which mature; the nervous system acts with greater energy, and the muscular system develops. In short, a period of the most active life sets in.

The physical vigor of the twelve-year-old and the thirteen-year-old child is only part of the explanation of the characteristic intellectual temper of this period. Just prior to this period the child, as we have seen, passes through an era of marked individualism. The unsocial tendencies of that period bring disappointments and new lessons, and finally the child is ready for a renewal of his contacts with the social group. He cannot now be purely imitative as was the primary child, for he has gained self-consciousness. He cannot be content with pure individualism, because his experience has broadened so that he sees his dependence on others. A new social era opens. With self-consciousness and with a desire to get back into society by accepting its ways and complying with its demands, the adolescent seeks, albeit somewhat clumsily, a new contact with his fellows. The awkwardness of this period, its lack of self-assurance, its eagerness for social recognition, are all perfectly clear to the student of human nature who has analyzed the case of a twelve-year-old pupil.

The New School adapted to Adolescence

Has the school met the legitimate demand for a suitable education of the adolescent? The answer is that the school has been slow in meeting this situation. The archaic form of school organization which attached the seventh and eighth grades to the elementary school has hindered greatly a proper recognition of the special needs of adolescence. The child of twelve or thirteen does not need a review of the elementary work so much as a preparation for the active life of adulthood. The adolescent needs to be given an insight into the organization of society. He needs to be brought into contact with the ways and languages of other peoples. Fortunately, the keener educational insights of the present day are bringing us to a recognition of these needs. The school for the adolescent is beginning to emerge out of the current reorganizations of the seventh and eighth grades.

In many schools these two grades have been gradually separating from the rest of the elementary grades. The teaching has been organized on the departmental plan; that is, a number of special teachers, each dealing with a single subject, replace the single teacher who has charge of the whole curriculum in the lower grades. Furthermore, the curriculum has been enlarged. Manual arts and household science have been introduced and, in some cases, other subjects which were formerly offered only in the high school. A new type of school, including the seventh, eighth, and ninth grades and known as the junior high school or the intermediate school, is appearing.

Where these and like changes have not been made in the seventh and eighth grades, criticism has made itself increasingly heard because the pupils do not get ahead in these grades. The reviews which are sometimes carried on at great length in preparation for promotion into the high school are a waste of time and energy and leave the pupils without enthusiasm for school work and without habits of concentration.

In an earlier chapter it was shown that the seventh and eighth grades came from Europe during the decade 1840-1850. Every line of evidence which is taken up points to the desirability of a complete reorganization of the work of these grades.

The spread of the junior-high-school idea has been remarkably rapid. This is due to the growing conviction that pupils in the seventh and eighth grades require a higher type of instruction and discipline than that which is supplied in the lower grades. The curriculum is being enriched by the addition of science, foreign language, mathematics other than arithmetic, and several of the practical arts. Instruction is being intrusted to teachers of broader training, and the individual needs of pupils are being more adequately met by the introduction of some elective courses.

Later Adolescence a Period of Specialization

The early part of the adolescent period which has been under consideration in the foregoing paragraphs is followed by a period which can be described as the beginning of specialization. The fact that individual differences here assert themselves and that individual outlooks determine the training demanded is clearly recognized in the adoption of the elective system by the high school. Special education has an adequate foundation in the work of the earlier years, and now the student must build his individual career on this foundation. He comes to a new period of individualism. He is not individualistic in the sense in which the fourth-grade boy is when he breaks away from imitating social examples. The boy of fifteen to eighteen has passed through the first period of individualism and through the socializing training of early adolescence; he now comes to a new type of individualistic effort which will fit him for his place in the social system.

The upper limit of this period, as set down in the foregoing discussions, coincides with the age at which a normal student is now supposed to finish high school. There can be very little doubt that with the readjustments going on in the seventh and eighth grades there will be far-reaching changes in the upper high school also. It is not too much to expect that with improved methods of teaching and with a better curriculum it will be possible for the normal student to complete at eighteen years of age the first two years of the college curriculum. The complete reorganization of the higher institutions is thus likely to follow the changes which are now under way in the high school.

The freshman and sophomore years of American colleges are at present filled with subjects which are essentially secondary in character. The reorganization suggested is therefore altogether legitimate.

The Reorganized School System

The scheme of school organization which is in keeping with the foregoing study of mental development is as follows: Three primary years are to be devoted to the rudiments of the social arts. Three intermediate years following the primary are to be devoted to gaining an outlook on the world. Three years covering the period now covered by grades seven, eight, and nine are to be devoted to social studies and a systematization of knowledge of the world. The three years from fifteen to eighteen are to be devoted to a completion of general training and to the beginning of specialization. After this will come complete specialization.

Not all students can go through the full training thus outlined. More and more, however, communities will provide for, and require the completion of, the whole cycle. If a student's training must be curtailed, there will doubtless be an increasing tendency to bring the higher stages down rather than to terminate education before preparation for life has been carried far enough to give specialized individual training.

EXERCISES AND READINGS

Considering the kindergarten and the first grade in the light of the discussions of this chapter, what are the characteristics of pupils which justify placing them in the one or the other? What is the present rule with regard to this placing? Should there be any systematic education of children in the home? If so, along what lines?

Make a detailed catalogue of the kinds of ability, both physical and mental, exhibited by a group of pupils in the first grade, and then attempt, by contrasting a third-grade group, to determine what pupils acquire in the primary years. Which of the new characteristics noted are consciously sought by the school?

What kind of reading matter should be offered to pupils in the fourth, fifth, and sixth grades? What grade of experience is required of teachers in the middle grades?

What readjustments is the student called on to make as he passes from elementary school to high school? From high school to college? Do the institutions concerned put forth any effort to help the student in making these transitions?

When should formal education stop? Should pupils be given a course in the methods of educating themselves? If so, at what school period?

Show in terms of earlier chapters what are the forces making for reorganization of the school system and the forces opposing this reorganization.

AMES, E. S. Psychology of Religious Experience. Houghton Mifflin Company. Like other books on the psychology of religion, this calls attention to the great importance of the changes that come with adolescence.

HALL, G. S. Adolescence. D. Appleton and Company. This is a somewhat erratic and often purely hypothetical description of the development of pupils at the beginning of the high-school age. It called attention, however, to the importance of the period and marked an epoch in the development of educational theory.

HALL, G. S. Youth. D. Appleton and Company. A brief summary based on the foregoing.

KIRKPATRICK, E. A. Fundamentals of Child Study. The Macmillan Company. This is the best summary of the child-study movement. It offers a treatment of the different periods of a child's life somewhat different from that in the text.

CHAPTER XIV

SYSTEMATIC STUDIES OF THE CURRICULUM

The curriculum based on authority versus the living curriculum. Older subjects products of long selection. Social needs and the curriculum. Systematic studies as devices for facilitating evolution of the curriculum. A study of representative adults. A study of current references. A study of the mistakes of pupils. Prerequisites for higher courses. Administrative studies. Need of broad, coöperative studies. Exercises and readings.

The Curriculum based on Authority versus the Living Curriculum

The six preceding chapters, which have dealt with the curriculum, make no pretense of presenting formulated courses which can be given to classes. Some reader may have been impatient because he did not find there an outline of arithmetic or geography or Latin or English. It has been the purpose of these chapters to deal only with general principles and general problems. The fact is that it would be absolutely futile to lay down a curriculum and say of it that it is the true curriculum. The curriculum of a school is a living thing. It is constantly undergoing readjustments. Its content is drawn from the social life to which it introduces pupils, and its arrangement depends on the ability of pupils of different ages and different capacities to grasp this constantly readjusted content.

There are some teachers who prefer to have the course of study handed down to them by some superior authority. There are many fifth-grade teachers, for example, who prefer to have the superintendent tell them just how many pages of geography to cover each week and how many minutes to devote to this subject. There are many Latin teachers who are satisfied to take from some college catalogue a statement of the number of pages to be read in Cæsar, to divide this number by the number of days during which the class meets, and then to plod through the assignments. The day of such teachers, unfortunately, is not yet past, but it is passing. The course in geography or Latin is not a quantitative matter; it is not a static affair; it is an organized body of material which grows and changes with the development of society. To the intelligent teacher a course of study is a subject of constant scrutiny and revision. Every detail must be weighed as to its importance and as to its relations to the whole series of topics and to the needs of pupils.

Older Subjects Products of Long Selection

Efficient teachers have always assumed toward the subject-matter of their courses an attitude of the type described. As a result there has been in every generation of schools some progress in organizing courses. Little by little experience has refined the practices of schools. Take, for example, Latin or any of the older subjects. Countless teachers have contributed to the organization of this subject. There is very little probability that pupils will encounter in first-year Latin anything that they ought not to be asked to learn, because the details have been tried out on successive generations of learners, and only that has been retained in first-year Latin which can be taught in that year. In the newer subjects, on the contrary, there is the greatest uncertainty. In his enthusiasm for the new ideas which come to his own mind, the teacher of biology rushes forward to generalizations which are too mature for his first-year classes. The subject-matter will have to be tried out and sifted before it is as well selected as is the course in Latin. The teachers of the new subjects will inevitably pass through a series of the same kind of sifting processes through which the teachers of Latin have passed. Even when some of the problems thus arising are settled, the new subjects will still be difficult of organization. Thus biology is changing by virtue of the evolution of the science at a rate which complicates the case very much more than it can ever be complicated in Latin.

Social Needs and the Curriculum

Further evidence that the curriculum is a living, changing institution is seen in the way in which courses are related to social demands. There was a time in the history of the secondary school and college when the course in Hebrew was regarded as universally desirable for every student of the social group which attended these institutions. That was in the period when the group was of a definitely vocational composition. For example, in the early days of Harvard College 70 per cent of its graduates entered the ministry, and Hebrew was a requirement. The later history of the student body explains why the requirement of Hebrew became obsolete. Two paragraphs from a recent bulletin of the Bureau of Education give some of the facts as follows:

> From this it is apparent that those who founded the institution primarily had in mind a theological seminary. The professions of the graduates for the early period bear witness to the fact that this was practically what the institution was. The ministry was the one profession most necessary, most demanded by the society of that time, and this profession more than any other required an advanced education. It is not surprising, therefore, to find this profession dominant during the early years of Harvard's history. This dominance continues for over a century, and not until the period immediately following the Revolutionary War does any other profession claim so many of the graduates as the ministry.
>
> The curve representing this profession has three distinct tendencies. The first part, extending from 1642, the date of the first

> graduating class, to 1720, is slightly downward, with rather wide variation. This stretch of 80 years shows a decline from 70 per cent for the first three years, a percentage never again reached, to 60 per cent for the last five-year period. The second tendency is seen in the period of theological unrest, marked off roughly by the years 1720-1775. Here the downward tendency is clearly defined. It shows a decline from 60 per cent to less than 20 per cent. The variations during this period are not so marked. The third tendency extends from the Revolutionary War to the present. This shows a slow, persistent relative decline reaching well below 5 per cent by the end of the nineteenth century. The variations during this period, particularly during the last half, are inconspicuous.[64]

Systematic Studies as Devices for facilitating Evolution of the Curriculum

The effect of this and like radical social changes is sometimes slow in actually modifying the curriculum because of the conservative tendencies discussed in earlier chapters. But the final effect is inevitable. The changing social order carries with it the school and its subjects of instruction.

The characteristic fact about the present generation of progressive educators is that they are undertaking certain studies which are designed to hasten the processes of selection. The curriculum is to be modified and improved, with every new accession of knowledge and with every new evolution in social life. How the improvement can be brought about most expeditiously and most productively is a problem which is engaging much of the attention and energy of school officers.

It will be noted that there is no opposition between the natural tendencies of growth and revision and the special investigations which are intended to hasten the process of adjustment. The purpose of scientific studies here, as in every other sphere, is to facilitate natural evolution and to give it rational guidance.

A Study of Representative Adults

One of the first methods of studying the curriculum is that of investigating the relation between school work and the demands of later life. The following description of a study made as part of a school survey teaches some very impressive lessons on the need of revision in the elementary curriculum:

> The most serious defect of the present course of study, including some of the suggested revisions now under consideration, is that it makes thousands of children waste tens of thousands of precious hours in the laborious acquisition of facts for which they will never have any practical use. While the survey was under way the staff attempted to test the practical value of some of the subject matter taught to children in the elementary grades.

[64] Bailey B. Burritt, "Professional Distribution of College and University Graduates," p. 15. *Bulletin No. 19*, United States Bureau of Education, 1912.

For this purpose short examinations were prepared from the material prescribed by the course of study and actually being taught in the upper grades in spelling, arithmetic, history, and geography. Through the coöperation of a woman prominent in social and intellectual circles of the city, 11 of the leading successful citizens were brought together one evening and asked to take these examinations. The object was to find out whether or not the material that the children of the upper grades were being taught was of the sort actually used by able men of affairs in the conduct of their daily business. For carrying out the test the most prominent and successful citizens were purposely chosen and in making up the examinations the most difficult material was purposely selected. The result of these examinations in spelling, geography, arithmetic, and history of the fifth, sixth, and seventh grades was that no one of the men examined made a passing mark in any subject. The reason is that the material on which they were examined, and which the children in the schools are daily learning, is of a sort that is seldom or never met with in the business of even the most successful men engaged in commercial and professional pursuits. The gentlemen who submitted to the examination were the following:

A state senator
A former lieutenant governor
The president of a manufacturing concern
The former superintendent of parks
A banker
A physician
A merchant
A lawyer
A newspaper editor
An efficiency engineer and a clergyman

The test in spelling consisted of ten words taken from the spelling lists of the seventh grade. These words were as follows:

1. abutilon
2. bergamot
3. deutzia
4. daguerreotype
5. paradigm
6. reconnaissance
7. erysipelas
8. mnemonics
9. trichinæ
10. weigelia

Among the 11 men taking the examination, one spelled six of these words correctly. Three succeeded in spelling four words, two got three words right, one got two, three spelled one word correctly, and one failed on every word. It is not surprising that they failed so completely for no citizen in any ordinary walk of life needs to know how to spell these words. When the rare occasion arises that he needs to write one of them, he looks it up in the dictionary. These words and scores of words like them are studied in the classrooms as well as found in the spelling book.

The test described above was suggested by the experience of the director of the survey who went into a sixth grade room where an examination in spelling was being given. He took the test with the children. It consisted of 20 words, and he failed on six of them. These six words are included in the ten-word list used in the examination of the business and professional men. Some of the children in the schools can spell these words correctly but while they are laboriously learning to do it, many of them are still unable to spell short and common words as "which," "separate," and "receive."[65]

A Study of Current References

Another method of comparing school courses with common social needs is set forth in the following quotation:

> At a meeting of the Committee on Economy of Time held in the fall of 1912 it was suggested that current literature could be profitably employed as a standard for determining the kind of geographical information that the school should provide. The proposal was to read current newspapers and magazines, record the geographical references, and determine from the frequency of these references the relative value of the various types of geographical information. Results of the application of the method presented at the meeting seemed to indicate that the content of geography as now taught in the elementary school would be greatly modified if materials were chosen upon this basis. . . .
>
> Miss Biester collected and classified the geographical and historical references and allusions in eighteen issues of the *Outlook* and the *Literary Digest*, representing a period of seven years ending with 1913. She found in these eighteen journals a total of 2,237 geographical references. The distribution was as follows:

	Per Cent
References to facts of location, size, direction, etc., which may be assumed to require for their understanding a knowledge of "place and location" geography	53.5

[65] Survey conducted by L. P. Ayres of the Russell Sage Foundation. "The Public Schools of Springfield, Illinois," pp. 86-88. Published by the Springfield Survey Committee, Springfield, Illinois, 1914.

References to political divisions and facts of government which may be assumed to require a knowledge of "political" geography	25.1
References to industries, commerce, products, etc., which may be assumed to require a knowledge of "commercial" geography	5.8
References to people, customs, religion, education, etc., which may be assumed to require a knowledge of "social" geography	4.8
References to places as scenes of historical events, which may be assumed to require a knowledge of "historical" geography	1.7
Other references primarily of local or transitory interest	8.9

A grouping of this sort is obviously subject to the errors or peculiarities of individual judgment, but it may be said that the classification just presented is quite consistent with those furnished by other readers. Except for the absence of explicit reference to physiographical principles, this grouping represents fairly accurately the distribution of emphasis in the textbooks ordinarily used in the seventh and eighth grades. The physiographical principles, however, are precisely the "general" principles to which we referred above; that is, their function is broadly interpretive and adaptive; they "cover" a host of particulars too numerous in the aggregate, and too insignificant separately, to warrant specific attention.

Another suggestive grouping is based upon the frequency of references to the various continents. If one is to read intelligently the journals which formed the basis of this test, one will find occasion to apply one's knowledge of the continents in approximately the following proportions (the maximum frequency of reference being represented arbitrarily by 100):

North America	100	Africa	4
Europe	73	South America	3
Asia	13	Australia	1

The principal European countries had an importance for the readers of the journals in question in the following proportions (giving England, as the country most frequently referred to, the arbitrary value of 100):[66]

[66] W. C. Bagley, "The Determination of Minimum Essentials in Elementary Geography and History." Fourteenth Yearbook of the National Society for the Study of Education, Part I, pp. 131, 134-135. The University of Chicago Press, 1915.

England	100	Italy	32
France	80	Turkey	30
Germany	70	Austria-Hungary	24
Russia	35	Spain	22

A Study of the Mistakes of Pupils

It is not merely the remoter needs of adult life which should be taken into account in determining the content of courses of study. Pupils in schools have certain urgent needs which should be met. A study was carried on in the schools of Kansas City, Missouri, which dealt with the needs of pupils in grammar. Teachers observed and noted the mistakes of pupils, and collected a body of written material which was carefully analyzed. The urgent needs of pupils were readily discovered and were found to be comparatively few. The following quotations give the gist of the matter:

> Table M, which is based upon the oral and written errors of the children of the community, displays the items to be included in a course of study for the elementary grades. It assumes that all types of error were found and reported. That this assumption is absolutely correct is not probable. That it is approximately correct seems reasonably certain. To verify its accuracy further other studies would need to be made in Kansas City.
>
> As the present course of study in grammar in the sixth and in the seventh grades of the Kansas City schools was materially simplified in the 1913-1914 session, it is now one of the simplest in the United States. Notwithstanding this fact, many items would be omitted from it upon the basis of Table K. These are included in Table L. The pages refer to "Grammar and Composition with Practical English," by Robins, Row, and Scott (Row, Peterson & Company, Chicago), the text now in use in the sixth and seventh grades.

Table M
Omissions From and Additions to the Present Elementary Course of Study in Grammar in Kansas City

Omissions:

1. Exclamatory sentence, p. 2.
2. The interjection, pp. 16 f.
3. The appositive, pp. 37 ff.
4. The nominative of address, pp. 39 f.
5. The nominative by exclamation, pp. 40 f.
6. The objective complement, pp. 53 f.

7. The adverbial objective, pp. 56 f.
8. The indefinite pronouns, pp. 69 f.
9. The objective complement, p. 91.
10. The objective used as a substantive, p. 91.
11. The classification of adverbs, pp. 94 ff.
12. The noun clause, pp. 107 ff.
13. Conjunctive adverbs, p. 116.
14. The retained objective, pp. 128 f.
15. The moods (except possibly the subjunctive of *to be*), pp. 135 ff. and 152 ff.
16. The infinitive except the split infinitive, pp. 145 ff.
17. The objective subject, pp. 149 f.
18. The participle except the definition and the present and the past forms, pp. 162 ff.
19. The nominative absolute, pp. 165 ff.
20. The gerund, pp. 168 f.

Additions:

1. The pronoun *what*.
2. Proper and numeral adjectives.

The first, second, and third of the omissions affect punctuation; the first and second, the exclamation point; and the third, the comma. The exclamation point is used at the end of the exclamatory sentence and after interjections to express an intensity of feeling greater than that expressed by the period, and it is doubtful if children have the nicety of experience to understand the difference. If the point is absent, its omission cannot be counted as an error because the reader has no way of knowing how intense is the feeling that accompanied the sentence. Strangely enough, the children used the appositive hardly at all. Instead of saying, "Bill, the bandit, killed a deer," they seem to prefer to say, "Bill was a bandit, and he killed a deer."

To the omissions, tabulated in Table M, should be added such sentences for analysis and parsing as are given to children solely because they involve subtle points in grammar. This is true because the errors made by children seem to occur in the commoner and more easily classified constructions, as may be seen by an examination of Table I.

POSTSCRIPT

The content of the course of study in elementary grammar in

> the Kansas City schools is not dealt with here. The problem is simply and solely to find out what the course of study would be *if it were based upon the errors of the children*. The problem of the content of the course of study requires such serious consideration that it can be determined only by practical experience and opinion aided by other scientifically conditioned studies.[67]

Prerequisites for Higher Courses

The problem of finding what is the best progression of studies within the curriculum is an important problem on which we have at the present time relatively little information. President Lowell of Harvard University collected some statistics on this matter which can be briefly summarized in three quotations from his article:

> Harvard University is singularly rich in material for determining the relation of college studies to the work of the professional schools, because nowhere in the world have so large a body of undergraduates been so free, for so long a period, as in Harvard College to study whatever they chose, and to make any combination of courses they pleased. With the exception of one required course in English, and sometimes one in another modern language, the election of courses has been almost wholly free for a quarter of a century, and in fact the variety of combinations made has been almost limitless. Moreover, the Law and Medical Schools have contained a large number of graduates of Harvard College, and this is essential for a fair comparison of the results. . . .
>
> The statistics here presented cover, therefore, only bachelors of arts of Harvard College who graduated afterwards from the Harvard Law and Medical Schools, and they comprise only men who took twelve courses, or nearly three years' work, in the college. . . .
>
> If, therefore, one can draw any inference from figures so small, the case of mathematics is singular. Unless some other element enters into the problem, such as an unusually high standard in the department, or an unusually vigorous intellectual appetite on the part of students who elect the subject, the result may be supposed to indicate, so far as it goes, that mathematics, altho rarely selected for the purpose, is a particularly good preparation for the study of law; perhaps because the methods of thought in the two subjects are more nearly akin than is commonly supposed.
>
> Leaving aside this possibly exceptional case, the conclusions to be derived from the facts presented in this paper would seem to be that, as a preparation for the study of law or medicine, it makes

[67] W. W. Charters and Edith Miller, "A Course of Study in Grammar," pp. 43-45. *Bulletin No. 2*, University of Missouri, Vol. XVI (1915).

> comparatively little difference what subject is mainly pursued in college, but that it makes a great difference with what intensity the subject is pursued—or, to put the same proposition in a more technical form, familiarity with the subject-matter, which can be transferred little, if at all, is of small importance in a college education, as compared with mental processes that are capable of being transferred widely, or with the moral qualities of diligence, perseverance, and intensity of application which can be transferred indefinitely. The practical deduction is that in the administration of our colleges, and, indeed, in all our general education, as distinguished from direct vocational or professional training, we have laid too much stress on the subject, too little on the excellence of the work and on the rank attained.[68]

Administrative Studies

Other studies of the curriculum have been made which may be called administrative studies. The most elaborate investigation of this type which has been carried out is reported in a volume entitled "The Supervision of Arithmetic."[69] Two of the leading students of the science of education have here reported an exhaustive study of the practices of various school systems in administering the arithmetic course. At the same time they have made an analysis of the textbooks which are commonly used in administering this course. Finally, they have supplemented this body of fact with numerous opinions from competent school people regarding changes which ought to be made.

It is not possible to take up in detail the various findings reported in this volume. One especially interesting set of facts, however, may be referred to as furnishing convincing evidence that the school curriculum is constantly in process of revision. The particular part of the book which shows this deals with the number of hours a week devoted to arithmetic in the course of study of various cities. If we compare the relative amount of time given to arithmetic in earlier years and at present, we shall have some indication of the movement which has been going on within the school curriculum. In 1888 New York City devoted 26 per cent of the total school time in the grades to arithmetic. In 1904 this had been reduced to 12 per cent, showing that the attention to arithmetic is in point of time less than half what it was at an earlier period. Boston, on the other hand, devoted to arithmetic almost exactly the same relative amount of time in 1904 that it did in 1888. In both cases about 16 per cent of the time of the course of study was given to this subject. Chicago shows a distinct increase in the amount of time given to arithmetic. In 1888 it was giving 9 per cent of its time to that subject. The time devoted to arithmetic in 1904 was 18 per cent, or just twice as much.

These statements confirm the remark repeatedly made in this volume that the course of study is constantly undergoing revision. The only intelligent way for the

[68] A. Lawrence Lowell, "College Studies and Professional Training." *Educational Review*, Vol. XLII (October, 1911), pp. 220, 221, 233.

[69] W. A. Jessup and L. D. Coffman. The Macmillan Company, 1916.

school system to deal with the problems of the course of study which are sure to come up is to make a careful examination of the movement which is under way, for this movement is usually guided by the personal judgment of some enthusiastic school officer or by the chance readjustments which arise out of the effort to bring new subjects into the curriculum. The result is a blind fluctuation, the magnitude and importance of which are wholly unrecognized until exact comparisons are set up.

Such general discussions as that summarized in the foregoing paragraphs are supplemented in the volume referred to, by detailed studies of such questions as the following: When should the teaching of fractions begin? How far should the elementary course deal with square root and cube root? What are the characteristics of a given textbook which make it available for a particular school system?

The kind of study which is here reported for arithmetic should, of course, be made for other subjects as well. The time allotment for the course in geography and the distribution of topics within that course are quite as important as the time allotment in arithmetic.

Need of Broad, Coöperative Studies

It would be a serious mistake to advocate any one of the investigations referred to in this chapter as the sole basis for reform in the curriculum. There must be a broad consideration of social and educational conditions if the school is to arrange its materials of instruction in the most advantageous form. Furthermore, the individual teacher cannot make all the studies involved. The problem is one which involves coöperation and the organization of scientific methods which will give to each school officer the benefit of the experience of many schools.

EXERCISES AND READINGS

The best type of exercise which can be suggested in connection with this chapter is the analysis of a series of textbooks by members of the class. The following suggestions will aid in the attack on three classes of texts:

First, let the student get several sets of readers, beginning with primers and running up to the books designed for the upper grades. Note among other characteristics such matters as the following: Are the selections in the primers equally interesting? Are the vocabularies the same? What devices in the primer are adopted as aids in explaining the words? Are the sentences of equal length? In the readers for the upper grades is the emphasis on poetry the same? Is the reading matter equally appropriate for boys and girls? Does it fit all localities equally well? Is there any suggestion that would carry the pupil out of the book itself to other books?

Second, let the student take several geographies. Are the maps equally good? Are the pictures equally helpful? What is the order of topics? Is the treatment equally detailed in the various books? Is the attention given to the United States satisfactory both in point of gross volume and in point of details taken up? What is the degree of emphasis on physical geography and on man's place in the world, that is, on commerce and civilization?

Third, take books in first-year Latin. What emphasis is given to vocabulary, to reading, and to grammar? How do books of this type differ from books on French and German? Is the choice of reading matter in the various books based on the same principle of selection? How far could the books be used by a pupil without a teacher? What is the contribution expected of the teacher; that is, what must the teacher know about Latin more than is given in the book? How are the pages of material related to assignments; that is, are assignments suggested by the text itself?

Bagley, W. C., and Rugg, H. O. "Content of American History as taught in the Seventh and Eighth Grades." *Bulletin No. 16*, School of Education, University of Illinois, 1916.

Minimum Essentials in Elementary-School Subjects. Fourteenth Yearbook of the National Society for the Study of Education, Part I, 1915. The University of Chicago Press. Other types of study than those suggested in the above questions are outlined in this yearbook.

CHAPTER XV

STANDARDIZATION

Tests and measurements of products. Earlier standards based on opinion. Objective and exact standards. Beginnings of the movement. Handwriting scales. Speed as a correlate of quality. Standards, personal and impersonal. Social standards versus imposed standards. Comparison through exact measurement. Records as a basis of standardization. Studies of oral reading. Studies dealing with other subjects. Mechanical aspects the first to be standardized. Standardization and the science of education. Exercises and readings.

Tests and Measurements of Products

There is a group of recent studies which affect the curriculum and all other phases of school organization so profoundly that a separate chapter must be devoted to an exposition of their character and aims. These are studies which aim to standardize school work through tests, measurements, and exact quantitative descriptions of the products of teaching.

For example, one of the efforts of the elementary school is to teach pupils to write. It is entirely possible after the school has done its work to find out by an examination of the results how well pupils can write. It is never expected that pupils in the second grade will write as well as pupils in the upper grades. In this sense, then, it may be said that the results expected in the second grade are of a lower standard than those expected higher in the school. Furthermore, there is a sharp contrast between rapid writing and slow writing. The pupil who writes one hundred and fifty letters in a minute with a quality or form of letters which is fair exhibits one kind of result, while the pupil who writes only seventy-five letters a minute but shows great regularity in his letters exhibits another kind of result. It is not easy in two cases such as have just been described to determine at once which result is better. It may be that speed should be encouraged in order to secure free, fluent movements even if quality has to be sacrificed for the time being.

Earlier Standards based on Opinion

One difficulty in dealing with the results of school work has been that schools have had no clear definition of what ought to be demanded. Opinion has been matched against opinion. Thus the parent often feels that he has a right to pass unqualified judgment on the progress of his child and on the teacher's methods of dealing with him. The employer demands of the boy whom he employs a certain proficiency in spelling and adding. The superintendent, in pursuance of his duties, tells the teachers that their work is satisfactory or otherwise and that the children do or do not read as well as they should. The teacher has a certain expectation, and the pupil feels sure that he is doing his work well. Each, according to his personal standard, is estimating the work done in the school.

Very often these standards differ when applied to one and the same performance; sometimes they differ so radically that social troubles follow. The parent says that his child is doing satisfactory work, while the teacher estimates the work as inferior. In such a case it happens, often after a controversy, that one standard ultimately prevails. It is a matter of record in some communities that the parent's standard has at times been asserted with enough energy to result in the removal of the dissenting teacher from office. On the other hand, it is more commonly true that the teacher's standard dominates, and the pupil either changes his ways or fails of promotion. In either case, it would have been better for all concerned if some exact standard could have been set up which would have been recognized as superior in its sanction to individual opinion.

Even teachers of experience disagree in grading the same examination paper. One demands correctness in every detail, while the other concentrates attention on originality and force of expression.

Objective and Exact Standards

The effort to lay down by investigation satisfactory standards of school work is one of the most productive lines of educational inquiry which has ever been instituted. Like all great movements, this movement of standardization has been misunderstood and opposed, but it is steadily gaining ground and promises to be the largest contribution of this generation to education.

In essence it consists of a careful, systematic measurement of what pupils accomplish. If there are at hand measurements of the actual achievements of pupils in various subjects in all the grades, it is safe to compare any single performance with the general average. It should be noted that this does not imply a demand that every pupil's work be like the average. There are pupils who do their work under unfavorable conditions, as, for example, pupils who have difficulty in reading because they hear no English at home. Their results should not be expected to reach the average, at least in the early grades. How far the results are from the average should, however, be definitely known. Explanation can then be given. Where conditions are not unfavorable the demand can be the more vigorously made that the average expectation be reached.

Beginnings of the Movement

The way in which this movement began and the rapidity with which it has progressed are vividly described by one of its chief exponents as follows:

> Eighteen years ago the school superintendents of America,

assembled in convention in Indianapolis, discussed the problems then foremost in educational thought and action. At that meeting a distinguished educator[70]—the pioneer and pathfinder among the scientific students of education in America—brought up for discussion the results of his investigations of spelling among the children in the school systems of nineteen cities. These results showed that, taken all in all, the children who spent forty minutes a day for eight years in studying spelling did not spell any better than the children in the schools of other cities where they devoted only ten minutes per day to the study.

The presentation of these data threw that assemblage into consternation, dismay, and indignant protest. But the resulting storm of vigorously voiced opposition was directed not against the methods and results of the investigation, but against the investigator who had pretended to measure the results of teaching spelling by testing the ability of children to spell.

In terms of scathing denunciation the educators there present and the pedagogical experts, who reported the deliberations of the meeting in the educational press, characterized as silly, dangerous, and from every viewpoint reprehensible, the attempt to test the efficiency of the teacher by finding out what the pupils could do. With striking unanimity they voiced the conviction that any attempt to evaluate the teaching of spelling in terms of the ability of the pupils to spell was essentially impossible and based on a profound misconception of the function of education.

Last month in the city of Cincinnati that same association of school superintendents, again assembled in convention, devoted fifty-seven addresses and discussions to tests and measurements of educational efficiency. The basal proposition underlying this entire mass of discussion was that the effectiveness of the school, the methods, and the teachers must be measured in terms of the results secured.[71]

Handwriting Scales

One of the earliest types of school work to be standardized was handwriting. Standard "scales," as they are called, have been prepared by several investigators, and their use has become very common.

The first scale was prepared by Professor Thorndike.[72] He secured a number of specimens of children's writing, and asked experienced judges to arrange these specimens in a series of descending degrees of excellence. By combining

[70] J. M. Rice, editor of the *Forum*.

[71] Leonard P. Ayres, "Making Education Definite." *Bulletin No. 11*, Indiana University, Vol. XIII (October, 1915), pp. 85-86. Published by the Extension Division of Indiana University.

[72] E. L. Thorndike, "Handwriting." *Teachers College Record*, March, 1910.

the judgments returned by the experts it was possible to secure an average judgment. Certain typical specimens were then set aside, representing equal steps in the descending scale. In practical use, a given sample of handwriting which is to be judged is compared with the successive steps in the scale until an approximate equality in degree of excellence is found. The sample to be judged is then marked with the grade agreed on for the standard specimen.

A second scale was prepared by Ayres[73] on a more objective basis. The specimens were arranged in a series, not in accordance with the judgment of experts, but according to the time which was required to read them.

A third scale, more elaborate than either of the others, was prepared by Freeman.[74] He first made an analysis of the different characteristics which enter into excellent writing, such as uniformity of slant, uniformity in the height and spacing of letters, and other like essential characteristics, and then selected specimens exhibiting decreasing grades of excellence in each of these characteristics. Since each characteristic of writing is capable of definite measurement, the specimens could be graded on the basis of direct measurements. Thus the slant of a number of specimens was measured letter by letter, and objective grades were established.

Finally, the preparation of scales of handwriting has gone so far that special scales or series of graded specimens for particular school systems have been prepared.

Speed as a Correlate of Quality

In the meantime the matter of speed in handwriting has also been a subject of careful measurement, and tables of average speeds for different grades have been prepared in a number of school systems.

A device for presenting in a single diagram both speed and quality and at the same time comparing several grades in the same school with each other was worked out in the Cleveland survey. The figure and a description of its meaning are given on pages 165, 166.

> The relative emphasis on speed and quality actually found in a number of different schools is set forth in the following diagram. The separate parts of this diagram are made up as follows: The average speed of a grade is represented by distances in the horizontal, and average quality by distances in the vertical, scale. Thus, taking the first section of the diagram, that of the North Doan School, the fifth grade has an average speed of 71 letters per minute, and an average quality of 41. The sixth grade shows progress in both speed and quality, though speed increases more than quality. The seventh and eighth grades show further progress in both speed and quality, the two changing at about the same rate. The diagram for the Kentucky School shows progress of a slightly

[73] L. P. Ayres, A Scale for Measuring the Quality of Handwriting of School Children. Russell Sage Foundation, New York.

[74] F. N. Freeman, The Teaching of Handwriting. Houghton Mifflin Company, 1914.

> different type. In this school the sixth grade, as compared with the fifth, shows progress in quality, but very little in speed. Progress from the sixth grade on is about equal in quality and speed. Memorial School emphasizes speed almost exclusively up to the eighth grade, while Mt. Pleasant emphasizes quality.
>
> The various schools which have been reported in the four upper sections of the diagram are all regular in the sense that each school shows steady progress from grade to grade in both speed and quality. Without attempting to comment in detail on the special cases, attention is called to the series of results presented in the lower part of the diagram.[75]

Before giving examples of standardization in fields other than penmanship, it will be well to indicate the full meaning of the foregoing paragraphs.

Standards, Personal and Impersonal

First, it will be seen that measurements are here substituted for purely personal judgments. It was the universal practice before this movement began, and it is the common practice to-day, for a supervisor to go from school to school, passing on the excellence and speed of handwriting. The supervisor has arrived at a personal standard through his experience. He expects a certain result in the fifth grade. He has in his mind a more or less clearly defined requirement and regards it as his duty to impose this on pupils and teachers. In the same way the teacher has a personal standard which is imposed on the pupils. It would be a mistake to describe these personal standards as arbitrary or unintelligent. The experienced teacher is usually approximately right in his expectations, and the supervisor usually does a great deal to raise and unify the level of work with which he comes in contact. But it is not possible in a complex social situation to rely on personal standards. Personal life and professional activity are too transient. How many schools have changed standards, to the great disadvantage of the penmanship, with each change of supervisors? Furthermore, personal standards are vague when one tries to transmit them to others. This is a serious matter when it is remembered that a very large proportion of teachers in each school are changing each year. If a supervisor is to systematize the work of his schools, he must constantly be bringing into agreement with his standards the standards of a large number of new teachers. For the sake of coöperation it is advantageous to turn a personal standard into one which can be described and defined. Finally, a personal standard grows up out of all the accidents of a personal career. The person of narrow experience may not have incorporated into his standards valuable elements which he would have accepted had he come in contact with them. The person of strong personal likes and dislikes may often be prejudiced. The person of broad experience may be inexact when it comes to details. To demand of all who teach handwriting that they rise above purely personal standards is not unlike the demand that the central government rather than the states mint our coins.

[75] Measuring the Work of the Public Schools, pp. 75-77. Cleveland Education Survey. Published by the Survey Committee of the Cleveland Foundation, Cleveland, Ohio, 1916.

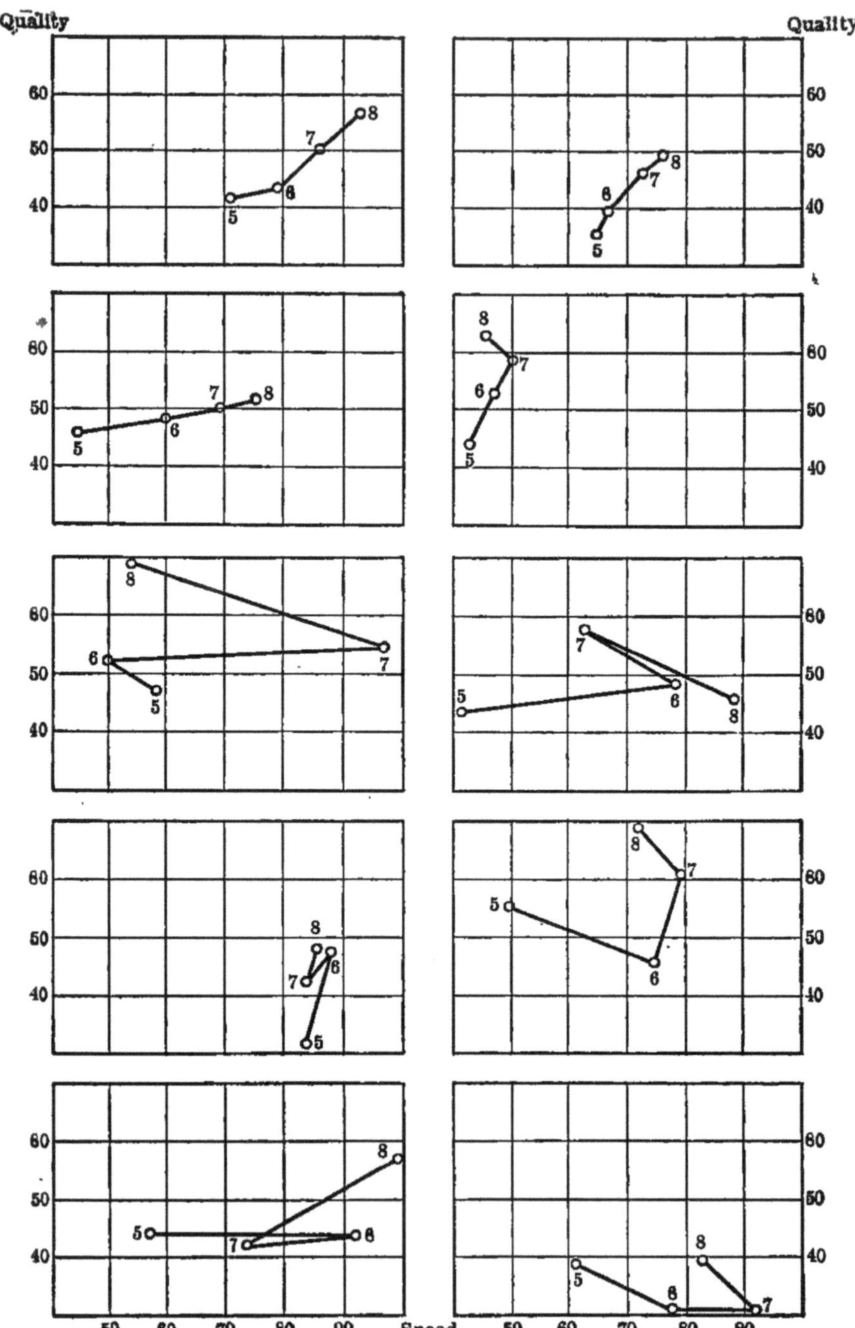

Fig. 14. Average quality and average speed of handwriting of pupils of the four upper grades in ten schools[76]

[76] Quality on vertical scale, speed on horizontal scale. The four schools referred to

Social Standards versus Imposed Standards

Second, the standards set up are derived from the work actually going on in schools. There is no dictation from purely theoretical and arbitrary sources. It is quite impossible to close one's eyes to the fact that in the past there has been a tendency to assume that the only standard of action is the perfect standard. Many a child has been taught penmanship from perfect copy and has been urged to imitate this copy at whatever cost of time and pains. The slow, painful effort to draw letters like those in the copy book is not an unfamiliar exhibition in the penmanship class. A standard derived from the school work itself is a social standard; it is based on what pupils really do. One need not be satisfied with present performances, but one starts from solid ground. Furthermore, out of actual measurements will come a clear idea of the range of variation. One of the most astonishing facts which have come out in the course of the study of standards is the fact that there are very wide variations in the same grade. There is, therefore, an easy possibility of finding for each grade high standards. These high standards have the further advantage of being standards actually realized by pupils. We are justified in describing the standards thus set up as natural standards. They do not limit the progress of any grade or aim at mechanical uniformity as do the arbitrary standards based on personal judgments.

Comparison through Exact Measurement

Third, standards measured and expressed in definite terms can be compared and can be made the basis of studies which are quite impossible so long as standards are not expressed in common terms. For example, when the speed of handwriting in a certain school is deliberately changed, what is the effect produced on quality? Heretofore it has been almost impossible to answer such a question. Every school reform has been enthusiastically hailed by its friends as accomplishing much. In the second generation most of these reforms are checked, if not actually dropped, because it is found that the good accomplished in one line is entirely lost in some other. To-day reforms are in a position to measure their effects in all directions. A change in the speed of handwriting may or may not be advantageous; it is the duty of measurement to so state results that some light will be thrown on this matter.

A concrete example will serve to show how studies of this kind may be carried out. Fig. 15 shows the relative speeds and qualities of handwriting found in various grades in a miscellaneous group of cities and the corresponding facts for St. Louis and Grand Rapids. It is seen that both of these school systems are ahead at all points in speed and behind at first in quality. Both cities have made a conscious effort to get away from the slow drawing of letters in the lower grades. In doing this quality has been sacrificed. It is not the purpose of this discussion to decide what methods of teaching handwriting are best; the value of this example is that it shows quality and speed reduced to terms where the two can be studied together

---

in the text are represented in the four diagrams in the upper part of the figure. North Doan is reported in the diagram in the upper left-hand corner. Kentucky is shown in the upper right-hand corner. Memorial is under North Doan. Mt. Pleasant is under Kentucky.

and with a high degree of exactness.

Records as a Basis of Standardization

Fourth and finally, measured standards show the direction in which pupils are moving, because they permit a permanent record of each step of the child's development. Schools have been slow to learn the value of records. On the one hand, school records have been piled up by the tome and no use has been made of them; on the other hand, they are usually so loosely thrown together that they are of very little value in guiding educational policy. Here is a form of record which can be duplicated and compared from year to year. Medicine has long since learned that exact records are the only safe means of guiding treatment. Modern agriculture has become scientific through the use of records and through decisions regarding experiments which these records make possible. Modern business has learned to make its accounting intelligent enough to guide policies. Finally, schools are beginning to see that records of a type permitting continuous comparisons are invaluable in determining at what point school work shall take this or that form.

Studies of Oral Reading

What has been done with penmanship has been paralleled in some other subjects of elementary instruction. The following quotations have to do with oral reading:

> A coöperative study of reading was organized during the month of September by the committee in charge of the grade-teachers' section of the Illinois State Teachers Association (Northeastern Section), which met at Elgin, Illinois, November 3 and 4. The purpose of this study was to secure a body of facts in regard to the achievement of boys and girls in reading in a number of schools represented in the Association. . . .
>
> The materials used in this study of reading were the standardized oral-reading paragraphs and the silent-reading tests which have been used in connection with the surveys in Cleveland, Grand Rapids, and St. Louis, as well as in a large number of investigations carried on in other cities. . . .
>
> The standardized oral-reading paragraphs consist of a series of twelve paragraphs arranged in the order of increasing difficulty. The tests were given to the pupils individually by a principal or by a teacher who had been previously trained for the work. As the pupil read the teacher recorded the time required to read each paragraph together with the number of errors which were made of the following types:
>
> (*a*) Gross mispronunciations, which include such errors in pronunciation as indicate clearly that the word is too difficult for the pupil to pronounce.

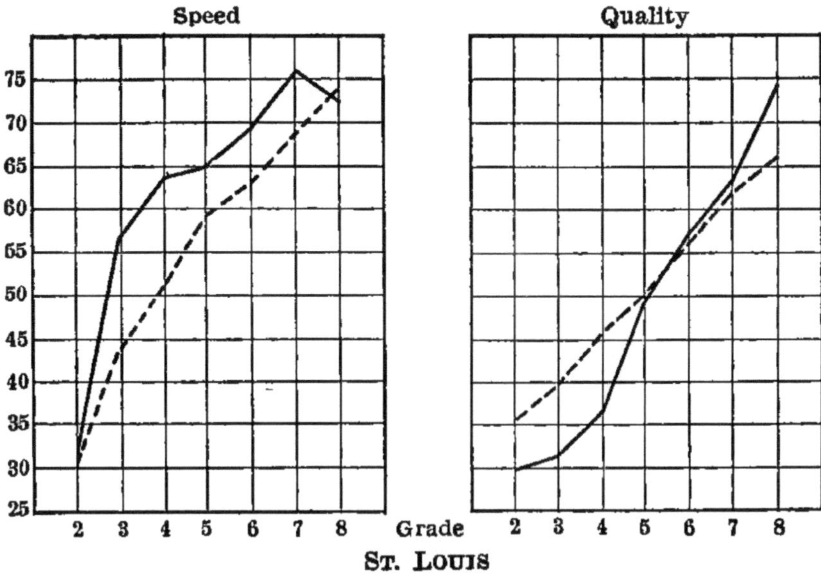

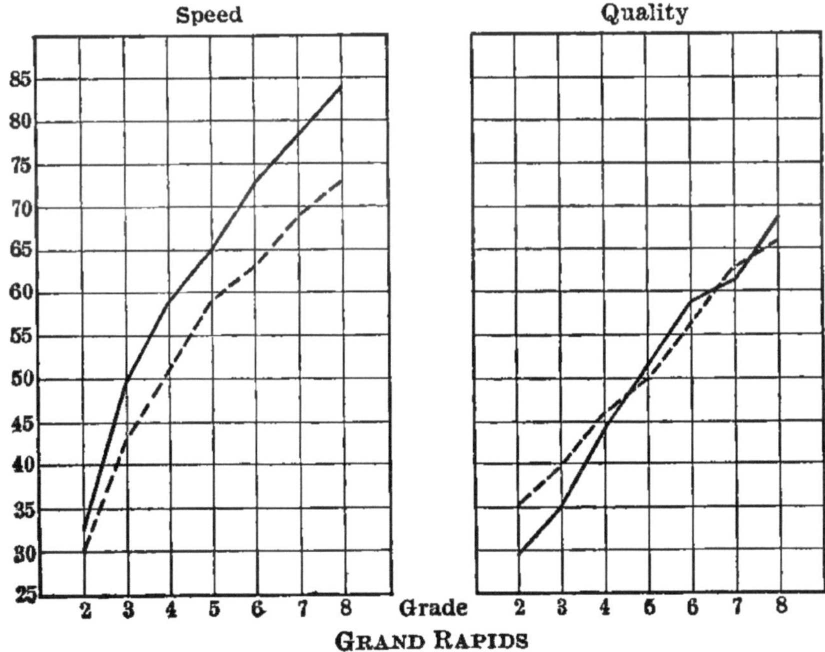

Fig. 15. Speed and quality of handwriting

Dotted lines indicate the level of achievement in various grades in fifty-six cities, the results from which were averaged; the full-drawn lines show the achievements in the two cities discussed (*b*) Minor mispronunciations, which include the pronunciation of a portion of a word, wrong accent, wrong syllabification, omission of syllables, etc.

(*c*) Omission of words.

(*d*) Insertion of words.

(*e*) Repetition of words or groups of words.

(*f*) Substitution of one word or group of words for another.

A pupil continued to read until he had made seven or more errors in each of two paragraphs. By means of a system of scoring based on the time required to read and on the number of errors which were made it was possible to represent the achievement of a pupil or a class in numerical terms. . . .

The upper section of the table [given below] gives the average number of seconds required to read paragraph 1 and the average number of errors made by three *poor* second-grade classes and by three *good* second-grade classes. Of the poor schools, School M made more errors and read more slowly than the average. School N read with fewer errors than the average, but read so slowly that the oral-reading score for the class was below the average. School O, on the other hand, gave sufficient emphasis to rate, but neglected accuracy to such an extent that the oral-reading score was low. An examination of the records made by the good schools shows clearly that consistent progress in both rate and accuracy is a prerequisite to a high level of achievement. The schools of northern Illinois vary widely in the amount of emphasis given to these phases of reading achievement. There is need, on the part of many teachers, for a continuous critical study of the specific character of the results which they are securing.

RATE AND ERRORS IN ORAL READING

PARAGRAPH 1—GRADE II

	Average	Poor Schools			Good Schools		
		M	N	O	X	Y	Z
Rate [seconds per passage]	42.2	65.0	64.1	39.1	27.2	32.8	37.9
Errors	1.4	2.0	0.5	2.4	1.1	0.9	1.3

PARAGRAPH **1**—GRADES II, III, AND IV

	Average	School A	School B	School C	School D
Grade II					
Rate	42.2	37.9	65.0	39.1	43.4

Errors	1.4	1.3	2.0	2.4	1.7
Grade III					
Rate	21.9	19.8	23.6	23.9	28.0
Errors	0.9	0.7	1.7	1.8	0.8
Grade IV					
Rate	18.6	18.0	21.9	16.0	27.0
Errors	0.8	0.6	1.3	0.5	1.5

Additional light is thrown on this problem when we follow certain schools through the second, third, and fourth grades. The average rate and number of errors for Grades II, III, and IV are given in the left-hand column of the lower section of the table. The records for School A show that second-grade pupils do better both in rate and in accuracy than the average. The same thing may be said of the third and fourth grades. Continuous, consistent progress of this type is very commendable. In School B, on the other hand, the pupils do less well in each grade in both speed and accuracy than the average. A question arises here concerning the general effectiveness of the classroom instruction. School C ranks low in accuracy in the second grade. Apparently this difficulty was realized in the third grade, and considerable progress both in speed and in accuracy resulted. In the fourth grade average results are attained which are above the average. This school represents consistent, continuous growth from grade to grade of a highly desirable type. School D, on the other hand, makes improvement in speed and accuracy in the third grade, but fails to increase its rate in the fourth grade, and makes a record in accuracy which is distinctly below the record made by the third grade. It is evident, if the records for the present second, third, and fourth grades are typical of the results secured from year to year, that there is need for more intelligent instruction and supervision in School D.

In this connection it should be said that objective standards of attainment for each grade should be defined. By means of tests given throughout a school or a city the present level of achievement can be determined. By means of comparisons with results secured elsewhere new goals of attainment can be defined. Each teacher should become familiar with the methods of giving tests. She should utilize them frequently in examining her work to find sources of strength and weakness. Through the co-operation of teachers and supervisors progressive revisions in standards of attainment and methods of procedure should be made. This type of co-operation is necessary because it is only when all the units of a school system work consistently together toward clearly defined ends that the most effective results can be secured.[77]

Studies dealing with Other Subjects

A great number of similar studies are being reported each year on arithmetic, spelling, and other aspects of the elementary curriculum. The high-school subjects are more complicated than those in the elementary school, but even these are beginning to be tested. There are satisfactory tests in algebra and the beginnings of measurements in Latin and English.

Mechanical Aspects the First to be Standardized

In all cases standardization begins with the mechanical aspects of school work. These are more susceptible to exact quantitative description and are the first to be taken up. Some writers have professed to find in this a reason for rejecting the whole movement toward standardization. There are, they assert, products of teaching which are subtle and intangible. These are the products which are most highly to be prized. Thoroughly to standardize penmanship and oral reading and algebra is to set aside these more important matters.

Two answers are to be made to this objection to the movement toward standardization. In the first place, the higher values of education are not secured by teachers who are negligent of the fundamental mechanical requirements. The teacher who successfully trains his pupil to study history will make of him a good reader also. In the second place, if it should prove to be desirable to give less time than is given at present to training in the mechanical aspects of school subjects, it will certainly be absolutely essential that the limits and restrictions be set up with discrimination. We shall never be able to deal intelligently with the mechanical aspects of education until we have studied them.

A third statement which can be ventured with assurance in the light of the recent history of this movement is that its limits cannot be set. Each year new aspects of school work are measured with exactness. It is certain that the ultimate conquests of measurement will push the opponents back into their own territory.

Standardization and the Science of Education

In short, standardization is nothing but a systematic effort to deal with educational problems explicitly and in the light of exact information. Whatever may be the limits of exact knowledge in educational matters, it is certain that we ought to secure as much knowledge of this type as possible.

EXERCISES AND READINGS

The exercise which will best serve to supplement this chapter is a series of tests performed on members of the class and worked out by them for purposes of comparison with other standard results. In the appendix of the volume of the Cleveland survey en-

[77] William S. Gray, "A Co-operative Study of Reading in Eleven Cities of Northern Illinois." *Elementary School Journal,* Vol. XVII, No. 4 (December, 1916), pp. 250-257.

titled "Measuring the Work of the Public Schools" a full set of standard tests will be found.

S. A. Courtis, 82 Eliot Street, Detroit, Michigan, furnishes tests in various subjects, especially arithmetic.

The following institutions furnish various tests:

College of Education, The University of Chicago, Chicago, Illinois.

Teachers College, Columbia University, New York City.

Bureau of Measurements and Tests, State Normal School, Emporia, Kansas.

The readings which are most useful in this connection are to be found in current educational periodicals. The student will find the latest scientific studies in such journals as the following:

School Review. Published by The University of Chicago Press. This is a journal dealing chiefly with high schools.

Elementary School Journal. Published by The University of Chicago Press. This contains very full reviews of elementary tests.

Journal of Educational Psychology. Published by Warwick and York, Baltimore, Maryland.

Educational Administration and Supervision. Published by Warwick and York, Baltimore, Maryland.

Educational Review. Published by the Educational Review Publishing Company, Easton, Pennsylvania.

School and Society. Published by The Science Press, New York City.

CHAPTER XVI

METHODS

Meaning of the term "method." Meaning of the term "device." Personal methods and devices. Supposed conflict between methods and subject-matter. Two examples of modern methods. Object teaching. Laboratory method in physics. Spread of the laboratory idea. Reaction against the question and answer method. Inefficient methods of study. Organizing a school for supervised study. Organizing subject-matter for supervised study. Experiments in method. Method as a subject of scientific tests. Exercises and readings.

Meaning of the Term "Method"

The problems of instruction are by no means solved when a subject has been selected and placed in its proper relation to the other subjects in the curriculum. There is still the problem of presenting the subject to the class in such a way as to appeal to the attention and interest of its members. The special term which is applied in educational writings to the organization of material for class instruction is the term "method" or "method of teaching."

In contrasting American schools with European schools it was pointed out in an earlier chapter that the American method is the textbook and recitation method, while the method of the European schools is predominantly the oral or lecture method. The subject-matter of instruction can be treated by either of these methods.

Meaning of the Term "Device"

Another term which has been used in educational discussions to distinguish between the more general modes of procedure and certain details of classroom work is the term "device." A classroom device is some special piece of equipment or some particular way of dealing with a class that can be described as appropriate to a single classroom situation or to some topic of a given subject. For example, if a teacher of Latin has verb forms printed on cards for the purpose of drilling his classes in the recognition of such forms, his cards are spoken of as devices. Again, if one calls the roll by assigning a number to each member of the class and then requiring each number to be given in its order, it is said that one has a time-saving device.

Personal Methods and Devices

Every teacher has methods and devices of presenting material to his or her classes. The experienced teacher behaves skillfully in the presence of a class because all the details of procedure have been tried, and those which proved successful have been retained. The inexperienced teacher is clumsy in his methods, just as is any novice in dealing with an unmastered social situation.

Supposed Conflict between Methods and Subject-Matter

It is sometimes pointed out that in the training of teachers there is danger that competition will arise between the demand for skill in methods and the demand for knowledge of subject-matter. The specialist in science scoffs at a course in methods of teaching, saying that all the prospective teacher needs is to know the subject thoroughly, and method will take care of itself. Furthermore, such a critic of methods often points out that the time required for a course in methods must be taken from time which the student ought to devote to subject-matter.

The school principal who is looking for a science teacher is likely to reply that he has had teachers thoroughly acquainted with the science but utterly unsympathetic with pupils. Such teachers do not know how to get the facts to the students. They are abstract, or speak too fast, or do not assign the lessons in such a way as to help the students see the important points.

There is no necessity of being one-sided in this matter. The successful teacher will ultimately have both knowledge of the subject-matter and methods and devices of presenting the subject-matter. If he is lacking in either, he will be in just that degree inefficient. There can be no doubt that a properly balanced appreciation of both is the sane and wise attitude to assume.

Two Examples of Modern Methods

It will, of course, be quite impossible to do more than illustrate the problems of method in this general introduction. The remainder of this chapter will be devoted to comments on two significant innovations in method which are characteristic of present-day teaching as contrasted with the teaching of two generations ago. The older of these innovations was the adoption of the laboratory method; the later general innovation is the movement in the direction of supervised study in all subjects.

Object Teaching

An appreciation of the laboratory method can be gained by reviewing briefly the history of this method in American schools. As far back as 1809 a follower of Pestalozzi, one Joseph Neef, conducted a school in Philadelphia, where he exhibited Pestalozzi's object method. Pupils learned by direct contact with things. Such teaching was in sharp contrast with the ordinary methods then in vogue, for at that time instruction consisted exclusively of statements, either oral or written, which the pupils were supposed to learn by heart.

The object-teaching movement made little progress until it was taken up in 1860 by Dr. Sheldon, the head of the normal school at Oswego, New York. From Oswego the movement spread, especially to the new Western schools, and had so wide an influence that the study of nature in the lower schools was vigorously advocated and extensively undertaken. The inductive method of direct contact with the facts was advocated in fields other than nature study. Dr. Sheldon's daughter took a vigorous part in the development of instruction in history based on direct contact with source material. The laboratory method in history, as it was sometimes called, spread and inspired enthusiasm for methods in all the literary subjects analogous to the laboratory work of the sciences.

Laboratory Method in Physics

In the high schools a parallel movement took place in the last third of the nineteenth century, leading to the adoption of laboratory work as a definite mode of instruction. On this subject one writer on the history of physics has given the following statements:

> Experimental work had not been entirely unknown in secondary schools even in the early part of the century, but no attempt had been made to bring the pupil into personal contact with its results. The Boston Grammar Schools were all furnished with a $275 set of physical apparatus as early as 1837, and most of the academies installed sets about that time, but the apparatus was for the use of the instructor only, the pupils not being allowed to handle it. And this condition existed to within about thirty years of the end of the century, when the agitation for individual laboratory work began.
>
> This period of agitation was marked by the beginning of some laboratory work and the discussion of the value of individual work and the inductive method by educators. But there was no general adoption of the plan till a later period. It was about this time that David Starr Jordan accepted the chair of Natural History in an Illinois college and attempted to establish a chemical laboratory. His attempt was promptly vetoed by the board of trustees. . . .
>
> In the report from the Albany, N.Y., City School, for 1882, the Superintendent recommended that a whole year be given to the study of physics with opportunity for daily experiments, the class participating in the experiments as far as practicable. The report of 1882-1883 from the Washington, D.C., High School, states that laboratories have been fitted up. Indianapolis reported in 1883 that the experimental method had been introduced and was meeting with approval from both teacher and pupil. Cincinnati reported in 1882 that physics was taught from a syllabus four hours a week during the third year. St. Louis reported physics taught through the second year of the high school. The reports show only quali-

tative experiments. . . .

The general trend of accumulated opinion in 1884 shows increased favor of the idea that mental discipline is the chief aim in physics teaching. There was a general notion that the study of physics ought to train the pupil to think, but as to what method should be used to bring about this result there was no settled opinion. Laboratory work meant anything from a few simple demonstrations by the teacher to a complete individual laboratory course, such as is given at the present day.

For the next fifteen years, physics teaching, in fact, science teaching in general, was in an experimental stage. In the effort to make science a disciplinary study, the laboratory method was coming into general use rapidly, but the old idea of making science include everything in reach—a remnant of the *Natural Philosophy* stage—had prevented its becoming a really disciplinary study. We find David Starr Jordan in 1889 lamenting the superficial way in which science was taught.[78]

Spread of the Laboratory Idea

The historical statements given above show how recent is the acceptance of the laboratory method even in science teaching. The enthusiasm for the method is as impressive as its youth. It would be impossible to turn the present generation of science teachers away from the laboratory method of teaching. In spite of its cumbersomeness of administration, its demand for expensive equipment, and the deliberation which it compels in teaching the results of science, the laboratory method is everywhere accepted as the true method. Indeed, as stated above, the literary subjects such as history and English, the latter especially in the teaching of composition, not infrequently adopt the term "laboratory method" in order to show their recognition of the effectiveness of the method worked out by the sciences.

Reaction against the Question and Answer Method

The second innovation in method of teaching, namely, supervised study, came as a reaction against the purely examination method of conducting class exercises which was formerly almost universal except in laboratory classes. The examination method is the familiar one of calling a pupil to his feet and then asking him one question after another to find out whether he has learned his lesson. If he answers well, he is marked with a high grade. If he answers badly, he is marked with a low grade, reprimanded, and told to do his work over.

The futility of some of this procedure is at once evident if one thinks of the student who has made an honest effort to learn his lesson, but has failed because

[78] David A. Ward, The History of Physics Instruction in the Secondary Schools of the United States. Unpublished thesis for the Master's degree in the Department of Education of The University of Chicago.

he adopted an inefficient and often a wrong method of getting the lesson. In such a case the pupil fails because he does not know how to get his lesson. It therefore occurred to some progressive teachers that it was their duty to inquire not merely into the results of the student's study but also into his methods of study. The moment this new idea is grasped, the function of a recitation will be seen to be something more than the examination of pupils. The recitation is now coming to be the place where pupils learn how to do intellectual work, how to attack intellectual problems, and how to guide their efforts into more economical and effective channels.

Inefficient Methods of Study

Observation of high-school pupils who are asked to study will always show the need of attention to methods of study. The following description of such observation is illuminating:

> To ascertain to what extent the other members of the class might have this difficulty, the following experiment was tried. In assigning the next lesson, suggestions were given with unusual care. The pupils were then told that the next fifteen minutes would be given to studying the lesson, and that they should begin the assigned home work immediately. The experiment showed at once that the pupils did not appreciate the value of limited time, for all were slow in beginning work. It took some of them the whole fifteen minutes to go through the technique of getting started. Several evidently were not in the habit of working alone, for they looked about helplessly and simply imitated the others. However, these same pupils had come to the classroom daily with the lessons well prepared. Very little was accomplished in the fifteen minutes indicating that the pupils very probably wasted much time in studying their assignments of home work. Although the class had been in the high school only a short time, the teacher had been presupposing a habit of study which did not exist. Much of the difficulty is due to lack of knowledge as to how to study and how to use time to advantage. The remedy in this case is, of course, definite instruction as to methods of study.[79]

Organizing a School for Supervised Study

The organization of a school to provide opportunity for supervised study is thus described by the principal of one of the first schools to undertake this type of work on a large scale:

> We took five minutes from each of the six recitation periods, which we have in our school day, and put these together to make a thirty-minute study period coming once a day. In order that each

[79] E. R. Breslich, "Supervised Study as a Means of providing Supplementary Individual Instruction." Thirteenth Yearbook of the National Society for the Study of Education, Part I, p. 45. The University of Chicago Press, 1914.

class might receive the benefit of this period, we arranged that the first period class use the time on Tuesday; the second period class on Wednesday; and the third period class on Friday; the following week that the fourth, fifth, and sixth period classes use the period for supervised study. On Monday and Thursday the teacher uses this study period by having come to her room for individual attention, such students as she thinks may need individual help. So much for the plan.

In regard to the results, we have found that the plan is of greatest advantage with the younger students, and in the first part of a subject. That is, the younger students need direction in method of study, and all the students find it helpful when learning the method of attack upon a new subject.

We find it necessary, of course, to keep some definite check upon the work of the students. This is done by setting for them certain concrete problems in their study. For instance, to work out a certain number of examples; to be ready to prove a given theorem; to pick out the topic sentences in a given paragraph; to determine the most important points of a certain topic in physics; to pick out the leading events in a given historical topic, etc. We find the method works very well in mathematics, science, and history. Some difficulty has been experienced in the study of an English classic, such as *Macbeth*, in making the work of the study period definite. We are working at this problem.

Besides teaching methods of study, we have found one decided advantage of this study period is that by reason of it, the teacher gets a considerable insight into the methods of study of the various students and can discover those who waste time, who have faulty methods of attack, etc.

Another point which we have found as a result of this work is that the teachers themselves are not at all clear as to definite methods of study.[80]

Organizing Subject-Matter for Supervised Study

One of the recent elaborate plans for supervised study is thus described by its author:

It has been erroneously assumed by many writers that supervised study was synonymous with effective study. It has been taken for granted that schools administering supervised-study schedules taught pupils how to study. There is a wide difference between *more* study and *effective* study. Supervised-study schedules may secure the former and miss the latter. Effective study de-

[80] F. M. Giles, late principal of the Township High School of De Kalb, Illinois. Thirteenth Yearbook of the National Society for the Study of Education, Part I, pp. 57-58.

pends upon many elements, among them proper time and place, concentration, reading ability, organization habits, questioning habits, and memory. Supervised-study schedules mechanically provide for the first two and more nearly secure the third than do other devices. The remaining elements involved in the technique of study are not necessarily concomitants of so-called supervised study. . . .

The origin of the plan I am about to describe grew out of study of the classroom exercise in typewriting. In the typewriting class pupils remain in the same group, but are individually apart. A pupil taking typewriting may stay out of school for two weeks and return to the same group in his mathematics, Latin, and typewriting. In the last subject he starts in exactly where he left off with a distinct realization that his muscular-mental co-ordination has been impaired, while too often in the first two subjects he takes up the advanced work with his classmates apparently without any particular sense of loss. Why should he, if he makes his grade? Does he not figure out a distinct gain?

Two things differentiate the mechanics of the typewriting exercise from the mathematics and Latin recitations: (*a*) consecutive, daily assignments which the pupil may follow without the guidance of a teacher; (*b*) individual responsibility and progress or an accounting for individual differences. Apply these same principles to academic subjects and it becomes necessary to provide printed daily lesson assignments and to check upon individual preparation of these daily assignments. One added factor, however, appears with the academic subject which uniquely distinguishes it from the manual, namely, the *expression* of the lesson ideas.

In typewriting the pupil during the exercise concretely and muscularly shows the teacher how well he understands the lesson. In academic subjects the understanding must first be tested by language expression. There is no machine yet invented for eliminating this language-expression exercise. Consequently for all academics there must always remain the recitation period. *Throwing one's ideas into a language mold is not the same as expressing one's ideas by mechanical means.* For this reason the recitation period must always be stressed. . . .

The laboratory-recitation plan is based on the fundamental idea that recitation groups should be organized on the basis of preparation. Pupils need not recite on the day's preparation, but the recitation for the day is upon work previously prepared and tested. The recitation teacher knows that when his group assembles each and every pupil has previously prepared and has been checked in the work to be recited upon, otherwise the pupil would not be in the group. This is accomplished by the following *modus operandi*:

Co-operating laboratory-recitation teachers. Forty or fifty pupils are assigned to a certain laboratory-recitation period operated by two teachers—one the laboratory, the other the recitation, teacher—in adjoining rooms. While the laboratory teacher is supervising the preparation of lessons during the ninety-minute period, the co-operating recitation teacher is conducting recitations with groups of pupils taken from the laboratory on the basis of their preparation. For illustration, each Friday the laboratory algebra teacher in the second period will give the co-operating recitation teacher of that class and period the advancement of the slowest pupil in each of two or three recitation groups previously determined on the basis of laboratory preparation. The recitation teacher prepares his work for the following week on the basis of this information. If there are three groups, the recitation teacher devotes thirty minutes to each group; if two groups, forty-five minutes. The pupil spends either one-half or two-thirds of each period in the laboratory, the time depending upon the number of groups into which the recitation has been divided, and the remaining time in recitation.[81]

Experiments in Method

The meaning of experiments such as have been described is not far to seek. The ingenious supervisor or teacher who has watched the ordinary recitation made up of a series of questions and answers recognizes the fact that such a recitation is very formal. His efforts to improve teaching will carry him into new types of class exercises. The laboratory type of exercise will serve better in certain cases; in others, the supervised-study type. Sometimes it is desirable to try other experiments. Without attempting to deal with these other experiments in detail, it may be well to enumerate some of the types of class exercise which have not been discussed in full.

The lecture method is common in higher institutions. In the primary grades this method has taken the form of story-telling and has been developed of late with elaborate technique.

The study lesson is a name which has been used to describe an exercise in which the pupils study new material on which they have not prepared in advance. The special forms of this kind of exercise may vary from a critical reading together of an advanced section of the textbook to a series of readings by members of the class of various scattered sources in collateral books.

A report lesson is a modification of the lecture method. The members of the class, rather than the teacher, furnish the lecture material; each student having

[81] I. M. Allen, "Experiments in Supervised Study." *School Review*, Vol. XXV, No. 6 (June, 1917), pp. 401-404.

prepared a part of the whole in advance has an opportunity to present his findings to the class, with the result that the subject is studied in full through the coöperative efforts of all.

The laboratory method may take on the form of field excursions in the geographical sciences and the form of gardening in agriculture. Whatever its form it is one of the most radical departures from the traditional class exercise.

Shopwork has become common in many lines. With the girls the class exercises in domestic science and domestic art are crosses between construction exercises and investigation exercises.

Drill exercises in mathematics and language consist in the performance under the teacher's supervision of a series of tasks which are designed to cultivate fixed habits in the fields to which they belong. Very often such exercises are conducted in such a way that each pupil works individually.

Written examinations ought to be included here. Whenever a class is given a series of review questions for the purpose of requiring a general review of a whole subject, the result of the exercise is to fix in the student's mind certain larger elements of the study and to establish certain broad habits of selection. Written examinations may be, from this point of view, devices of training, not merely tests of results. The examination method as a training method has, accordingly, an important place.

The coöperative recitation is one in which the pupils ask the questions. The teacher withdraws as far as possible, and allows the members of the class to initiate the discussions. When this kind of exercise is first introduced, the pupils are likely to follow as closely as they can the manner of questioning which they have seen exhibited by their teachers. If the experiment is carried out persistently, the pupils will ultimately become quite independent and spontaneous in their questioning.

Method as a Subject of Scientific Tests

Class exercises are thus seen to differ in form and in results. When the student of standards begins to make his tests and measurements, he finds an inviting field for study in the different effects which follow the various types of exercises enumerated above.

EXERCISES AND READINGS

Methods can be discussed from various points of view. Let the student consider methods in relation to the different subjects of instruction. How will the method of teaching manual training compare with the method of teaching Latin or arithmetic or music? Again, let the relation of method to the maturity of pupils be discussed. What can be done in a high-school class in English that is not possible with an elementary class? In this connection what are the methods of teaching adults? Does a preacher exhibit method in his preaching? What is the method of a writer in a newspaper as distinguished from the method of a writer of novels? Methods can be considered from the point of view of the teacher's personality and equipment. Are there any natural differences between the methods of men and women in teaching? Classify teachers with respect to the aggressiveness of their methods of attack. Some are very quiet and require the pupils to do most of the talking; others are not.

In the Appendix will be found a list of questions designed to aid in the observation of classroom methods.

CHARTERS, W. W. Methods of Teaching. Row, Peterson & Company, Chicago.

EARHART, L. B. Types of Teaching. Houghton Mifflin Company.

MCMURRY, C. A. The Elements of General Method. Public School Publishing Company, Bloomington, Illinois.

PARKER, S. C. Methods of Teaching in High Schools. Ginn and Company.

STRAYER, G. D. A Brief Course in the Teaching Process. The Macmillan Company.

STRAYER, G. D., and NORSWORTHY, N. How to Teach. The Macmillan Company.

CHAPTER XVII

CLASSROOM MANAGEMENT

Intellectual progress and social conditions. Social training general. Types of social organization. Social control through anticipation. Organization of routine. Punishments and rewards. Larger social organization. Attempts to classify unruly members of the social group. Impersonal discipline. Exercises and readings.

Intellectual Progress and Social Conditions

The last chapter dealt with the intellectual side of class exercises. The recitation has for its final purpose the conveying and fixing of certain ideas and methods of thinking. But this end can be reached only when the social conditions within the class are properly under control. The teacher is concerned, therefore, not alone with intellectual instruction; he is concerned also with what is sometimes called school government or school discipline. If the class is in a riot, it is impossible to make any headway with history or arithmetic. Young and inexperienced teachers are often ineffective because they do not know the art of social management. They know the subject-matter which is to be impressed on the minds of the pupils, but they do not understand the serious social distractions which are sure to arise at times in a group of immature human beings.

Social Training General

The social conditions necessary for successful classroom work are often dependent on the general discipline of the whole school rather than on the momentary situation. If the general social tone of a school building is low, the best teacher is likely to find himself handicapped. If, on the other hand, the social management outside the classroom is efficient, a given teacher who is not skillful in organizing his class may get on without serious disturbance.

There is another sense, also, in which the problem of management is a general one. The effect of class management on the pupil's life is profound. The school coöperates with the home and often outweighs the home in determining the pupil's ideals of social life. These ideals are not so much matters of intellectual training as of social habit. The influence of a teacher over his pupils is often due quite as much to the way in which he manages the class as to the subject-matter which he teaches.

Types of Social Organization

A social situation can often be anticipated and conditions can be prearranged so as to direct all the participants into lines of activity which are desirable. In considering classroom organization it is important that we recognize, first, the possibilities of prearrangement. The more experienced a teacher becomes, the more he can anticipate situations.

Second, there are forms of class organization which facilitate social coöperation, such as arranging pupils in line. This is recognized outside the school, and it is a common practice to arrange people in line, when, for example, they are securing tickets. The management of groups of people can best be carried on by the adoption of such forms. There need be nothing artificial about the forms if they are not overdone. The skillful teacher often uses formal routine to keep the class moving as a unit.

Third, there is no social group which does not at times profit by a critical review of situations after they are over. Punishment is meted out by society to those who have failed to conform to social demands. On the other hand, rewards are given to those who have promoted in conspicuous ways the interests of the group. Both punishments and rewards are to be recognized as educative devices, and should be used in the school only when they are such. The future welfare of society is what should be in mind in every expression of judgment on past performances.

Briefly put, social management deals first with conditions before the group comes together; second, with the forms necessary while the group is together; and third, with the rewards or punishments which should follow an act in the interests of future behavior.

Social Control through Anticipation

Examples of anticipatory arrangements are not difficult to find. All the material equipments of the school contribute to class management. The division of the building into small classrooms provides for the division of the school into manageable groups. The arrangement of seats and the precautions against the noise and distraction which result from the shuffling about of furniture are further examples of preparation in advance for the management of classes.

In like fashion, the program for the day is worked out in advance by the wise administrator. This program provides for a distribution of work and recreation such that there will be no undue tax on the child. The third-grade pupil, for example, cannot sit still for thirty-five minutes at a time, so the teacher changes the character of the exercise at the end of every twenty or thirty minutes.

Anticipatory measures of the type here pointed out are usually not thought of by the inexperienced teacher as devices of class management. Class discipline is usually assumed to be a matter of the moment. If one will learn to look ahead, it is surprising how far most situations can be anticipated. The first day a teacher meets a class it is possible to foresee that it will be safer to require certain members of the group to sit apart. It is better to arrange their seats at once rather than to wait until an overt act precipitates a separation as a punishment.

The fact is that unfavorable social situations usually grow out of conditions that are remote and cannot be dealt with adequately at the moment. The disorderly boy is often one whose physical condition is unfit. The school is beginning to recognize the importance of proper feeding and proper hours of sleep, and is taking steps to see that pupils receive at home and at the luncheon hour the kind of hygienic attention which will prepare them for the work of the class. The social situation in the classroom is thus anticipated by a whole series of preparatory moves which at first sight seem remote from the teacher's direct task of meeting a class.

The attitude which is encouraged by a study of anticipatory measures is the same as that which is coming into the practice of medicine. There was a time when the physician regarded it as his chief duty to deal with disease after it had actually appeared. To-day the far-sighted practitioner is an advocate of what he calls preventive medicine. He aims to get the community interested in preparing in advance wholesome conditions which will conduce to health. The teacher's task ought not to be that of constantly penalizing pupils who have done wrong; it should be rather that of preparing conditions which will reduce disorder to a minimum and promote to its highest degree orderly procedure in the class.

Organization of Routine

The anticipation of social needs passes insensibly into the organization of regular forms of routine to be followed in the class exercise itself. The class exercise is not different in its essentials from any social gathering. It has been found necessary in meetings of any type to require one who would speak to secure the floor. It would lead to social chaos if everyone in an assembly spoke his mind according to his own personal impulse.

The difficulty in applying this analogy to the classroom and the difficulty in general about all fixed routine is that free discussion is often defeated by formality. The teacher is anxious, if he understands his task, to draw out the enthusiastic response of every member of his class. How to do this and at the same time avoid confusion which will disturb the whole group is a nice problem of adjustment. Formal methods should be required and adhered to far enough to insure the smooth operation of the social life of the class, but spontaneity should be prized and conserved.

Another and perhaps more fortunate example of routine to avoid confusion is to be found in an effective beginning of a class exercise. When a recitation is about to begin, it is a matter of major importance that the teacher be ready with something which will attract the attention of the whole class. Some instructors accomplish this with the first question; some resort to such a device as the announcement of the next assignment; some begin with a summary of the last lesson; some have the members of the class write for a few minutes. In sharp contrast with these methods which indicate that the instructor is ready and knows what he wants done are the aimless wanderings of some instructors who look over their desks for a book which seems to be lost in the débris, or the time-consuming roll call indulged in by others.

A third type of illustration of orderly procedure is the systematization of methods of passing in material. If pupils arrange their written work or their books or other material in a regular fashion, there will be no disorder in handling them. The social group will move as a unit, and this common movement will itself make for social solidarity.

There is much sanction in social psychology for this emphasis on routine. The customs of primitive peoples take on the character of sacred rites, so essential are they to the common life of the social group. Even in civilized society the demands of the group are paramount. There is in the family a fixed time for eating meals, not because hunger coincides in its reappearances with the movements of the clock but because the joint activities of a social group proceed better when they are systematized.

The routinizing of school work can go too far. The requirement has been imposed within the memory of this adult generation that pupils sit in their seats through long recitation periods with their hands behind their backs. Marching in lockstep from class to class has sometimes been required. The list could be lengthened indefinitely. The trouble in most of these cases is that the teacher loses sight of the educational motive of all discipline and begins to think of so-called order as an end in itself.

Punishments and Rewards

Even after a situation has been as carefully organized as is humanly possible, there are sure to come social emergencies. These furnish occasions for a type of discipline which is valuable not so much for the effect which it produces on the present situation as for its effect on the future. Furthermore, there is often very little expectation that the future will bring an exact repetition of the particular situation which has just passed. The discipline is therefore general in its type rather than specifically applicable to the present.

Viewed as a general preparation for the future, the social condemnation or approval of an act is often very important. For example, a boy breaks something through sheer carelessness. Shall the teacher pass the act without comment, or shall the act be made an occasion for punishment? Some people are disposed to determine what kind of treatment shall be given in terms of the value of the object broken. This is evidently to make of the specific act a specific issue. It is better, if it can be done, to detach attention from the specific act and note the general consequences of carelessness. Educationally, the accident furnishes an opportunity to warn, not against breaking that particular object again, but against being careless. If the lesson is well taught, it will tend to keep the boy from rushing about in the future without regard for his surroundings, whatever those surroundings may be.

Commendation, like blame, is useless except as it sets up in the pupil's mind true canons of judgment. To praise a child for a particular act, merely concentrating attention on that act, is to neglect the opportunity of cultivating a general virtue.

So complicated are the issues touched on in the last few paragraphs that many teachers feel that the safest course is to avoid praise and blame as far as possible and allow natural consequences to open the eyes of children to the virtue or error of their ways. Social approbation and social condemnation are thought of as something highly artificial and to be avoided. Experience does not justify this view. Social life has its rewards and its punishments, and the child will miss a large part of his education if he does not come to understand the importance to him of social values.

Let us consider a concrete case. A group of small boys in the fourth grade hid the rubbers and umbrella of a little girl in their grade one rainy noon, so that the girl was much delayed in starting home for luncheon and was much distressed. What could be done? The range of ordinary school punishments seems very limited. In earlier days there was a form of punishment capable of the nicest gradations and of universal application for every offense. But corporal punishment has gone, and if, from among the remaining possibilities, properly adjusted punishment is to be administered, it must be devised with ingenuity and regulated in quantity. The teacher in the case referred to hit on the plan of making the three little boys serve the girl for a week. They brought her coat and hat to her after school. She sent them on errands to the library. They learned more under the careful observation of the class about how boys should treat others, especially girls, than they could possibly have thought out in long months of freedom from the bonds of service.

Legitimate praise is perhaps harder to administer with equity than punishment. The teacher holds up a child's drawing and calls attention to its excellences. The danger is that the child will become self-conscious and conceited. A boy is polite and the teacher remarks on the fact. The other boys in the class who have not of late merited such praise make a virtue of their freedom from the taint of the teacher's praise.

The difficulty of laying down any principles regulating punishment and praise is that cases cannot be discussed intelligently without reference to the general social situations in which they find their setting. It may be said, indeed, that when an act is performed, it is too late to deal with it adequately in any case. The only effective form of classroom management is that which anticipates the act and develops a social atmosphere in which condemnation or approbation is naturally and spontaneously contributed by the whole group.

It is sometimes said that good school discipline is to be found only where there is no discipline. This remark is true only when discipline is thought of as synonymous with punishment administered; it assumes that the administration of such punishment is the chief or only form of discipline. In a larger view of the situation one should recognize that the best school discipline is that which guides the social group at all times and controls its attitudes toward all acts. The spirit of a class is no accident of the moment. That teacher has the best discipline who has planned and prepared the social situation so carefully that a departure from the established order brings an instant and wholesome response from the whole group.

Larger Social Organization

With this larger view of discipline in mind, one may legitimately introduce into this discussion a reference to those forms of elaborate organization of the school group which are sometimes attempted in the school-city or the school-state. Under these plans the pupils of a school are organized into an imitation city or state patterned after the adult corporation. The purpose of such an experiment is twofold. First, the conduct of a miniature organization prepares the pupils for participation in later life in the duties of citizenship, and second, there grows up a feeling of responsibility for the conditions in the immediate social group. The officers of the school-city are more active than they would otherwise be in restraining their fellows from possible disorder and in promoting acts which redound to the advantage of all.

These elaborate organizations are educational devices which often stimulate great interest and serve their twofold purpose admirably. In general, it must be remembered that a sense of responsibility cannot be cultivated in a day and is not the natural possession of an immature mind. Unless there is constant supervision the school-city is likely to go on the rocks even as a real municipality suffers from the tendency of human nature to backslide. The teacher must bring to the school-city those experiences and those social stimulations which will train and keep alive the community spirit.

It is a mistake to assume that social organization exists only where it finds expression in some such elaborate form as is discussed in the foregoing paragraphs. Social attitudes of some kind are always present. The teacher who leaves the matter to mere chance runs risks. The teacher who overdoes organization suffers from the reaction which commonly follows restraint. The teacher who deals with the situation with plan and foresight may mold the social group into a helpful agency contributing greatly to the work of the school.

Attempts to classify Unruly Members of the Social Group

However carefully the social whole has been organized, there comes a time when an unruly member appears. The teacher's task is then to defend the group and bring the eccentric member if possible under the influence of the social order.

In a very interesting chapter in his volume on "School Discipline" Professor Bagley has supplied the evidence that no classroom can be regarded as free from the appearance of unruly types of students. Even good teachers of long experience who in general are free from difficulties with the discipline of their classes find it necessary to give special attention to the troublesome types. These types are described by Professor Bagley as including the following: the stubborn pupil who makes difficulty because he is constantly refusing to fit into the social order; the haughty pupil who is not merely conceited but in his ordinary performances disturbs the regular social routine by his overbearing attitude both toward his fellows and his teacher; the self-complacent pupil who cannot be aroused to activity by any of the ordinary inducements that are presented by the school. Other types include the irresponsible pupil, the morose pupil, the hypersensitive pupil, the deceitful pupil, and the vicious pupil.

This collection of unmanageables fortunately does not turn up in any single class at one time, but, as Professor Bagley remarks, it would be unwise for us to leave young teachers with the idea that the appearance of any one of these types is due to the teacher's inefficiency. Many an efficient young teacher is baffled at the outset by the difficulties of dealing with one or another of these types of students. Professor Bagley made inquiry of some of the best teachers whom he could locate, and found that it is inevitable that pupils of these types are to be found sooner or later in every school. The wise teacher does well to plan in advance for the reception of the particular specimen that is sure to fall to his lot with every ten or twelve pupils.

Impersonal Discipline

The final comment which may be made in this connection is that the teacher must recognize that school discipline is a professional and educational problem, not a matter of purely personal relations between pupil and teacher. The teacher is dealing with a problem of group organization; he cannot allow the fractious pupil to pull him down to the level of a personal controversy. It is difficult at times to keep from the strong emotional reactions which blind the teacher to this objective view of school order, but the efficient teacher will see to it that the group idea and the needs of the social whole guide every act of discipline and reward.

EXERCISES AND READINGS

Distinguish between pupils of different ages with reference to the form of discipline appropriate. Does the first-grade child have any sense of responsibility? How far can a class in a high school be trusted to take care of its own order?

A commission in New York City, after studying the cases of disobedient pupils, recommended a return to corporal punishment. What can be said in favor of such a move? What are the evils of corporal punishment?

Society as a whole has taken an entirely new attitude in modern times toward the matter of punishment. The prison policy of modern nations is different from the older policy. What can be said with regard to prison education? What is the relation of crime to physical conditions?

With regard to the matter of rewards and prizes, what can be said for and against exemption from examinations as a reward for good work? Should medals be given for high scholarship? What is the attitude of society at large outside of the school in regard to rewards? For example, what does society do for the painter, the author, the successful plumber and carpenter? Is the example of society at large capable of direct translation into school practice?

BAGLEY, W. C. School Discipline. The Macmillan Company.

MOREHOUSE, F. M. The Discipline of the School. D. C. Heath and Company.

PERRY, A. C. Discipline as a School Problem. Houghton Mifflin Company.

SPENCER, HERBERT. Education. Chapter III on Moral Education. D. Appleton and Company.

CHAPTER XVIII

SELECTED ADMINISTRATIVE PROBLEMS

Programs and marks. The total school day. The class period. Physiological fatigue. Conditions like fatigue. Practical precepts based on study of fatigue. Administrative considerations controlling length of the class period. Adjustment of work within the period. Adjustment of credits. The problem of grading. Experiments with grading systems. The study of marks as an introduction to a study of the school system. Exercises and readings.

Programs and Marks

The regular and orderly movement of a social group depends on the adoption of a program. The daily program of a school is an indispensable formal device for maintaining that type of solidarity which was discussed in the last chapter. A second formal device of school control is the marking system, under which the pupil's status is determined and in accordance with which all his relations of an official type are regulated. The marking system may be treated as a conventional plan for distributing social rewards and punishments. Together, the daily program and the marking system are so much more significant than any other devices of social organization that they may properly be selected for special treatment.

The Total School Day

The arrangement of the daily program involves, first of all, the determination of the total amount of time available in the school day. Reliable information on this matter is at hand for a large number of the smaller cities of the United States, as indicated in the following quotation:

> The following statistics show present conditions regarding the length of the school day. Of 1,270 cities reporting, 338 have a school day of from four and a half to five hours; 521, from five to five and a half hours; 411, from five and a half to six hours. Of 1,310 cities reporting, 1,242 have two daily sessions, and 68 but one daily session. The tendency is toward a longer school day, especially in the grammar grades and in the high school. The opinion of most school men is that a high school of two sessions is superior to a high school of one session. With the one-session

plan, but little time is available for study periods. It is evident that four recitations, the number generally required, demand more than one or two 45 or 50 minute periods for study. The theory is that with the one-session plan pupils will prepare their lessons at home in the afternoon. The experience of the superintendents who have tried the one-session plan has generally been similar to that of the superintendent of schools at Detroit, Minn., who says:

> The one-session plan which I found in vogue in this high school was retained for the present year so that its workings might be studied. It is fine in theory, but a failure in practice. Asking the pupils to be ready for work at 8:30 caused much tardiness. It was impossible for those who came by the bus or train to be on time. Then the fact that the high school had one time schedule and the grades another, while occupying the same building, caused endless confusion. During the afternoon, when students came back only for shop and laboratory work or to consult teachers, there was further annoyance from students passing to and fro through the halls. There was too much idling about the buildings for the good of the grades in session or of the high-school students themselves. Of course, the fine theory was that students would spend the afternoon studying in the quiet and freedom of their homes, but they didn't. Too many of them roamed the streets and came to class unprepared the next day. The plan also kept the industrial teachers waiting until afternoon before they could begin their work. They were compelled to do it when pupils were tired and nervous. This work ought to be interspersed through the day to relieve the tension of the other work.
>
> One argument advanced in favor of the one-session plan is that many students work their way through school by using the afternoon. The facts are otherwise. This year only three boys have worked afternoons, and possibly the same number of girls.
>
> Next year we shall return to the "long day" and lengthen the time devoted to each subject, so as to give teachers a better chance to teach it thoroughly. Each student will also have a longer time at school to study under the supervision of the principal.[82]

At Gary the eight-hour school day with variations in the program to secure play, shopwork, class work, and entertainment is the ideal toward which the system is working. In some other quarters the reduction of formal school work has

[82] W. S. Deffenbaugh, "School Administration in the Smaller Cities." *Bulletin No. 44*, United States Bureau of Education, 1915, pp. 40-41.

been advocated on the assumption that outdoor work and play can be supplied by the home or some other agency enough to fill up the pupil's waking hours. Whatever the form taken by the discussion, one leading tendency appears everywhere: the child's work should be organized throughout the day. In most communities this means that the school will be called on to extend its control to most of the hours.

The Class Period

When the length of the school day has been determined, the problem of subdividing the day presents itself. The subdivision must first of all recognize the claims of various subjects. The type of problem which arises at this point was discussed at length in the chapters on the curriculum, and we need not here discuss further the claims of subjects. We turn now to the general problem of class organization which can be formulated in the question, How long can a student profitably try to concentrate his attention on a single form of activity?

Physiological Fatigue

The pupil's ability to work is determined by certain physiological conditions which should be understood by every teacher. These conditions can be described in a brief study of the physiology of fatigue.

Any animal tissue, as, for example, a muscle, is a storehouse of energy. Through nutrition the muscle tissue is kept in condition to contract. Whenever the muscle contracts, it uses up its own substance; it burns up its tissues to a limited degree. In the process of thus consuming its material the muscle gradually becomes clogged with waste products. It is the business of the circulatory system in a living organism to carry away this waste material and thus free the muscle from the effects of its contraction. The circulatory system also brings new materials in the form of nutrition to restore the depleted tissues. The restoration of the tissue through nutrition is not the demand which is most urgent in the case of a muscle which is called on to contract for a long period of time. Sooner or later the muscle must, indeed, be brought back to its normal state of nutrition, but during actual contraction the most immediate physiological problem is to keep it clear of its own waste products. If these waste products are not removed, they tend to interrupt further contraction by preventing the nerve fiber which enters the muscle from discharging motor impulses into the muscle. If stronger nervous impulses are sent through the nerve fiber, the muscle, even though it is somewhat clogged, will be found in a condition to contract with its original vigor; but if the nervous impulses are not increased, the contractions gradually diminish in intensity. This is a condition of muscular fatigue, and is to be distinguished from exhaustion, which does not set in until the substance of the muscle has been used up to a point which endangers the tissue.

Fatigue is nature's effort to protect tissues against any possibility of excessive use. Fatigue sets in at a period long before danger to the tissue is at hand. The overcoming of fatigue is dependent in all cases on the power to dispose of waste products. The athlete, for example, becomes a better runner chiefly through a training of his organism to carry away waste products. The untrained individual grows stiff and sore from exercise, not because his muscles are used up, but because his muscles are clogged with waste substances.

This description of muscular fatigue lays the foundation for an understanding of the problem of nervous fatigue. The nerve cells, like the muscles, get clogged by the products of their own action. They then fail to carry nervous impulses freely, and the individual can do his mental or physical work only with excessive effort. Fatigue of nerve cells means that nature has limits of work in these cells. Fortunately, the limit is reached long before exhaustion or other real dangers set in.

Conditions like Fatigue

Matters are complicated by the fact that physical conditions other than ordinary use produce fatigue-like effects in nerve cells. Excitement of any kind rapidly changes the condition of nerve cells, and sometimes foreign chemical substances get into the blood, as in fever or infection, and produce a condition that is in effect the same as fatigue.

Still further, as a fact of large importance in determining capacity for work, the nerve cells pass each day through a kind of internal cycle of conditions. At certain hours their condition is such that they transmit nervous impulses freely, and work is easy; at other hours work drags because the nerve cells are not prepared to be active; their internal chemical condition is such as to obstruct transmission of impulses. Thus, one is usually very energetic in the middle of the forenoon, but is logy at noon and sleepy at a late hour in the afternoon. Marked individual differences appear, making this statement merely a general statement. Furthermore, personal habits can be changed to some extent through the adoption of new habits of life.

Finally, there are all sorts of pathological conditions which profoundly affect the life and action of nerve cells. Anæmia and malnutrition may render nerve cells utterly incapable of continued action.

Practical Precepts based on Study of Fatigue

Enough has been said to make it clear that no simple formula can be applied to a group of pupils when one tries to determine for purposes of the daily program how long their nerve cells can be kept at work on a single task. The wisest course for the teacher to follow is to be alert, and when a class reaches its limit of profitable work to introduce a change. On the other hand, the teacher should be very discriminating and should understand that fatigue is not a dangerous symptom. For example, suppose that the athlete always stopped his exercise just as soon as he began to feel the necessity of sending stronger nervous impulses down to his muscles. He would lose the best results of training, for these results consist in the acquisition of the power to overcome fatigue. So also with the pupil. The acquisition of the power to overcome fatigue is a most important part of the pupil's training.

Keeping the principles suggested in the foregoing discussion in mind, it is relatively easy to arrive at certain practical rules of program administration.

First, maturity ought to mean greater power of endurance. The older classes should—and usually do—have longer periods of work.

Second, the period should be long enough to stretch the pupil's powers. Regulation of work within this period should be left to the teacher, and teachers should train themselves to recognize the symptoms of fatigue and to judge when training has gone as far as it can in overcoming fatigue.

Third, there should be variety in the program. The nervous system is made up of many different centers. The variation of occupations brings different centers successively into play and gives to each the opportunity of relaxation which is most wholesome. A long school day with much variety is eminently more rational than a short session of work of a single type concentrated into a few hours.

Administrative Considerations controlling Length of the Class Period

When recommending variations in the program we collide with what may seem at first to be an insuperable difficulty. It is impossible from an administrative point of view to have class exercises of irregular lengths. Imagine what would happen if the mathematics teacher should dismiss his class after a recitation of twenty-seven minutes, and the Latin teacher should hold his for fifty-three minutes. For administrative reasons class periods must be measured by the clock.

This leads to certain absurdities in school organization. For example, in order to regularize credits in high schools a unit of credit has been defined as a certain number of hours of class work. A moment's consideration makes it perfectly clear that an English class consisting of thirty freshmen will do less intensive work in a forty-minute period than will an advanced senior class of four students in trigonometry. The administrative fiction of uniformity when like credit is given for these two classes is grotesque.

The assignment of a double period to laboratory classes is likewise a concession to administrative convenience rather than a carefully weighed arrangement. It is easier to make up periods in multiples of the standard recitation time. But it is by no means clear that the sciences can profitably use double periods. The internal adjustment of laboratory work needs more careful study than it has received in the past. The laboratory method, as shown in an earlier chapter, is one which has excited great enthusiasm. Many a laboratory assignment which does not fill the time allotted to it is tolerated because of the vague general enthusiasm for the method and the formal arrangement of double periods.

Adjustment of Work within the Period

Such examples as these show from a new angle the importance of the movement for supervised study which was described in an earlier chapter. The teacher in charge of the class must ultimately have at hand various devices, some intended to give play to individual differences, some intended to promote social coöperation. Then, while administrative necessity dictates a uniform period for the class exercise, the educational needs of the students can be met by variations in the content and method of instruction.

Adjustment of Credits

Such a formula as this dictates also the recognition in an administrative way of the differences between the work performed by different students. There has been of late an increasing recognition of the justice of giving pupils different degrees of credit for work which they do in one and the same course. The student who carries a course in algebra with a high grade undoubtedly learns more than the student who does low-grade work in the same class.

The Problem of Grading

The proper distribution of credits opens up the complex problem of grading systems. The grading system is the basis of academic rewards and penalties. Yet it is recognized by pupils and teachers alike to be full of pitfalls. The ordinary system uses letters such as *E* for excellent, *P* for poor; or percentage designations such as 100 for perfect, 60 or 75 for just passing; or some other similar symbolism.

The ambiguities in the system arise in part out of the fact that individual teachers have the most divergent notions as to the meaning of each of the symbols.

Let us assume the case of a new teacher who has just come to a given school trying to find out what the other teachers mean by their marks. This teacher will be told that 100 per cent means perfection. But what is perfection in a subject? Is the student perfect when he tells what is in the textbook, or is there a demand for original thinking? Still more doubtful is the meaning of 90 per cent. Does this signify nine tenths of what a student might know, or is it a kind of vague statement meaning that the student is in the upper part of the class?

The new teacher will be very likely at this point, if he is intelligent about marking systems, to ask how many students in a class usually get 100 or 90. This question is based on a conception of the meaning of marks entirely different from that which was referred to in the last paragraph. Marks may refer, and often do refer, not to the degree of perfection in knowledge but to the relative position of the student in his class. Some teachers mark the best pupil 100 and then try to grade the rest from this standard.

Experiments with Grading Systems

Examples could be multiplied indefinitely, showing that there is great vagueness in regard to the meaning of marks. We are, however, more interested in the efforts which are being made to overcome these unsatisfactory conditions.

First, teachers are being informed by comparative diagrams what the relation of their own marking system is to the general average of their colleagues. A few years ago the president of Harvard sent to each member of the faculty a chart showing the curve of distribution, reproduced in Fig. 16, and, superimposed on this, the curve of the individual instructor's marks. The standard curve was derived by averaging the marks from eight large courses.

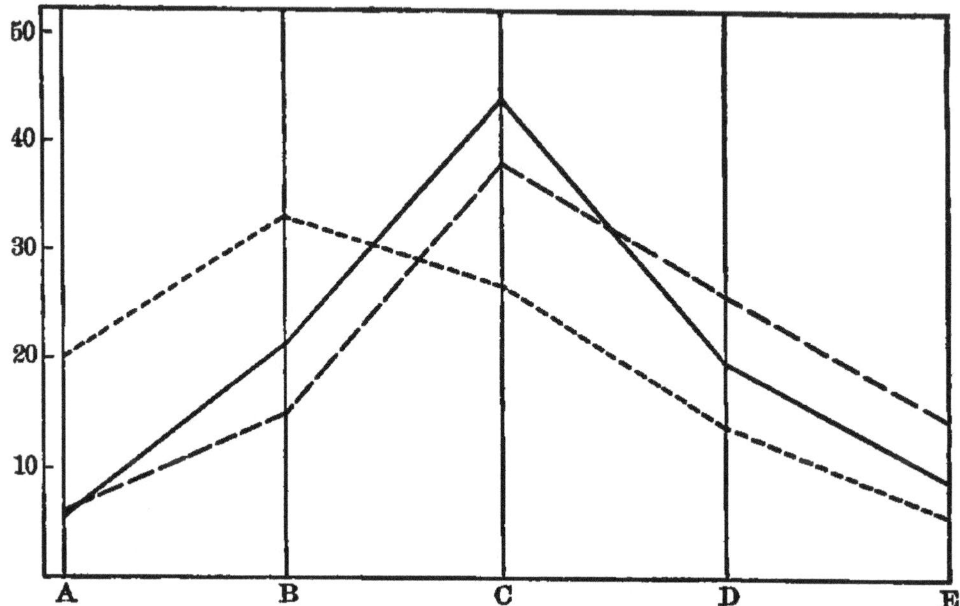

Fig. 16. Distribution of grades in various Harvard classes

The full-drawn line shows the average percentage of grades in eight large elementary courses. The dotted line and the broken line represent two departures from the average practice by instructors in two different departments

Second, the University of Missouri[83] has frankly given up trying to determine whether students are 100 per cent perfect in a subject or only 80 per cent. All students in all classes are arranged in the order of their excellence in their classes. The marks, in other words, are relative. When all the marks of the institution are compiled, there are a few students who are relatively very high, many who are mediocre, and a few who are low. The low ones are dropped, the high ones get honors, and the mediocres get the reward due the average student. On the basis of this kind of a classification the University gives to a student who stands in the uppermost 5 per cent of his class 1.2 credits toward graduation. The student in the next lower 20 per cent gets 1.1 credits. The 50 per cent who are mediocre get the normal credit of 1.0, while the lower ranks are penalized from 0.1 to all credit.

A third effort to improve the situation is being tried in the high school of Kansas City, Kansas.[84] In each classroom is posted a conspicuous chart telling students what they must do to get high grades. One may pass with a *C* if one does

[83] Max F. Meyer, "The Administration of College Grades." *School and Society,* Vol. II, No. 43 (October, 1915), pp. 577-589.

[84] See article by W. A. Bailey, *School Review,* Vol. XXV (May, 1917), pp. 305-321.

the required work taken up in a sixty-minute combination recitation and study period. If one is to receive *B*, it is required among other virtues that one be sufficiently well prepared to recite without prompting from the teacher. Furthermore, one must do outside work and report on it. The *C* pupil does his work in the class, but that is not enough for a *B*. The *A* pupil must fulfill even higher requirements. Each department is allowed to post, in addition to the general statements made for the whole school, special regulations which obtain for the work of that particular department.

This system is a kind of public definition of the marks, and has the great advantage of clearing up in the minds of the students what often seems to them to be an unjust and mysterious scheme.

The Study of Marks as an Introduction to a Study of the School System

The study of grading systems has attracted much attention of late among the students of the science of education. It is an excellent subject with which to illustrate scientific methods, because the records being in quantitative form lend themselves to easy and exact statistical comparison.

There is no better body of material for a principal to employ in arousing his teachers to a recognition of the fact that they are factors in a system. Marks are a kind of technical language used in the school system. Their successful use calls for some comprehension of the meaning and problems of the system as a whole.

EXERCISES AND READINGS

Let members of the class make up a school program. Let there be in a certain high school eight teachers, one well qualified in each of the following subjects: English, mathematics, Latin, physics, biology, modern languages, domestic science, and manual arts. There are seven classrooms and a study room. There are 400 students, distributed as follows: 140 freshmen, 110 sophomores, 90 juniors, and 60 seniors. The school is in session from 8.45 A.M. to 12 noon and from 1.30 to 3.30 P.M. Make up a program of classes. Record all the questions that are not answered in the above statement of conditions. Supply answers yourself, recording explicitly the answer which you give in each case. Let the members of the class then compare programs.

What is the difference between such a problem as above defined and the problem of making out a program for an elementary school?

A very good exercise under this chapter is to give a written exercise to the class and then ask the writers to mark each his own paper after the question and its possible answers have been discussed by the class. In like manner let each member of the class mark a certain English composition or a recitation made by some member of the class. Let the members of the class rate the various members of the class in regard to their work. After each of these markings make a general table showing the distribution of grades and note the differences between the different markers.

There is very little written on detailed administrative problems. A very good reading exercise at this point can be made up by referring to Monroe's "A Cyclopedia of Education" (Macmillan) and requiring the student to find ten strictly administrative topics and ten which have to do with methods. For most of the articles in the "Cyclopedia" reading references are given.

CHAPTER XIX

PLAY

Motives for cultivation of physical powers. Earlier attitude toward play. Play as natural behavior. Periods in the development of play. Play as natural education. Social necessity of recreation. Play as physical education. The school and play. Surveys of children's play in cities. Systematizing instruction in play. Survey of recreational facilities. Play as part of the regular school program. Slow spread of modern attitude toward play. Exercises and readings.

Motives for Cultivation of Physical Powers

Recent educational practice has laid great emphasis on the cultivation of children's physical natures as well as their mental powers. This new emphasis on physical training is due in part to a recognition of the wisdom of extending education so as to include all sides of the individual. It is due in part also to the conviction that the only way to deal successfully with the ordinary work of the classroom is to provide the kind of change and relief which comes from physical exercise. Regular opportunities for play are accordingly provided in the schools of to-day, and an elaborate system of physical supervision is being developed in all the leading school systems. Some review of these movements will be appropriate by way of supplement to the general survey in earlier chapters of the activities of the school system.

Earlier Attitude toward Play

The school of a generation ago retained a good deal of the Puritan attitude toward play. One has only to recall the pandemonium which used to break loose at recess and at the time of dismissal to realize that there was a sharp distinction between school and play. In school one sat up straight and still; when one was free from school one let out all the pent-up inner impulses. The kind of play that was exhibited under these conditions was riotous, irregular, and aimless. Furthermore, the kind of play which was cultivated under these conditions did not carry over into later life. There was no system, no progression, in that play, and no cultivation of the inventiveness so necessary if the recreations of later life are to be intelligent.

Play as Natural Behavior

The change in attitude from that of the old-fashioned school to that of the modern school is traceable in part to practical experience and in part to a general and fundamental change in the philosophy of life. To-day there is the profoundest respect for all that is natural. The theological attitude of medievalism and of the Puritans that the body is the baser part of self has disappeared with the development of the biological sciences. The social sciences, too, have contributed the lesson that all human behavior is in accordance with certain natural laws. The philosophy of naturalism thus accepted has profoundly modified the views of parents and teachers with regard to the play impulse in children.

Periods in the Development of Play

Not only is play natural, but numerous scientific studies reveal the fact that in the animal world and in man's life play contributes in no unimportant degree to the individual's development. These scientific studies have shown that play follows definite lines of development. There is first the play of early infancy, which consists in the rhythmical movement of the limbs and in the grasping after objects which satisfy the senses. This is the period of the rattle. There is at this stage no regard for others, no social interest. Then comes a second stage, where play is made up of imitative acts. This is the period of the girl's doll and of the boy's kit of tools. The child's attention is now centered on others and their doings, and this outward attention furnishes the individual with his models of action. Then come the plays of contest and competition, when the child, now of school age, matches himself against his companions in speed or strength. This is the period of running games. Imitation has ripened into the kind of rivalry which helps the individual to realize his personal powers. Following competition comes the period of team play, in which social union with some of one's companions is combined with contest against others. The adolescent child is now becoming aware of the uses of social sympathy and co-operation. At each of these stages some of the earlier forms of play survive, and all ripen into the form of play characteristic of adult life, where the competitions are against intellectual obstacles more than against physical. Adult play demands skill and intellectual mastery of complex problems.

When one has learned that there is a natural and orderly evolution of the play impulse, one realizes that it is rational to follow this natural order in promoting individual development. Play takes on a dignity that it never had in the days when it was looked on as an uncurbed attribute of infancy to be tolerated only because there seemed no possible way of eradicating it.

Play as Natural Education

Indeed, the scientific discussions have gone much further than merely to trace the course of the development of play. They show why play is to be recognized as a necessary phase of life. At first the immature instincts of the child tend to express themselves in activities that are irregular and ill-coordinated, but aimed unmistakably in the direction of the later serious activities of adult life. The kitten chases the ball in preparation for the later activities of the hunt. The explanation of this form of early play is that in the young animal's nervous system there are inherited paths which are ripening into action. The impulses of life tend to flow down these inherited paths; it is nature's method of helping the nervous system to mature to the point of full action.

When nature's processes have matured the nervous system, the lines of behavior of which the individual is capable are diverse. Each serious activity of life engages some of the individual's energy and brings to the point of fatigue a certain group of his possible activities. When one part of the nervous system has been fatigued, there will always be other parts which have not been used. For example, a man who reads for four hours does not use his arms and legs. At the end of the four hours his reading powers will be fatigued, but his arms and legs will be over-ready for action. There must be some change in activity and some relaxation from serious work. Play is nature's answer to this demand.

Social Necessity of Recreation

In addition to the scientific studies of the nature and function of play appears the sociological fact that the growth of leisure has created a new demand for well-regulated play. Furthermore, the conditions of urban life are unfavorable for some of the simple plays which in an earlier stage of civilization furnished an outlet for the natural impulses. If the environment is artificial, there must be a deliberate and intelligent effort to supply what nature demands but civilization has made inaccessible.

The danger in a congested city where natural play is not possible is a moral danger. There are vicious agencies which are not slow to take advantage of the strong natural demand for recreation. The result is that for the sake of gain appeals are made to the baser impulses of human nature. The success of these unsavory forms of amusement attests the presence of a strong natural demand. The way to meet the danger is to provide forms of recreation which are wholesome and elevating.

Play as Physical Education

Finally, all the arguments in favor of play are reënforced by the general demand that the physical condition of children in school be made a matter of especial concern. Play is the form of exercise which serves better than any other to keep the physical system in good tone. Hence the conclusion that play is as indispensable as it is natural.

The School and Play

In the light of these scientific and sociological studies it is evident that the school has a task before it. Briefly stated, this task is as follows: Nature intended that the child should play; play is a phase of the child's natural education. The conditions of life in cities have deprived children of the opportunity for the free development of play. The educational system must take the children in hand and train them back into nature's ways.

Surveys of Children's Play in Cities

Evidence that the situation needs attention is furnished by studies which have recently been made. The following quotation supplies one such body of evidence:

> In the hour and a half following the close of school November 10 and 18 careful observations were made in all parts of the town at the same time, by four adults selected for the purpose. They were instructed to look carefully through the streets, vacant lots, yards, parks, and playgrounds and make a notation of every child or young person up to the age of 21, observed. The information sought was what each one was actually doing, at play or otherwise, and where he was doing it. They were also asked to estimate the ages of the children observed. On November 6 a preliminary sounding was made by the investigator. Each observer was assigned definite territory so as to avoid duplication and all worked at exactly the same time. The results of these "soundings" have been carefully tabulated and summarized.
>
> Altogether 696 children, 447 boys and 249 girls, were observed. Of the total number, 262 or almost 40 per cent of the children and young people were doing nothing. Especially significant is the fact that 168 of the 262 idling boys and girls were idling in groups. Here is where mischief usually starts. A majority of those walking (203) were in reality idling. Fifty-six or eight per cent of the children were playing football and baseball and 22 or a fraction over three per cent were occupied with other games. A play life the two chief features of which are idling and walking indicates that the community is not discharging its plain duty with respect to the boys and girls.[85]

A like result is reported in the Cleveland survey.

> A play census, taken June 23, 1913, under the direction of the Chief Medical Inspector and Assistant Superintendent in charge of Physical Education in Cleveland, seemed to show this same lack of relationship between the school and the out-of-school activities of children. The results of this study are shown in the following table. [Page 272]
>
> **CONCLUSIONS DRAWN FROM THIS CENSUS**
>
> 1. That just at the age (under 15) when play and activity are the fundamental requirements for proper growth and development 41 per cent of the children seen were doing nothing. The boy without play is father to the man without a job.
>
> 2. Fifty-one per cent of all the children seen were in the streets, in the midst of all the traffic, dirt, and heat, and in an environment

[85] Howard R. Knight, Play and Recreation in a Town of 6000 (A Recreation Survey of Ipswich, Massachusetts), pp. 7-8. Russell Sage Foundation, New York City.

conducive to just the wrong kind of play.

RECORD OF 14,683 CLEVELAND CHILDREN

		Boys	Girls	Total
Where they were seen	On streets	5,241	2,558	7,799
	In yards	1,583	1,998	3,581
	In vacant lots	686	197	883
	In playgrounds	997	872	1,869
	In alleys	413	138	551
What they were doing	Doing nothing	3,737	2,234	5,971
	Playing	4,601	2,757	7,358
	Working	719	635	1,354
What games they were playing	Baseball	1,448	190	1,638
	Kites	482	49	531
	Sand piles	241	230	471
	Tag	100	53	153
	Jackstones	68	257	325
	Dolls	89	193	282
	Sewing	14	130	144
	Housekeeping	53	191	244
	Horse and wagon	89	24	113
	Bicycle riding	79	13	92
	Minding baby	19	41	60
	Reading	17	35	52
	Roller-skating	18	29	47
	Gardening	13	14	27
	Caddy	6	0	6
	Marbles	2	0	2
	Playing in other ways, mostly just fooling	1,863	1,308	3,171

3. That only six per cent of the children seen were on vacant lots despite the fact that in most of the districts vacant lots were available as play spaces. A place to play does not solve the problem: there must be a play leader.

4. That even though 36 playgrounds were open and 16 of them

with apparatus up, only 1869, or 11 percent, of the children seen within four blocks of a playground were playing on playgrounds. Last Friday 6488 children played on playgrounds.

5. That of the 7358 children reported to have been playing, 3171 were reported to have been playing by doing some of the following things: fighting, teasing, pitching pennies, shooting craps, stealing apples, "roughing a peddler," chasing chickens, tying can to dog, etc., but most of them were reported to have been "just fooling"—not playing anything in particular.

6. We need more and better playgrounds and a better trained leadership.[86]

Systematizing Instruction in Play

What is to be done in dealing with this situation? Three answers have been given. First, plays must be arranged in a sequence which will follow the natural order of children's development, and when this play course is properly organized, children must be given training in play. The training should be of the same kind as that given in any line, namely, such as to stimulate self-activity and full utilization of the teacher's suggestions. Specialists in the field have found it advantageous to revive folk games and to call attention to the interest which children exhibit in festivals and dramatic representations. In other words, the discovery of plays suitable for children is nothing but the extension into the field of recreation of the type of educational resourcefulness which has enlarged the curriculum in every division of the school. The enriched course of training in play should be used for the improvement of adults as well as children, thus making education for play a part of the movement of educational extension.

Survey of Recreational Facilities

Second, the available resources of the community for play must be canvassed and must be intelligently utilized. In the quotation from the Cleveland survey given above it was pointed out that there are vacant lots which are not used. A study of the play facilities of the community will also show the necessity of curbing those forms of recreation which are undesirable. A survey of this kind should deal not only with the community's equipment for play among children but also with the play of adults. Such a survey has been made for the city of Madison, Wisconsin, and there is now going on in the city of Cleveland an extensive examination of all forms of recreation and amusement together with an investigation of their effects on the people.

A few extracts from the Madison survey will show the kind of findings which are turned up by such an inquiry:

A study of the various sections of this survey shows that play

[86] George E. Johnson, Education through Recreation, pp. 48-50. Cleveland Education Survey. Published by the Survey Committee of the Cleveland Foundation, Cleveland, Ohio, 1916.

or recreation occupies a great place in the life of the city. The time, effort and money put into it is enormous. Practically every social organization, as well as the individual and home, is involved in it. A very large percentage of the business section of the city and many outlying business places are directly or indirectly, wholly or partially, devoted to it, as is a large area of the whole city territory. Its influence is far reaching. . . .

The study of children's activities in connection with the map survey shows that there is an enormous amount of play forced into the streets, even in well-to-do sections of the city, and in other cases into the worst of environmental conditions. There is no leadership or supervision of this play and there are no public playgrounds except Burr Jones Field and two park playgrounds and inadequate, unsupervised school playgrounds, where there is no attractive organization or play to draw the children from the streets to more wholesome activities and influences on the playgrounds. This is physically dangerous and a menace to morals.

The study of commercial recreation shows that the large number of children are involved in passive amusements indoors during the few hours free for outdoor, health-giving activities or when they should be in bed. This is bad from the standpoint of health, the educational efforts of the school, and general social habits or ideals.

The study of environmental influences and a neglect of play show that some of this street and unsupervised play results disastrously, even in delinquency, and supports the claim of many observers that most of the bad habits of children develop in play under bad influences.

If the play of children is to be wholesome and generally developmental rather than inactive or detrimental, they must have wholesome places to play in, equipment, companionship, and at least a part of the time organized play and leadership. In so far as the home cannot supply these demands most of the time—and the larger number of homes cannot—public interest in the welfare of the rising generation demands that the play be centered in a community playground under proper supervision. The supreme need of children of Madison is playgrounds under trained directors.

The recreational needs of the young men and women of the city requiring public attention are of three classes, all of which require places, organization and leadership. (1) They need athletic and aquatic activities, athletic organization and leadership. These activities are wholesome and increase efficiency rather than decrease it. (2) The young men and women need facilities and organization for more wholesome social activities, such as dances. They need to be under the auspices of the best influences rather than the questionable, and it is just as easy to have the best as the questionable. (3) Young men and women need opportunities for, and direction in, the more constructive use of their leisure time. They need places for their club meetings that have a distinct educational value as well as organization and general leadership. Individual use of museums and libraries also needs organization. The facilities for these activities are meager and an effective organization and leadership are totally lacking.

The needs of adults in the way of activities and facilities are so complicated that it is almost impossible to summarize them. From the standpoint of public effort, the main points are provisions for the essentials in the way of facilities, organization, promotion and direction that cannot be supplied by individuals or small-group initiative or enterprise. This requires a public body that can study and deal with these needs. There is still a great body of adult individuals, largely of the untrained, laboring classes, without recreational resources and unprovided for by any recreational agency except, perhaps, the saloon. These men are recreational outcasts; they seriously need a place where they can find clean opportunities for their toilet and bath and wisely organized recreation. The provision of organization is the way to a simple, constructive use of leisure time by at least some of the younger of these men; here is a demand for a new type of men's club, or a new type of organization of men who have no recreational resources. It is a need practically untouched by social agencies, yet one that must be faced frankly if these men are to gain or maintain any semblance of self-respect and not be a menace to democratic institutions.[87]

Play as Part of the Regular School Program

Third, the work of the schools should be so adjusted that play will take its place with other subjects as a regular and essential part of the curriculum. This implies not only that play will be given time in the program but also that the same kind of expert guidance will be provided for play as is provided for the other activities of the day. The great value of a varied program is evident to all who have watched the process which has been going on very rapidly in recent years of opening up the school hours so as to include many different types of activity. Play needs not only to be organized as play and to be equipped with proper facilities, but it needs also to be incorporated into the regular systematic program of the school. This statement may be reënforced by extracts from the conclusions reached by the Cleveland survey.

Some reorganization of the educational corps should take

[87] Madison Recreational Survey, pp. 97-99. Prepared by a Special Committee of the Madison Board of Commerce, 1915.

place with a view to efficient administration of play and recreation from a broad educational and social standpoint. This would lead to a far greater influence of the school upon the out-of-school life of the community. Through lack of greater influence of the school during out-of-school hours, there is a great social leakage for which the city must pay.

The school is the natural and logical agency for the safeguarding of the great fundamental interests of children and youth. Each year discloses more and more clearly that the school is the one institution we have yet conceived that is best fitted adequately to conserve these interests and utilize them for educational and social progress. Opportunities that came as a matter of course to children a generation ago do not come to many children now unless they are specifically planned for by some agency other than the home. Met wisely by the community, this seeming handicap may, in the end, result in a great and new-found social strength.

Play is more than recreation. If its educational significance is real in the kindergarten period, it is real in every subsequent stage of growth and development. Rightly conceived, play is a most efficient method of education for life, for work, for social service. The fact that we do not yet know how to make full use of play in education need not and should not prevent the utilization of play, to the full extent to which we are prepared, for the tremendous social service it can render.[88]

Slow Spread of Modern Attitude toward Play

The suggestions just given, if acted on, would completely reverse the attitude of the Puritans, with whom our school program originated. To them play was a distraction, an evil to be avoided during the few serious hours which are to be devoted to self-improvement. This Puritan attitude is contrary to experience, unsupported by science, and disadvantageous for the school and society. To reverse it has required long centuries and will require a more general recognition than now exists in the minds of most people of the possibility and importance of incorporating play as an integral and systematic part of the educational scheme.

EXERCISES AND READINGS

Let the class undertake a survey of the recreation facilities of the town or a survey of the play activities in which its members actually engage in the course of twenty-four hours.

A whole series of questions arise with regard to athletics. Is professional baseball a form of recreation, or is it work? Is atten-

[88] George E. Johnson, Education through Recreation, pp. 91-92. Cleveland Education Survey. Published by the Survey Committee of the Cleveland Foundation, Cleveland, Ohio, 1916.

dance on the theater a form of play? The early students of the theory of play spoke of literature as play. What can be said in support of this view? How late in life do animals play? How does play relate itself to business?

Play when considered in connection with school work is undoubtedly in some cases a distraction. Is it for this reason to be criticized? Under what conditions are play and study at odds with each other? Are there methods of adjusting the relation without giving up play?

On the administrative side such questions as these arise: Should all the teachers take part in the teaching and supervision of games, or should a special teacher be employed to have full charge of this part of the school program? Should there be any effort on the part of the school to supervise play after school hours?

Groos, K. Play of Man. D. Appleton and Company.

Groos, K. Play of Animals. D. Appleton and Company.

Third Yearbook of the National Playground Association. Playground Association of America, New York City. This contains an elaborate syllabus on play and also a full bibliography.

CHAPTER XX

HEALTH SUPERVISION

The relation of health to school work. Treatment of pathological cases. School luncheons. Control of home feeding. Public attention to nutrition of children. Control of contagion. The school health department. Difficulties of introducing health instruction. Health as a subject of instruction and as a mode of life. Exercises and readings.

The Relation of Health to School Work

Ordinary school work is so dependent on health that one wonders how teachers of an earlier generation could have failed to see the absolute necessity of systematic supervision of health. When we think, for example, of the consequences of absence from class exercises because of illness; when we think of a child's sense organs unable to carry to his mind the full message brought by the sounds and sights of the schoolroom; when we think of the nervous system dull and unresponsive because of malnutrition or hunger,—we begin to realize that the school is concerned in a very vital way with the problem of supervising health.

Treatment of Pathological Cases

In order to exhibit something of the scope of the present movement toward complete supervision of health, we may begin with the extreme cases. In progressive school systems the children who are tubercular or anæmic or otherwise seriously affected are taken out of the regular classes and put where the whole educational program can be subordinated to the one consideration of bringing them back to physical vigor. Often these classes are conducted in open-air rooms, and often the equipment of the rooms includes cots on which the pupils may rest as a part of the regular school exercise.

School Luncheons

A second line of treatment deals with nutrition. The importance of one aspect of this matter is brought out in the following paragraphs:

> Long ago Horace Greeley, in an address before a convention of teachers, called attention to one of the most perplexing social and economic problems of the age—a problem which still confronts school authorities of to-day.

> "In vain," he said, "shall we provide capable teachers, and comfortable school rooms, apparatus, libraries, etc., for those children who sit distorted by the gnawings of hunger, . . . or suffering from the effects of innutritious or unwholesome food."
>
> Medical inspection is forcing upon public attention *this* appalling fact—that a large percentage of children in school are in no physical condition, because of malnutrition, to profit by the present generous outlay of public money for school purposes. Practical educators, everywhere, are agreed that even the most patient, thoughtful effort to train under-nourished children is attended with but partial success. Out of their experience comes this plea—give the under-nourished child *body food* first, before offering him the wisdom of ages.[89]

In view of the condition in which many pupils come to school, it has been found important for school authorities or philanthropic organizations to provide luncheons. These have been most successful where a small price is charged for the food.

Control of Home Feeding

The influence of this experiment in feeding is important not merely because of the positive nourishment given to the pupils but also because of the example which it sets in proper standards of eating at home. Many families do not know how to feed children. The son of a truck driver who breakfasts with his father on coffee, sausage, and griddle-cakes will spend the morning trying to digest the food which is appropriate to his father's occupation but not to the sedentary life of the scholar.

Public Attention to Nutrition of Children

The importance of the whole problem of nutrition can be made clear by quoting from the work of a specialist. The paragraphs selected are the more impressive because they show that other nations as well as ourselves are confronted by these problems.

> Recently there has been an increasing tendency to make the report on nutrition of different children the basis of the entire medical-inspection report. This is because it has been demonstrated again and again that the occurrence of disease and physical defects is largely conditioned by nutritional disturbances.
>
> In Paris medical inspectors have charge of the school canteens and are required to report on the nutrition of each child. They are further expected to follow up any child with impaired nutrition and to administer tonics and special care.
>
> In England, since 1907, compulsory medical inspection has

[89] Sarah Webb Maury and Lena L. Tachau, A Penny Lunch, p. 8. 1915.

included inspection of nutrition. Beginning with 1909, the chief medical officer of the National Board of Education has reported yearly on the nutrition of the children throughout the country and on the work of the school feeding centers. In Scotland the medical inspectors are required to see that children suffering from malnutrition are fed properly either by the school or by the parents. As a result of this systematic work British school doctors are developing methods of technique and standards for judging malnutrition, which, on account of its complex and interwoven causes, is very difficult to estimate accurately. . . .

In American cities no record of the nutrition of the entire school population has been made. In 1907 in New York the Committee on Physical Welfare of School-Children reported 13 per cent of 990 children, selected as typical of the whole city, to be suffering from malnutrition. A similar investigation of 10,090 children in Chicago in 1908 revealed 12 per cent badly nourished in all grades, the proportion decreasing from 15 per cent in the kindergarten to 6 per cent in the fifth grade and above. Wherever an attempt has been made to include all classes of children in the examinations, the percentages found suffering from acute malnutrition run from 10 to 15. Where only schools in the poorer districts are included, the percentages are far higher, and vary between 20 and 40. However, it must be remembered that children from the poorer districts far outnumber those in other schools, so that in point of figures the actual proportion of children suffering from malnutrition is probably nearer the second estimate. Doctor Thomas F. Wood, of Columbia, gives 25 per cent as the estimate for the school population of the whole country.

"The longer a medical officer remains at school inspection," remarks Doctor Hope, of Liverpool, in a report for 1912, "the more severe becomes his standard of nutrition, and the less readily does he pass a child as being well nourished."[90]

One reason that health conditions in rural schools have been so long neglected is because of the common idea that country children are naturally vigorous and healthy. "This ought to be so but unfortunately is not," says Doctor Ernest Hoag, in a recent government report. He finds that, "in general, food is not as well prepared in the country as it is in the city; the available variety is smaller." Bad methods of ventilation and heating at home and at school, exposure to wet in the long walks to school, and overdressing in the house—all are inroads on the already badly nourished bodies. Investigations show that malnutrition and its

[90] Louise Stevens Bryant, "School Feeding." Educational Hygiene (edited by Louis W. Rapeer), chap. xvi, pp. 286-287, 289. Charles Scribner's Sons, 1915.

accompanying diseases are quite as frequent among country as among city children.[91]

Control of Contagion

Turning from nutrition to another aspect of the physical condition in schools, it is easy to show that the school must control contagion. The bringing together of hundreds of children increases so greatly the probability of spread of disease that the health authorities always welcome the arrival of the summer vacation as a relief from the most strenuous of their duties.

The School Health Department

The kinds of demands described have led to the development of health departments in many school systems. The various functions served by a school health department have been described by Dr. E. A. Peterson, a health officer in one of the largest cities of the country, in a report from which the following paragraphs are extracted:

> The problem of checking contagion is an acute problem in the schools. The facts show that in the early years of a child's school life he has more of the diseases of childhood than at any other period, especially more than he had when he was at home during the period immediately preceding school. Furthermore, as soon as school breaks up for the long vacation, contagion subsides. The bringing together of large groups of children in schools is one of the most prolific methods of spreading contagion. . . .
>
> But the school health service soon developed far beyond this first stage of merely policing the schools. Indeed, one sees the real justification of a separate school health department if he follows this health department into what may be called its second, third, and final stage of evolution. . . .
>
> Examinations by physicians within the last decade indicate that as many as five per cent of school children suffer from defective vision to such an extent that they cannot see lessons on the board unless they have the services of expert oculists, that one in every hundred cannot hear what the teacher is saying, that ten in every hundred are so "stopped up" by adenoids that attention to school work is nearly impossible until the science of medicine gives them relief.
>
> This drew the attention of the educational world to the necessity of ridding children of these defects in order that they may take advantage of the educational opportunity offered in the schools. . . .
>
> One characteristic development shown at this second stage of

[91] Ibid. p. 285.

school health organization is the employment of the school nurse. The school nurse marks the growth of the health era away from its first or merely policing stage. The school nurse is at once a medical officer and a teacher. She teaches the parents in the home and she teaches the children. She becomes a most important link between the home and the school. Her methods are those of persuasion, not those of the emergency police officer. . . .

Once the idea of making health a matter of intelligent interest took root, it was sure to grow. Correction of physical defects is itself a tardy method of dealing with the situation. Why not prevent the defects? This kind of thinking turned attention to the environment of the child and the necessity of making it as conducive to health as possible. . . .

Finally, it is by no means satisfactory that we should stop with the negative work of preventing disease and unfavorable conditions. We must be positive in our treatment of health. We want more health, more vigor, more efficiency. The fourth stage of medical inspection may properly be called the health development stage and has to do not only with the teaching of hygiene but with the development of higher ideals of wellness, with the raising of the standard of normality, with taking a person who is well and making him "wellest.". . .

The department must constantly assume new functions without dropping any of the old. If it is to be an efficient department, it must carry on all of the activities suggested in the summary which can be made up from the foregoing study.

First stage—Inspection

1. Inspection of children for contagious diseases

Second stage—Discovering and correcting defects

2. Physical examination of all children

3. Follow-up work in the home to get corrections

4. Maintenance of school clinics

Third stage—Prevention

5. Sanitary inspection:
   - Hygiene of building
   - Hygiene of curriculum
   - Hygiene of instruction
   - Special schools for special cases

6. Examination and inspection of principals, teachers, janitors and other employees

Fourth stage—Health development

7. Health teaching at school and at home
8. Establishing health habits by means of
    a. Toothbrush drills
    b. Handkerchief drills
    c. Bathing, etc.
    d. Health clubs[92]

Difficulties of introducing Health Instruction

Health work in the schools, as it has risen to the level of a subject of instruction, has encountered the kind of obstacles met by every new school subject. Teachers are ignorant on medical matters, and the doctors who come into the schools are ignorant of methods of teaching. The result is that the instruction given by teachers is sometimes formal and unscientific, while the work of the doctors does not prove as effective as it might because it does not reach the pupils. A partial corrective for this difficulty can be supplied through a better system of training teachers.

The following extracts from a paper by Dr. Allison show how one state is attempting to cope with this problem:

> In this tremendous but not superhuman task of teaching health, there seems to me no more effective method than to commit it to those who are and are to be the teachers. Progress in these matters cannot be made without an intelligent understanding on the part of the teacher. It is therefore important to teach the teacher. It is said that the normal school is historically the only institution in the country which has aimed to deal with the teaching problem.
>
> The Board of Regents of the normal schools of Wisconsin felt the need of making the normal schools of the state instruments of public health and in 1912 appointed a physician for this work. The work as organized consists of: (1) exclusion of the physically unfit among the normal-school students; (2) detection of remedial physical defects with suggestions in regard to same; (3) instruction in preventive medicine.
>
> 1. The term "physically unfit" is very elastic, but we should have some physical standard. The public has not been in a position to protect itself against those physically unfit in the profession, but it is beginning to make certain demands. For example, what community will now tolerate a teacher who is known to be tuberculous? It is well to enlighten these physically unfit, and stop the source of the physically undesirable, as we would the intellectually undesirable.

---

[92] Dr. E. A. Peterson, "Medical Inspection." Survey of the St. Louis Public Schools, Vol. VII, Part II, pp. 41-45. Published by the Board of Education, St. Louis, Missouri.

My experience with several thousand young men and women during the last three years has shown me that the health habits of teachers need improving. . . .

2. In the normal schools of Wisconsin a health-record card for each student is on file in the department of physical training. The side filled out by the physical-training teacher consists of a record of height, weight, and lung capacity, the neck, chest, and hip measurements, and a detailed record of posture. The physician's report includes a record of the past medical history, personal history, sex history, family history, and the present condition of nutrition, skin, eyes, ears, nose, throat, teeth, glands, lungs, heart, and elimination. Each student is advised in accordance with the conditions which are found. . . .

3. Instruction in preventive medicine consists of individual advice and classroom instruction as follows:

(*a*) Personal hygiene. This supplements what they have studied from the text and what they have received from the instructors of hygiene and physical training.

(*b*) A couple of lectures are given on the physical examination of school children. Teachers should be taught the essential facts about defective vision, defective hearing, adenoids, catarrh, diseased tonsils, nervousness, and mental defects. . . .

(*c*) Lectures are given on the cause, avenue of infection, mode of transmission, period of incubation, symptoms, complications, results, and prevention of the following communicable and preventable diseases: measles, scarlet fever, chicken-pox, smallpox, mumps, whooping cough, grippe, pneumonia, tuberculosis, diphtheria, meningitis, and infantile paralysis.[93]

Health as a Subject of Instruction and as a Mode of Life

A movement such as that described in the paragraphs just quoted shows perhaps better than any general description the strength of the demand that the schools teach and train for health. Health must be acquired as well as thought of in abstract terms. The school methods of dealing with it require a rational combination of the work of the physical-training department with that of the school physician and the teacher. The movement is therefore one of those broad movements in education which require the introduction of new materials of instruction but also call for a general and constructive administrative policy which shall support instruction by opening the way for an enlargement of school work of a practical type.

---

[93] Elizabeth Wilson Allison, "The Teacher's Field in Public Health Work." *Proceedings of the National Education Association,* pp. 676-678. Published by the Secretary of the Association, Ann Arbor, Michigan, 1915.

EXERCISES AND READINGS

What devices other than school luncheons can the school adopt in the effort to make people intelligent about the feeding of school children? What are the symptoms exhibited by children who are badly fed at home? What are the different types of difficulty which arise in the matter of nutrition?

Are the public-health controls in the city adequate to take care of contagion in the school? Should the school be dismissed in time of contagion? It is noted that pupils have a great many contagious diseases when they first come to school. This is sometimes explained by saying that the age from 6 to 8 years is more susceptible to disease. Is any other explanation to be offered? At what time in the year is contagion most common?

Would children's health be endangered by continuing school during the summer? Are physical examinations of pupils justified in public schools? What objections are raised to such examinations? Who should make them? It is sometimes argued that the expense of medical inspection and physical examinations is too great. Is there any answer?

Here, as in the case of play, the administrative question arises, should all teachers have a part in the health supervision, or should the task be assigned to specialists? Argue the case.

Gulick, L. H., and Ayres, L. P. Medical Inspection of Schools. Charities Publication Committee, New York City. This is the book which contributed very powerfully to the beginnings of the movement for school departments of health.

Wood, T. D. National Welfare and Rural Schools. *Proceedings of the National Education Association*, Vol. I-IV, 1916. Report of investigations of country and city children.

CHAPTER XXI

SCIENTIFIC SUPERVISION

Evolution of the demand for supervision. The principal. Other supervisory officers. Lack of public appreciation of central problems. Managerial training in relation to democracy. The purpose of the present discussion. Studies of the community. Selection and management of teachers. Standardization by measurement of results. An example of public recognition of the need of efficiency measurements. Scientific studies and central supervision. Scientific supervision. Exercises and readings.

Evolution of the Demand for Supervision

In the days when the school system was simple in its equipment and in its course of study no distinction was drawn between the problems of teaching and the problems of organizing the school. The teacher did everything that was done in the school. The teacher made the program, promoted the pupils, consulted with the town officials and parents, conducted the classes, and in not a few cases swept the floor and built the fire. There was, to use a phrase of the business world, no overhead management.

The course of study has grown complex. The work of the classroom is absorbing, and yet its success depends on equipment and organization that need to be studied and intelligently arranged. The work of one school must be correlated with the work of the schools in neighboring communities. The public must have authoritative information about the fiscal needs of the school and about the outcome of the public investments in education. The demand has arisen for a new type of school officer—the supervisor. This officer is not a teacher but a manager. His duty is one of organization and central adjustment.

The Principal

The new demand here referred to can be described by means of an example which exhibits one of the greatest weaknesses of our present school system. Schools of all grades which have grown large enough to employ three or more teachers commonly have an officer who is known as the principal.

In the small school the principal spends most of his or her time in teaching. In larger schools the principal does no classroom work. In both cases the principal is universally selected for a special position in the school because of his or her success in teaching. The work of the principal is thought of as that of a head teacher. The fact is, however, entirely at variance with this idea; the work of the principal is not that of teaching. Principals ought to be managers and central organizers. They ought to know the system as a whole and ought to devote time and thought to problems of a managerial type. The weakness of our present school system is that most principals are in no sense equipped for this central managing task. They do not know how to use profitably the release from classroom work which attaches to their office and title. The result is that they drift, often with the full cognizance of the board of education, into the habit of spending time on trifling clerical tasks which are wholly unworthy of the special position which they are supposed to occupy in the system. It is a deficiency of our educational system that while there are institutions for the training of teachers there are only a few general courses for administrative officers.

There certainly can be no objection to experience as a teacher in the classroom as preliminary training for the person who is to occupy a school principalship. But the moment the experienced teacher leaves the ranks and takes up the office of principal, a wholly new set of central problems should come within his view. He should recognize the fact that from this time on his task is one of a broader type, and the successful execution of that task will require a kind of study which is demanded at most in very minor degree of the teacher.

Other Supervisory Officers

What has been said of the principal is true also of assistant superintendents and of the superintendent of the school system. It is true also of departmental supervisors who have general oversight of certain subdivisions of the work. All these officers ought to become expert in a type of study and a type of management which are not expected of the individual teacher.

Lack of Public Appreciation of Central Problems

In general, it is evident from a study of American school systems that emphasis has not been laid on central organization. Cities have employed a superintendent when they had a population of five thousand inhabitants and have expected a single officer to continue to perform all the duties of that office when the population has increased to one hundred thousand. A principal is put in charge of a high school of two hundred students and continues to have full responsibility for the school when it increases to eight hundred students. Boards of education have refused to give supervisory officers clerical assistance, and have thus required a principal or superintendent receiving the highest salary of any person in the system to do work which a clerk could do more economically and quite as efficiently, thus interfering with the performance of important central duties for which no time is left.

Managerial Training in Relation to Democracy

The training of a large number of persons who will be competent to take up managerial functions is especially important in the school system of a democracy because the problems of each community are in some measure local problems to be solved at the point where they arise. In a school system which treats every child and every community exactly alike administration is simplified through uniformity. In a school system which is as complex as ours there must be an intelligent adaptation of organization to particular ends, and every device which will promote such adaptation is economical.

The Purpose of the Present Discussion

The general discussion of supervision will be clearer if we take up for brief description some of the problems which should be dealt with by central officers and some of the methods of solving these problems. It will not be the purpose of this discussion to attempt anything like a complete enumeration of such problems or methods, but merely to suggest their type.

Studies of the Community

First, there must be a study of the community. To some extent the individual teacher must take a share in this study. The character of each pupil and the facts about his home surroundings are important to the teacher in carrying on class work. But there must be some agency which can devote time and attention to a systematic collection of facts. The teacher has a right to expect that the school system as a system will make information readily available which it would be difficult for an individual to collect. The central officers should make such a study.

The making of a school census is a duty of the central officers who have in hand the enforcement of the compulsory-attendance laws. When these officers recognize their task as a large educational task, they will make the census not merely a formal basis for compelling attendance but a means of collecting a body of facts on which educational adaptations can be based.

It has been pointed out in earlier chapters that the community should be studied with a view to discovering the needs of pupils. Up to this time such studies have been made as special undertakings in a few isolated communities. For example, the industries of Richmond, Virginia, of Minneapolis, Minnesota, and of the state of Indiana have been studied by special commissions and reported at three annual meetings of the National Society for the Promotion of Industrial Education. What is needed is a constant study of these problems in every community. Again, teachers cannot meet the demand. This problem is a central problem, and the central management must be equipped to get information which the teachers need but cannot collect.

Selection and Management of Teachers

A second group of central problems have to do with the selection of teachers and their continued training while in service. It used to be very generally assumed, and in some quarters it seems to be assumed to-day, that in the teaching profession there is no need of training beyond the initial normal course or the initial college course that brought the candidate through the first requirements. A kind of persistence in professional efficiency on the part of teachers is assumed.

The day of such easy-going neglect of professional requirements is over. Score cards of teachers' qualifications are being worked out. The relative importance of such personal qualifications as a pleasant voice and manner as compared with such products of training as knowledge of the correct forms of English expression and knowledge of geography or Latin must be determined with direct reference to the particular duties which are required of the teacher. The development of methods of correcting deficiencies in the equipment of a teaching corps, the proper distribution of the time and energy of a group of teachers, and the proper method of keeping the records of the work of teachers are all central problems. As the teacher stands in a central relation to his or her class, so the supervisor stands in a central relation to a corps of teachers.

Of all the problems touching teachers, that of their training in service is perhaps the most important. There is a great deal of very blind and ineffective effort expended each year in futile attempts to meet this problem. A great deal of required reading is done by teachers, and a great many meetings are attended which could be turned to better account if there were well-organized systems of training in service and of parallel promotional requirements.

Standardization by Measurement of Results

A third group of problems are those which have been referred to in the chapter on standardization. The results of classroom work must be evaluated and comparisons must be made on a large scale to guide the future work of the pupils. In some measure this is a problem for teachers. But so far as the individual class teacher is concerned, there will have to be dependence on central agencies for the collection of material which can be used in comparisons.

At the present time a large share of the standardizing material is being collected by private agencies. Men and women who are interested in the promotion of educational science are making individual studies and are bringing together bodies of comparative material. This is entirely legitimate so long as the movement of standardization and quantitative treatment of results is in what may be described as an experimental stage. As soon as the utility of measurements has been proved, it becomes a public obligation to provide agencies for this work.

The growth of the movement toward the addition in all large school systems of one or more officers whose duty it shall be to measure results has been commented on in earlier connections. There is a national organization of school-efficiency officers with a membership including representatives of some twenty of the leading systems of the country. This shows in a concrete way that the demand for central officers of standardization is beginning to be met.

An Example of Public Recognition of the Need of Efficiency Measurements

A single example of a personal type may serve further to impress on the reader the character of this movement. Mr. S. A. Courtis, who is widely known as the author of a system of arithmetic tests, began his work in testing as a teacher in a private school for girls, the Liggett School of Detroit. He devised tests to find out how well his pupils were doing their work. He found at once that he needed comparative material because he saw that the success of his classes was in a measure a comparative matter. He published his first findings, and secured the coöperation of other interested teachers and school officers. Soon he became a center for arithmetic tests. He was compelled to give up more and more of his time and energy to a task which was broader in its scope than the task of teaching his classes. The school was intelligent enough to recognize this general service to all schools and gave him time and assistance in organizing his tests. The individual work of a scientific student thus began to develop. He was called to all parts of the country to discuss his methods and results, and centers of interest were established where his tests were used.

Ultimately Mr. Courtis was called to assist in the survey of New York City and in the surveys of other systems, notably Gary, Indiana. He was also asked to organize for the city of Detroit a department of investigation as a permanent division of the administration of the city schools.

Scientific Studies and Central Supervision

Example after example could be given of the organization of public supervision on the basis of private scientific investigation. These examples are important not only as exhibitions of the demand for more central supervision but also as demonstrations of the demand that all the larger problems of the school system be approached in the scientific spirit. The school system of this country, like all public institutions, has passed through the period of first organization. This was a period of urgent practical demands. Work had to be done by any means that came to hand. The situation was like all pioneer situations. In many cases teachers who were meagerly trained had to administer unorganized courses of study, and the public had to be satisfied with results which were, to say the least, uncertain. The pioneering period is not altogether passed yet, but there is wealth enough in most communities to support a more deliberate type of organization. There is a perfection of the instruments of education, an organization of the agencies of education, and a standardization of results which were impossible in earlier days.

The business of the central officers in a school system can be defined in terms of this discussion as the collection and distribution of scientific information and the administration of the system in keeping with the scientific information thus collected. Such a formula can be carried over to problems other than those enumerated thus far in this chapter. The problems of promotion and of the course of study, even the problems of class management and instruction, have large supervisory aspects with which the central school officers must deal.

Scientific Supervision

Such a statement gives a view of the principalship or superintendency of schools which is wholly different from that which is expressed by applying to these offices the title "head teacher." In England the chief officer in a school building is the head teacher or the head master. These names imply merely an extension of the teaching function and fail to recognize the necessity of a scientific study and administration of the schools.

The view advocated in this chapter is also at variance with the conception expressed in the titles of the chief school officers of German schools. There the head of a school is a rector or director. His personal authority is large. He continues in many cases to teach; his administrative influence as implied in his title arises from the fact that he represents the state. His task is that of dictating school policies, not that of organizing the school on the basis of a complete scientific study of the educational situation in the community in which he works.

It cannot be asserted that the American principals of schools are everywhere devoted and competent students of the science of education. There is, however, a freer opportunity in our schools than in those of any other nation for a complete realization of the scientific ideal. There is comparative freedom of organization, and there is comparative adequacy of equipment. There is at hand a body of broadly collected information. With this background there is every prospect of a more intelligent use of all the opportunities which are gradually being evolved for intelligent scientific supervision.

EXERCISES AND READINGS

The study of community needs has been carried on most vigorously in trying to answer the question, What industrial training do pupils in cities need? The National Society for the Promotion of Industrial Education has organized three extensive surveys, one in Richmond, Virginia, one in Minneapolis, Minnesota, and one in the state of Indiana. One of the best exercises which can be suggested is for the class to study the needs of a community after the model of one of these surveys.

A second exercise that may be suggested is that of examining the operations of a school building in detail. How does a building get its supplies? How many janitors are there? Who supervises the janitors? How much time does a principal spend in visiting rooms? What reports does a principal have to render? What reports do the teachers render to the principal?

The volumes of the Cleveland survey, including those which deal with industrial education, are models of exposition of community needs. (Copies may be secured from the Russell Sage Foundation, New York City.)

There is a body of sociological material with which students of this chapter ought to become acquainted. See the *Survey* (New York City), a journal devoted to the discussion of sociological problems.

CHAPTER XXII

THE SCIENCE OF EDUCATION

Scientific methods of studying schools. Definition through enumeration of methods. The history of educational theory and practice. Courses in psychology. Educational psychology. Statistical studies. The experimental method. Extension of use of psychological methods. Studies of retardation. School experiments and laboratory studies. Examples throughout earlier chapters. Studies of administrative problems. Method of comparison. Records necessary to scientific study. Subdivisions of the science of education. Rapid expansion of the science of education. Definition of the science of education. Exercises and readings.

Scientific Methods of studying Schools

Each of the preceding chapters has aimed to set forth certain practical school problems and to suggest the sources of information on the basis of which these problems are to be solved. Some of the information to which reference has been made is confessedly incomplete; some of it is in a form which renders very difficult exact and final inferences as to its meaning. Taken in the aggregate, however, the body of information at hand regarding schools is so great that we are justified in speaking of a science of education. Furthermore, the use of the term "science" would be justified even if we were in possession of fewer solutions of school problems than we now have, for the essence of science is its method of investigation, not its ability to lay down a body of final rules of action.

A complete transformation of the method of approaching school problems has come about in recent years. The time was when opinion, especially if it was backed by even a little practical experience, was urged as sufficient reason for all kinds of school practices. To-day it is only the rashly ignorant who talk about education or aim to influence actual school operations without informing themselves through a study of known and recorded facts. A host of practical school officers and special students of school problems have carried out laborious investigations and have created a technical literature which promises to reach every phase of school work.

Definition through Enumeration of Methods

It is not too early, therefore, to define the scope and methods of the science of education. Such a definition need in no wise limit the further development of the science, while it may serve to stimulate more exact formulation of its problems and methods. Our effort to frame such a definition naturally leads us to review the courses which have commonly been given to teachers-in-training.

The History of Educational Theory and Practice

The historical method of studying education was the first which was cultivated in institutions which undertook the training of teachers. The history of education divides readily into two branches: one deals with the history of educational theories, the other with the history of actual school practices. The history of theories is the easier of the two branches to cultivate because it consists chiefly in a review of the writings left behind by writers who discuss educational problems. Thus the earlier histories of education laid great emphasis on the writings of Plato and Quintilian, of Comenius and Locke, of Rousseau and Pestalozzi. Reviews of earlier writers were, however, of little real influence in molding modern practice, and the history of theories had only a very indirect influence on teachers.

More significant by far is the recent movement which studies practices in schools, especially the schools of one's own country. The development of arithmetic or grammar in American schools is illuminating as showing both the direction in which we are moving and the kinds of forces which operate in reformulating the course of study. Earlier chapters have aimed to suggest the value of such studies, especially Chapters II and III.

Courses in Psychology

Along with the study of the history of education there has commonly been prescribed in training schools for teachers a course in psychology. Herbart pointed out more than a hundred years ago the importance of the study of mental processes as a basis for the proper direction of educational practices. The science of psychology has also by its own developments encouraged the practical educator to expect help in the solution of school problems. There was a period when so-called child psychology flourished in this country and aimed to contribute to the development of school methods as well as to the solution of problems of the curriculum and school management.

Educational Psychology

A friendly alliance will always exist between the science of psychology and the science of education. Psychology has given to education certain methods and such special results as it has worked out with regard to memory and learning and the nature of behavior; education has taken the psychological material and developed a special branch of science under the name "educational psychology."

There are two fruitful psychological methods which have been borrowed in this way and put to work for education. These are the statistical method and the experimental method.

Statistical Studies

An impressive example of the statistical method is given in the studies of individual differences. For example, Thorndike has made a careful study of the degrees of likeness between twins, and between brothers and sisters who are not twins, for the purpose of defining more fully the meaning of the term "individual differences."

The Experimental Method

The experimental method has been employed in many ways. Thus, Freeman has recorded with the aid of suitable apparatus the rate at which one writes long and short letters. This study he has made with individuals of various ages and degrees of training and under different conditions. One result which he derived from these records is the fact that a given writer's rhythm of movement is the same in letters of different sizes and becomes more regular and more fixed with increase in skill.

Extension of Use of Psychological Methods

In taking over the methods of psychology and applying them to the solution of educational problems, a secondary advantage of the greatest importance has come to the science of education. These methods are capable of adaptation to a much broader range of problems than psychology would have attempted to solve. Both the statistical method and the experimental method have accordingly been carried over in the science of education to the widest possible range of applications.

Studies of Retardation

One of the first and most fruitful statistical studies made in education dealt with the retardation of pupils. Those who fell behind their grade were counted, and the problem which they presented was stated emphatically enough to bring about the organization of all kinds of special devices for the training of retarded individuals and groups.

School Experiments and Laboratory Studies

The experimental method was carried over and applied to whole classes. For example, two parallel classes were measured with reference to the effects of supervised study.

The experimental method has also been productively applied in detailed, analytical studies of particular subjects. Thus, to recall an example presented in an earlier chapter, reading has been investigated in the cases of slow and fast readers when they were reading orally and silently, when they were trained by the ordinary methods of the school, and when they were trained by special methods adapted to their individual cases. Like studies have been made of the movements performed in writing and of the stages passed through in various learning processes.

Examples throughout Earlier Chapters

Further examples will, however, be unnecessary for the reader who has had the patience to go through the earlier chapters of this volume. There are numerous illustrations in those chapters of statistical and experimental investigations of educational problems. These investigations show the extent to which the new science has borrowed from the old and the extent to which a new structure has been erected which has a right to claim an independent name and rank among the social sciences.

Studies of Administrative Problems

The recognition of the science of education as a separate discipline can be urged on the ground that the scientific methods which were first applied to the problems of mental development have opened up every aspect of school organization to scientific study. Thus, in the field of administration more than in any other field the value of scientific studies has been recognized. The promotion of pupils, the grading system, the construction of buildings, and the organization of financial systems are all spheres in which exact scientific methods have in recent years worked most important transformations in practice.

Method of Comparison

In many investigations the method of comparison has been brought to a degree of perfection which justifies reference to it as a special method of scientific research. All the previous discussions of standardization show how a single school system profits by the effort to evaluate its own practices in the light of the experiences and results of other school systems.

Records Necessary to Scientific Study

The scientific methods which have been referred to imply as their necessary basis a series of detailed and accurate records. Some of these records, as, for example, those which show school attendance and those which deal with expenditures, are kept in ordinary routine. Some have to be made especially for the purposes of scientific studies. Here belong all those records which are made through tests. Tests are merely devices for showing clearly and explicitly how far educational practices have succeeded in special cases.

Subdivisions of the Science of Education

The subdivisions into which the science of education naturally breaks up are dictated in part by the needs of different individuals within the school system and in part by the methods which are employed. Thus the supervisor needs a different type of training from that which is required by the classroom teacher. Again, the functions of the different supervisors are so different that some require full information on problems of school finance, while others are in more direct contact with the problems of promotion and of the curriculum. A second line of cleavage is that which is described most fully in this chapter and results from the use of different methods of investigation. Thus, laboratory studies of reading and writing naturally separate themselves from statistical studies of administrative problems.

Another line of division is that dictated by school organization. High-school problems are likely to be considered in special courses, elementary-school problems in others.

There is no need in a general introduction of the type here offered of attempting to consider these subdivisions. Our purposes are adequately served if we can show what the science as a whole is by referring to typical examples of scientific work undertaken in several of the subdivisions.

Rapid Expansion of the Science of Education

Furthermore, it is to be understood explicitly that the science of education is in process of rapid expansion. Any effort to describe its methods and content in full would of necessity fail. The rapid enlargement of the science and its methods in recent years is the most impressive fact which can be recorded in a chapter describing the scope and purpose of such a study. A simple definition within which there is wide room for expansion is therefore the only definition which is appropriate at the end of this introduction.

Definition of the Science of Education

The science of education aims to collect by all available methods full information with regard to the origin, development, and present form of school practices and also full information with regard to social needs. It aims to subject present practices to rigid tests and comparisons and to analyze all procedure in the schools by experimental methods and by observation. It aims to secure complete and definite records of all that the school attempts and accomplishes. The results of school work are to be evaluated by rigid methods of comparison and analysis. To direct studies of the school the science of education must add full studies of the social life of which the school is a part and of the individual nature which is to be trained and molded through the educational processes. In the light of such studies the science of education is to suggest such enlargements and modifications of school practices as seem likely to promote the evolution of the educational system.

This program is so comprehensive in its scope that it becomes evident at once that the science of education is a composite science requiring the coöperation of many investigators. In its formulations it may deal in a broad way with general problems, or it may break up into numerous subdivisions appealing to the specialist.

It would therefore be more accurate to describe it as a group of specialized studies rather than as a single discipline.

EXERCISES AND READINGS

This chapter furnishes an opportunity to study the contributions of other sciences to the study of educational problems. What does biology contribute? In this connection Spencer's first essay is perhaps one of the clearest examples of application of biology to education. Stanley Hall has carried to an extreme the use of biological hypotheses ("Adolescence," D. Appleton and Company). Fiske in his essay on the "Meaning of Infancy" (Houghton Mifflin Company) furnishes another example. The student should raise pointedly the question whether biological principles apply without modification to human education.

The discussions of biology pass directly into the consideration of psychology. James's "Talks to Teachers on Psychology" (Henry Holt and Company) is a very good beginning of readings in this line. One of the most recent and productive books is Freeman's "The Psychology of the Common Branches" (Houghton Mifflin Company). There are many general psychologies. The student will be led by a study of some of these books to the problem of distinguishing between general psychology and educational psychology.

Another type of related science is to be found in the mathematical sciences which contribute to educational studies. Thorndike's "An Introduction to the Theory of Mental and Social Measurements" (Science Press) was the first systematic effort to put statistical methods into form for educators. A much more satisfactory treatment of statistical methods is to be found in H. O. Rugg's "Statistical Methods applied to Education" (Houghton Mifflin Company). Numerous examples have been cited in earlier chapters of applications of statistics to education. To that list might be added Ayres's "Laggards in our Schools" (Russell Sage Foundation, New York City) and the statistical volumes of the reports of the Commissioner of Education, which both in the facts presented and in the summaries represent the most elaborate collection of educational statistics in any report on schools anywhere in the world.

By way of an independent exercise under this chapter let the student describe a particular scientific study which it would be appropriate to require each of the following school officers to carry out: a superintendent, a supervisor of drawing, a principal of a high school, a principal of an elementary school, a high-school teacher of Latin, a teacher in charge of a third grade.

CHAPTER XXIII

PROFESSIONAL TRAINING OF TEACHERS

Increasing demand for professional training. American normal schools. American demands on secondary-school teachers. German training of secondary-school teachers. New courses in colleges and universities for secondary-school teachers. The requirements of a standardizing association. The California requirements the most advanced in the United States. Continuation training of school officers. Specialized training for administration. Contributions to the science of education. Exercises and readings.

Increasing Demand for Professional Training

It has been the aim of the preceding chapters of this volume to make it clear that the teacher of the future must be able to cope in a large and intelligent way with problems which are not discussed in courses dealing with the subject-matter ordinarily taught in schools. The compensations offered to the trained teacher are fortunately more adequate than formerly, and increasingly justify the demand that the teacher bring to his or her task a more complete professional training.

American Normal Schools

The proper content of a professional training is a matter on which there is no general agreement in the United States. For a little more than seventy-five years there have existed in this country normal schools for the training of elementary-school teachers. These institutions have in some cases required graduation from high school as a prerequisite for admission, but more commonly not. Their courses of study have in some schools consisted chiefly of reviews of elementary-school subjects supplemented by a modicum of methodology or discussion of how to teach the subjects. In other cases the courses of the normal school have been general, of the type commonly offered in colleges or high schools. Sometimes the normal school has given its students large opportunity to teach children in so-called practice schools or model schools. Sometimes, on the other hand, the students in normal schools have had no direct contact with classroom management, but have gone out into the schools equipped only with the theory of teaching.

The situation with regard to these institutions is set forth in the following paragraphs from a bulletin of the United States Bureau of Education:

> Normal schools differ from each other very widely in orga-

nization, in admission requirements, in courses of study, and in modes of instruction. The explanation of this lack of uniformity is to be found in the fact that normal schools have never been a part of the system of higher education evolved in this country. Normal schools have grown up in isolation. While the colleges have been in the closest touch with each other through the organization of entrance examination boards and accrediting institutions, while high schools have been brought together by standard definitions of units, normal schools have stood apart. The typical normal school derives its financial support from legislative appropriations, receives its students without competition from a territory over which it exercises exclusive control, and has no difficulty in placing its graduates in positions which they regard as satisfactory. Furthermore, so urgent has been the demand in the country for teachers that school boards and superintendents have not been able to make rigid selections, with the result that standards of training have not been forced upon the normal schools from without.

In a situation where relative isolation has not compelled normal schools to define themselves to others there has been the largest opportunity for the play of personal influences. A strong president has often dominated the policies of a normal school to a degree that is almost unbelievable. The faculty sometimes has little or no voice in determining the courses or the modes of admission. There is no State authority in most of the States which is strong enough to determine what shall be done in normal schools. The result is that within a single State there are the widest variations. One president with the ambition to develop his institution into a degree-granting university goes on his way, while his neighbor uses the funds granted by the same legislature to develop a normal school which loudly announces its objection to granting degrees and limits its activities rigidly to the training of elementary teachers.

In recent years a number of causes have begun to break down the isolation of the normal school. First and foremost is the desire of normal graduates to enjoy the advantages of higher education in universities and colleges. The growth of summer schools at universities and the frequent transfer of normal-school graduates to college and graduate courses show with clearness the desire of teachers to enjoy the advantages of all kinds of higher education. Normal schools, drawn into the current of higher education, have been called upon to announce more definitely their requirements for admission and to describe the content of their courses. What is a course in methods of teaching arithmetic? Is it a review of the course given in an elementary school or is it a discussion of the pedagogical principles on which such courses are arranged? What is a course in practice teaching? Does such a course require of the student any study of material, and does it afford him any adequate critical discussion of his work? There has been a sharp and at times unfriendly clash between normal schools and colleges in the effort to secure answers to such questions. The normal school often takes the position that it administers only high-grade courses, while the colleges express a frank doubt as to the value of these courses for mature students.

Perhaps the disagreement between normal schools and colleges can best be illustrated by the widespread dispute regarding foreign languages. The normal school has been historically related to the vernacular school, and its officers have had little patience with classical or even literary courses. The traditions of the college are of a totally different type. So long as no students passed from normal schools to colleges the normal schools were at liberty to hold to the vernacular, but as soon as normal-school graduates sought admission to higher institutions the controversy was on.

A second reason why normal schools have been called upon to define themselves arises because colleges and universities have in recent years entered the field of teacher training through the organization of departments of education and colleges of education. In the State universities the demand for preparation of high-school teachers has been heard, and generous provisions have in many cases been made for the work of preparing such teachers. The normal schools have looked upon this organization of teacher-training courses as undesired competition. Conversely, the university authorities have been critical of the courses in the normal schools, and the issue has been sharply drawn. Incidentally it may be remarked that college departments of education have usually been subjected to the closest scrutiny and sometimes to violent criticism by other college departments because of their supposed inferiority. It may even be admitted that entrance requirements in the departments of education have sometimes been lower than those for other college departments in the hope of meeting the competition of normal schools, and courses of inferior standard in the college have been tolerated for like reason. All of these disputes and efforts at adjustment have aroused a general inquiry about teacher-training courses which a generation ago would have been without interest except to a small group of specialists. Now the problem is known to all who are interested in education, and the discussion must go on until some satisfactory conclusion is reached.[94]

[94] Charles Hubbard Judd and Samuel Chester Parker, Problems involved in Standardizing State Normal Schools, pp. 7-9. *Bulletin No. 12,* United States Bureau of Education, 1916.

American Demands on Secondary-School Teachers

If the situation with regard to the training of elementary-school teachers is chaotic, the situation with regard to secondary-school teachers is more so. Until very recently there was little or no effort in the state laws defining requirements for teachers' certificates to distinguish between elementary teachers and teachers in high schools. The candidate for a position in Latin found himself taking the same examination that would have been required if he had been about to teach a third grade. Of course in practice the school officers who employed the Latin teacher took steps to assure themselves that he had studied that subject, but practice in this respect has never been standardized.

German Training of Secondary-School Teachers

By way of setting up a contrast we may review the system which prevailed in Germany before 1914. The German system was the most highly developed system of training secondary-school teachers in the world.

> Candidates for positions in the secondary schools must first of all have completed the course of one of the secondary schools. In the second place, the candidate must have attended a German university for at least six semesters. Here an exception is made in the case of those candidates who expect to teach in the sciences. They may take half of the university courses in one of the technical institutions rather than in university lectures.
>
> After this preliminary training is completed, the candidate presents himself for an examination. Usually the period of training is much longer than the minimum above described. Indeed, in most cases candidates take the university doctor's degree before they come up for the examination. The examination consists of two parts. First, there is a general examination covering those subjects which are supposed to be essential as training for all departments; and, second, there is a special examination given in the particular subject in which the candidate is preparing to teach. Both examinations include written and oral divisions. . . .
>
> The examinations are formidable ordeals. They are conducted by special commissioners. On these commissions are university professors, officers of the education department, and representatives of the secondary schools. The candidate is first required to present two elaborate theses, one on some phase of the general subjects and one in the subject in which he has elected to take a complete examination. At the discretion of the commission the candidate's doctor's dissertation may be substituted for one of these theses. A period of 16 weeks is allowed for their preparation, and they are intended to show the ability of the candidate to carry on independent research in his selected field, and his ability to formulate material in a clear and systematic fashion. After the

presentation of these theses there follows a written examination, followed in turn by an oral examination.

After the examination the successful candidate now has before him two years of contact with the schoolroom before he can become a teacher with a regular position. The first of these trial years is known as the Seminar year and the second as the Trial year. During both of these periods the candidate is connected with one of the secondary schools and is under the general direction of the principal or director of this school. . . .

After a candidate has been assigned to a particular school, it becomes his duty, first of all, to participate in the activities of that school in any way that he can. He is usually assigned to some teacher, whose reports he helps to prepare and whose classes he has to visit with regularity. In addition, he is expected to visit all of the classes in the institution, so as to observe different methods of instruction and class management. It is required that the candidate meet with the director two hours a week for special training. At this point in particular the greatest diversity of practice appears. . . .

Sometimes the meeting is conducted as a demonstration lesson; sometimes it is a discussion; sometimes it is a series of reports by candidates; sometimes a lecture by the director or one of the teachers of the school. . . .

After the candidates have gone through a part of the first year's training and have become somewhat familiar with the methods of instruction in the classes which they visit and through the advice which they receive in the weekly meetings, they are allowed to give instruction. At first this instruction is limited to single class exercises under the immediate supervision of the regular teacher. The candidate is expected to prepare fully for such an exercise, so that he may carry on the work of the students in accordance with the general plan adopted by the regular teacher. The regular teacher remains in the class during the instruction given by the candidate, and after the class has been dismissed the teacher gives the candidate the benefit of such criticism as he has to make. Opportunity for these criticisms is presented by the school program, which is uniformly so arranged that 45 minutes of class work are followed by 15 minutes of recess. The criticisms are in some cases very helpful, especially where the teacher is interested in developing better methods of instruction upon the part of the candidate. On the other hand, the criticisms are often very severe and sometimes even caustic. In any case, the candidate learns through the comments given him by the teacher how far he has failed to conform to the expectation of the school. . . .

Several weeks before the close of the seminar year each candidate is called upon to prepare a thesis on some concrete pedagogical or didactic problem set for him by the director. This thesis constitutes part of his preparation for the teaching profession and may be the outcome of his readings or the outcome of his observation. Not uncommonly the candidate makes an elaborate study of some of the pedagogical literature related to his subject. It is to be remembered that many of these candidates have already completed the work for the degree of doctor of philosophy in the university and are for that reason trained in the methods of research and in the preparation of theses, while all have prepared elaborate theses in connection with the examinations which admitted them to the seminar year.

At the end of the seminar year the director, with the coöperation of the other teachers who have observed the work of the candidate, makes a report to the school authorities, and if the work of the candidate has been satisfactory he is now advanced to a higher grade and enters upon the trial year.

During the trial year he is required to teach six to eight hours a week without compensation. If he is especially fortunate, he may receive some compensation for substitute teaching which is needed by the school. In the main, however, he is called upon to carry a heavy burden of work without any compensation from the school. The director may also use his services for other purposes, such as the preparation of reports, the checking of lists, and other duties which need to be attended to for the purpose of administering the school. During this trial year the regular teacher is not required to attend the classes conducted by candidates. The candidate, therefore, gradually acquires independence in his conduct of the classes.

At the end of this trial year another report is made of the activities of the candidate and the judgment of the teachers in the school with respect to his success. If this report is favorable the candidate is now put on the eligible list and may be appointed to a permanent position. The length of time which it is necessary for him to wait for this permanent appointment is determined wholly by the needs of the schools. If there are no vacancies, the candidate may wait a relatively long period of time, in some cases as long as four or five years. On the other hand, for some years past it has been possible in most cities for candidates to receive appointment almost immediately on completion of the trial year.[95]

[95] Charles H. Judd, The Training of Teachers in England, Scotland, and Germany, pp. 74-82. *Bulletin No. 35,* United States Bureau of Education, 1914.

New Courses in Colleges and Universities for Secondary-School Teachers

The example of Germany is instructive as showing something of the amount of professional training which may be deemed necessary properly to qualify a teacher of secondary schools. It is not at all likely that the particular method adopted will be followed in the United States. Indeed, there is a rapidly developing movement in American colleges and universities to provide training for such teachers. The state universities especially have developed in recent years series of courses, both in subject-matter and in professional lines, designed to train secondary-school teachers. These, like the normal-school courses described above, are very little standardized, but are promising as a nucleus for the final organizations which will solve the problem.

The following paragraph indicates the existing conditions:

> The significant fact is that 21 of 24 universities report teachers' courses. This means that in some way the academic departments are professionally coöperating with schools or departments of education in furnishing to intending teachers the special methods and peculiar technique, as well as more fundamental educational principles and distinctive values of the actual subjects the students will teach when they take positions in the schools. The proper coördination of the university forces contributing to teaching efficiency is the curriculum problem for the immediate future in university administration. At present the solutions are about as numerous as the institutions concerned.[96]

The Requirements of a Standardizing Association

The standardization of the requirements will require legislation or the action of central standardizing associations. This movement is now under way. The North Central Association of Colleges and Secondary Schools sets as its standards for approval of high schools the following:

> All teachers teaching one or more academic subjects must satisfy the following standards:
>
> *A.* The minimum attainment of teachers of academic subjects shall be equivalent to graduation from a college belonging to the North Central Association of Colleges and Secondary Schools requiring the completion of a four-year course of study or 120 semester hours in advance of a standard four-year high school course. Such requirement shall not be construed as retroactive.
>
> *B.* The minimum professional training of teachers of academic subjects shall be at least eleven semester hours in education. This should include special study of the subject matter and ped-

[96] Charles Hughes Johnston, "Progress of Teacher Training." Report of the Commissioner of Education, 1913, Vol. I, chap. xxiv, p. 520.

agogy of the subject to be taught. Such requirements shall not be construed as retroactive. (For the succeeding year the Board will interpret courses in education as the same courses are interpreted by the colleges or universities offering them.)

C. If a teacher, new to a given high school, does not fully meet the requirement of the above standards but, in the opinion of the inspector, possesses the equivalent of the training prescribed, the inspector shall submit, to the Board of Inspectors, a statement concerning the training, experience, and teaching efficiency of the said teacher, together with his recommendation. The Board shall, on each case presented, make a decision.[97]

The California Requirements the Most Advanced in the United States

The qualifications required by the State Board of Education in California are the highest required in any state. They are as follows:

REQUIREMENTS

High school certificates may be issued by county and city and county boards of education under the provisions of section 1519, subdivision 5 (*a*); section 1775, subdivision 1 (*a*), and section 1792 of the Political Code of California, to candidates who meet all of the following requirements, to wit:

(1) *Requirement of Bachelor's degree.* Each candidate shall have received a Bachelor's degree from a standard college requiring not less than eight years of high school and college training.

(2) *Requirement of one year of graduate study.* Each candidate shall submit evidence that in addition to the academic and professional courses required for the Bachelor's degree, he has completed at least one year of graduate study, doing full regular work, though not necessarily a candidate for a degree, in an approved graduate school as hereinafter defined. Such graduate study shall include at least one full year course of advanced or graduate work in at least one of the subjects in which candidate expects to be recommended for certification.

(3) *Requirement of fifteen units of work in education.* Each candidate shall also submit evidence that he has completed in undergraduate or graduate standing, or the two combined, not less than fifteen units (semester hours) of work, in courses listed in the department of education in the institution in which the graduate work is completed, or courses in other departments of that or other institutions accepted as preparation for teaching by the

[97] Proceedings of the Twenty-first Annual Meeting of the North Central Association of Colleges and Secondary Schools, 1916, p. 94.

department of education. These fifteen units of work shall include the several courses in education hereinafter prescribed.

* * * * *

Required work in education. The required fifteen units of work in the department of education shall include the following courses:

(*a*) A course in school and classroom management, or equivalent work—a minimum of one unit.

(*b*) Work in actual practice of teaching, with conferences—a minimum of four units.

(*c*) A teacher's course in at least one subject in which the candidate expects to be recommended for certification, if such course be given in the institution and be accepted by or listed under the work in education—a maximum of three units for all such courses.

(*d*) A course in secondary education, presenting particularly the purpose and attainable goals of high school work—a minimum of two units.

(*e*) Such other courses relating to the theory, function and administration of public education, as are needed to complete the required fifteen units.

Practice teaching. The work in practice teaching shall be done under the general supervision of the department of education of the institution in which the year of graduate work is taken, and may be done in schools of elementary, intermediate or secondary grade, though preferably in secondary school work of the kind the candidate is preparing to teach, and under the direction of competent instructors in such work. The work in practice teaching may also be done in connection with the training school of any California state normal school.

Teachers' courses. Each teacher's course shall be a *bona fide* teacher's course and shall be made as concrete and practicable as possible, and shall have for its purpose the preparation of teachers to give intelligent instruction in the subject in the high schools of this State.[98]

Continuation Training of School Officers

The requirements which have been discussed up to this point have to do with admission to the teaching profession. Beyond that point there is nothing that can be described as sufficiently common to be regarded as typical. There are voluntary and compulsory gatherings of every kind and variety intended to keep teachers

[98] "Revised Rules governing High-School Certification," pp. 3-5. *Bulletin No. 5,* California State Board of Education, 1915.

intellectually alert and to inform them of progress in educational matters. There are institutes, so called, where teachers hear lectures. There are extension lectures, provided sometimes by boards of education, sometimes by teachers' associations. There are meetings of teachers called by the superintendent or by the supervisor of a special subject or of a special grade.

The miscellaneous activities which are indicated by such a list as the above all recognize the necessity of continued study on the part of teachers in service, and many boards of education are requiring study in addition to success in teaching as an essential prerequisite to promotion or to increases in salary.

The most significant movement which has ever been witnessed in the training of teachers in service is the summer-school movement. All the leading institutions of learning in the country are filled during the long summer vacation with teachers who are pursuing courses in education or in the various subjects which they teach.

Specialized Training for Administration

Two phases of continuation study on the part of teachers deserve special discussion. First, the form of promotion which carries a teacher into school administration, that is, into a principalship or superintendency, is being hedged about with very definite demands for advanced study on the part of candidates. This advanced study must take the form of readings or courses on administrative problems. Such problems have been exemplified in earlier chapters which have dealt with costs, promotions, and the like. It can be safely asserted that the time is not far distant when a special preparation will be required for entrance on administrative positions.

Contributions to the Science of Education

Second, the study of school problems by teachers in service has contributed powerfully to the creation of bodies of organized knowledge bearing directly on school matters. When education courses were designed chiefly for candidates for teaching positions, these courses survived even if they had no close relation to school work. To-day the situation is entirely different in character. Teachers in service come to the study of education with urgent problems to be solved. The abstract statements of the older courses will not satisfy such students. The impulses toward the development of scientific information about schools which arise out of a demand for efficiency and economy are powerfully reënforced by the demand within the teaching profession itself for definite and constructive studies of school problems.

EXERCISES AND READINGS

The training of teachers is so closely related to state legislation that this chapter suggests the possibility of introducing the student to the methods of looking up state laws. How does one go about finding school laws? Why is education a matter of state legislation rather than a matter of national legislation? What are some of the striking differences between the educational laws of different states?

Second, since the economic conditions which control teachers' salaries are of importance in determining how much training teachers shall be required to secure, the question of salaries is an important one. This matter may be looked up in the two bulletins referred to below.

Coffman, L. D. Social Composition of the Teaching Population. Teachers College Publications, 1911.

The Tangible Rewards of Teaching. *Bulletin No. 16,* United States Bureau of Education, 1914.

A Comparative Study of the Salaries of Teachers and School Officers. *Bulletin No. 31,* United States Bureau of Education, 1915.

APPENDIX

CLASSROOM OBSERVATION

In connection with the study of the foregoing chapters and collateral readings it is desirable that students visit classrooms and make systematic observations of the work there under way. In order that such observations may be productive it is necessary that the student have definite ends in view, otherwise observation will be scattered over many phases of that which is seen. The questions below are intended to furnish guidance.

It is recommended that each student in the course be required to spend at least three hundred minutes in observation and that he or she prepare a written report.

GENERAL DIRECTIONS

Before going to the classes for observation determine which of the topics outlined below you are going to make the subject of special study. It will be advantageous for you to learn the questions.

Go prepared to take notes. Confine your attention after the first general observations outlined below to the particular topic on which you are to report. Take down facts and definite individual observations. You are at liberty to talk with teachers if you can do so without imposing on them, but your report is not to be based on what they say but on what you see. Do not quote from books on the subject of your study.

Prepare a report of not less than two thousand words.

GENERAL QUESTIONS TO BE ANSWERED IN EACH REPORT

1. In what school or schools did you make your observations?

2. How many visits did you make, and how long was each? (Give dates and minutes.)

3. What was the grade of the class, and what was the subject of instruction?

4. Report on the physical conditions of each room. What was the condition of the temperature, of the lighting, of the ventilation? What kind of furniture was used? Did you see signs of fatigue on the part of teacher or pupils?

After noting these general external conditions, turn your attention to one of the problems outlined below and prepare your report with reference to that single topic.

I. GRADING

Attend a class several times until you come to know something of each individual member; then form a judgment as to the desirability of holding the group together. Suggest changes such as the putting forward or putting back of certain individuals.

1. Are the students alike in their physical development, or are some oversized?

2. Are the mental differences parallel with the physical?

3. Do you observe symptoms showing that some children frequently do not understand the class work and therefore are to be regarded as below the grade?

4. Do you see evidences that children are not fully occupied because the work is too easy for them?

5. Children differ in their willingness and ability to take part in class work. How far should this be considered in grouping children?

6. How far does the grouping of students in a class help or hinder the development of an individual? Give definite cases.

7. Should the class be changed in size to provide for the best teaching?

8. In certain schools the effort is now being made to organize more individual instruction. What do your observations lead you to conclude about the desirability of such a plan?

II. METHODS OF DISCIPLINE

For observations under this section visit a number of different classes and note the general restlessness or quiet of the groups. Note in detail how the "order" is maintained, and try to determine (1) what is the teacher's notion of order in each case, and (2) what devices he employs in securing what he wants.

1. Are there formal rules? For example, must the pupils sit in a certain way? Must they ask questions in a certain way?

2. Does the teacher talk about order?

3. Does he have other devices that are evident, such as pausing and looking at some member of the class?

4. Does he inflict penalties?

5. Does he have devices that are less obvious, such as varying the character of the work or calling on a member of the class who is disorderly?

6. What is the relation of order to the subject of instruction?

7. Does the teacher neglect disorder which you would correct?

8. Of all the cases which you observed, which do you regard as the best kind of order?

III. PREPARATION ON THE PART OF THE TEACHER

Visit several different teachers and contrast their methods. It may be advantageous after a first visit to go back to observe again teachers who are radically different.

1. Distinguish between a teacher's general preparation or broad knowledge of a subject and his special preparation for a particular class exercise. What evidence is there that the teacher prepared for this particular exercise?

2. Does the teacher seem to have in mind a fixed order in which the lesson is to proceed?

3. What is the relation of economy of the time and energy of the class to the teacher's preparation?

4. Has the teacher anything to contribute outside of the textbook material?

5. Does the teacher know how to fit the work to the class period so as to make a complete exercise?

6. Is there evidence that the teacher has made specific preparation for the next exercise?

IV. PREPARATION ON THE PART OF PUPILS

One of the best ways to get material for this section is to go first to the high-school study room or to the general library and take note of the way in which people study. The kind of question which should be raised in these observations of study periods is illustrated in V (*B*) below. After making these preliminary observations go to some recitations and see if there are evidences in the individual recitations of the way in which the work of preparing the lesson has been done. The purpose of this particular section is to discuss the methods of judging preparation from the recitation.

1. What proportion of the class has thought about the lesson as well as learned what is in the book?

2. When a student fails try to determine whether his failure is due to lack of study or to bad methods of study. For example, if a student has learned his lesson by heart, and forgets, he is very different from the student who has not tried either to understand or to learn by heart.

3. How far is the recitation an examination, and how far does it teach students to think? What is the effect of the teacher's method on the future study of the pupil?

4. How far do students show initiative in carrying forward the work?

5. How many questions do they ask?

6. Girls generally get better marks than boys for their class work. Why is this? Do boys contribute anything that girls do not?

7. Is there any difference in intellectual maturity exhibited by different members of the class?

V (*A*). ATTENTION DURING RECITATION

This section will be of special interest to those who wish to observe in the lower grades. Productive observations can be made, however, in every grade. The chief business of the school is to train in concentration. Observe individual pupils closely.

1. How long does a child keep his attention fixed on one thing?

2. What distractions does a schoolroom present?

3. What concession does the teacher make when pupils do not keep up concentration? For example, does he repeat questions?

4. What positive devices are adopted to keep up attention?

5. What are the physical symptoms of attention and its absence?

6. What individual differences are to be noted?

7. Do you note differences in attention at different times in the day or at different periods of the recitation?

V (*B*). ATTENTION DURING PERIODS OF STUDY

For this section go to the study room or to some class that is engaged in individual work, as, for example, the laboratory.

1. Note the way in which a student goes about his work. Is he ready to begin at once, or does he have to get matters together deliberately after he sits down?

2. Note whether he reads continuously from the book which he is studying.

3. Pay attention to the sort of thing that the student does when he looks away from the book. Does he turn his attention to other objects, or is he trying to think about the book itself? In general, what are the distractions that seem to take his attention from the work? When he comes back to his book, where does he take up the work?

4. Is his rate of work evidently slow or rapid? This can be judged by watching him long enough to see how much time he spends in reading a given page.

5. Note, if you can, the different ways in which students study different subjects. For example, is their work in history different from their work in mathematics? If so, which one seems to you to secure the highest degree of attention? Is the writing of notes apparently of value in keeping them at work?

VI. QUESTIONS AND ANSWERS

A comparison of different teachers and of different subjects of instruction will bring out most clearly the distinctions here aimed at.

1. What part of the recitation is consumed in asking questions?

2. Are the questions such as to require answers of more than a single sentence?

3. Are the questions based directly on the text?

4. What is the mode of assigning the question to members of the class for answer?

5. Give examples of good questions with reasons for your selection.

6. Contrast different subjects of instruction with reference to the questions which they permit.

7. Give examples of questions which seem to you too general or otherwise vague.

VII. MOTOR PROCESSES

The gymnasium, the sewing class, the cooking class, and the manual-training shop furnish the best opportunities for observations on this topic. Penmanship classes and almost any lower-grade exercise will, however, serve.

1. What are the characteristics of a clumsy movement?

2. Point out certain instinctive elements of behavior; that is, forms of movement which do not have to be learned, but are natural. Are these always helpful in the learning process?

3. Note the prevalence of rhythm in many forms of behavior. Is the rhythm more striking where the behavior is natural and instinctive or where it is being acquired as a special habit of skill?

4. Comment on the *educational* value of repeating acts which seem to have reached a high degree of perfection, such as taking stitches or swinging Indian clubs.

5. Are individual differences in rate and grace of movement capable of elimination through class training?

6. How far is skill dependent on knowledge?

VIII. RELATION BETWEEN SUBJECTS TAUGHT

For purposes of this section follow a class for a whole forenoon. If the class observed is one of the lower grades, the organization which places this class largely in the hands of one teacher favors a close interrelation of subjects. In the upper grades and high school, on the other hand, organization makes interrelating difficult.

1. What cases did you observe in which the teacher consciously tried to illuminate one subject by reference to another?

2. Did the pupils ask any questions or make remarks which showed that they were thinking about other school topics?

3. Within a given subject there is sometimes opportunity to relate topics which are remote from each other in the textbook. Did the classes visited show any examples of such relating of topics?

4. What opportunities for interrelating subjects did you observe in addition to

those taken advantage of by the class?

5. Sometimes the contrast produced by change from one topic to another or from one classroom to another is important in arousing or depressing a class. What contrasts did you observe?

INDEX

A

B

C

D

E

F

G

H

K

L

M

P

S

U

V

W

9 789361 382994

Printed by Libri Plureos GmbH in Hamburg,
Germany